D0572483

BLUE BEETLE

ROAD TRIP

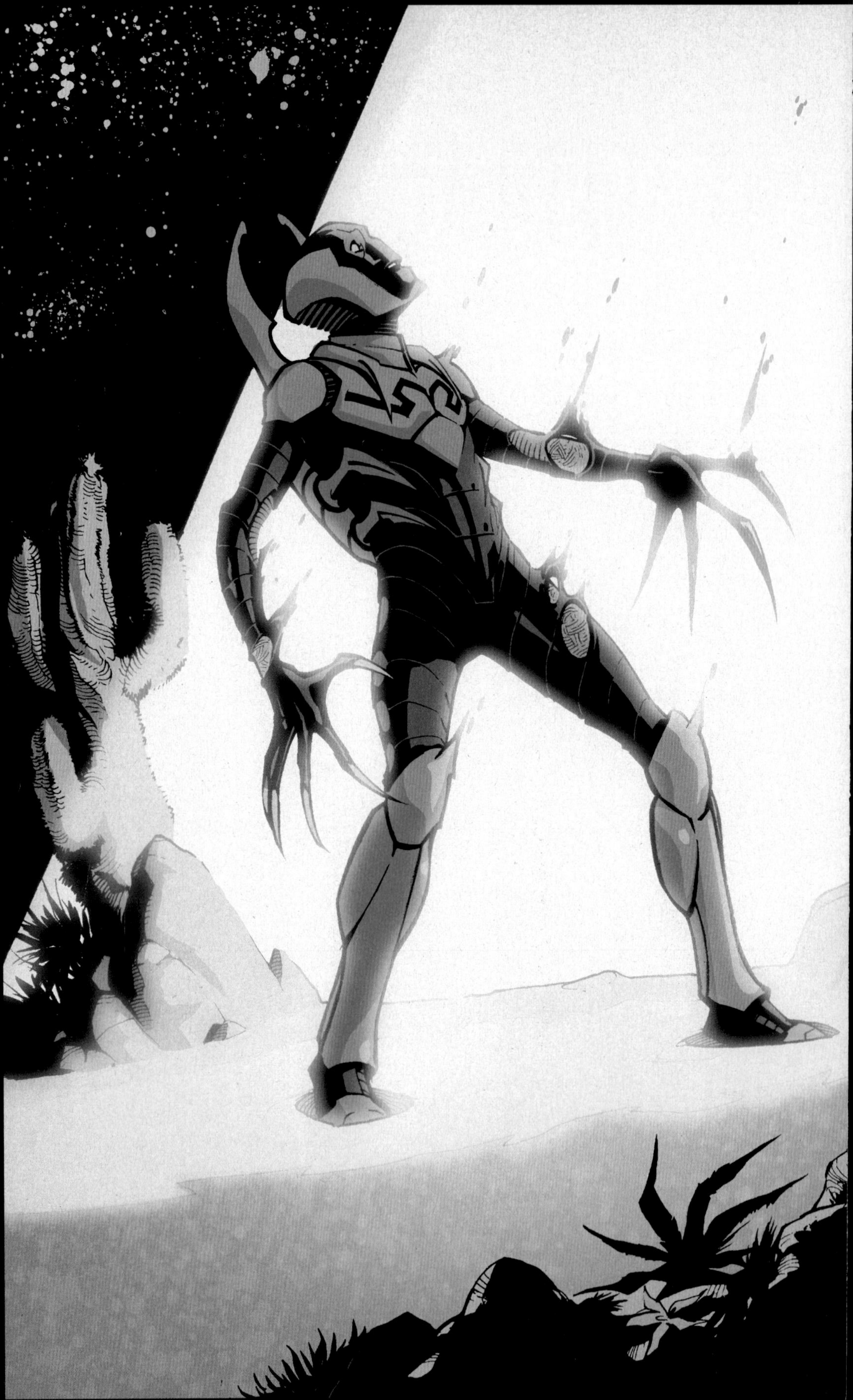

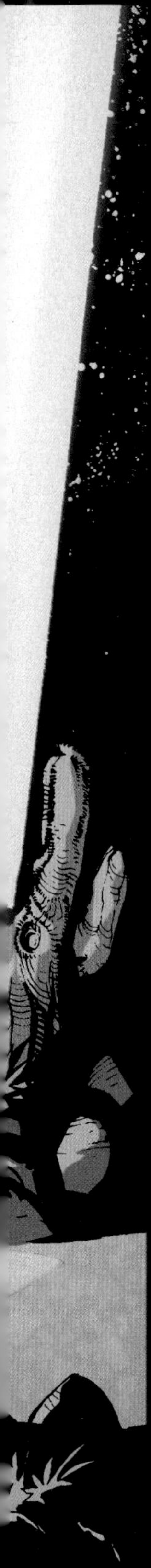

JOHN ROGERS & KEITH GIFFEN
WRITERS

CULLY HAMNER
RAFAEL ALBUQUERQUE
DUNCAN ROULEAU
CASEY JONES
ARTISTS

GUY MAJOR
COLORIST

PHIL BALSMAN
PAT BROSSEAU
JARED K. FLETCHER
LETTERERS

DUNCAN ROULEAU
CULLY HAMNER
ANDY KUHN
RAFAEL ALBUQUERQUE
ORIGINAL COVERS

BLUE BEETLE ROAD TRIP

DAN DIDIO Senior VP-Executive Editor

JOAN HILTY Editor-original series

RACHEL GLUCKSTERN Assistant Editor-original series

ANTON KAWASAKI Editor-collected edition

ROBBIN BROSTERMAN Senior Art Director

PAUL LEVITZ President & Publisher

GEORG BREWER VP-Design & DC Direct Creative

RICHARD BRUNING Senior VP-Creative Director

PATRICK CALDON Executive VP-Finance & Operations

CHRIS CARAMALIS VP-Finance

JOHN CUNNINGHAM VP-Marketing

TERRI CUNNINGHAM VP-Managing Editor

ALISON GILL VP-Manufacturing

HANK KANALZ VP-General Manager, WildStorm

JIM LEE Editorial Director-WildStorm

PAULA LOWITT Senior VP-Business & Legal Affairs

MARYELLEN MCLAUGHLIN VP-Advertising & Custom Publishing

JOHN NEE VP-Business Development

GREGORY NOVECK Senior VP-Creative Affairs

SUE POHJA VP-Book Trade Sales

CHERYL RUBIN Senior VP-Brand Management

JEFF TROJAN VP-Business Development, DC Direct

BOB WAYNE VP-Sales

Cover by Duncan Rouleau
Publication design by Amelia Grohman
Logo design by Brainchild Studios/NYC

BLUE BEETLE: ROAD TRIP
Published by DC Comics. Cover, introduction and
compilation Copyright © 2007 DC Comics. All Rights Reserved.
Originally published in single magazine form in BLUE BEETLE
7-12. Copyright © 2006, 2007 DC Comics. All Rights Reserved.
All characters, their distinctive likenesses and related
elements featured in this publication are trademarks of DC
Comics. The stories, characters and incidents featured in this
publication are entirely fictional. DC Comics does not read or
accept unsolicited submissions of ideas, stories or artwork.

DC Comics, 1700 Broadway, New York, NY 10019.
A Warner Bros. Entertainment Company
Printed in Canada. Second Printing.
ISBN: 978-1-4012-1361-9

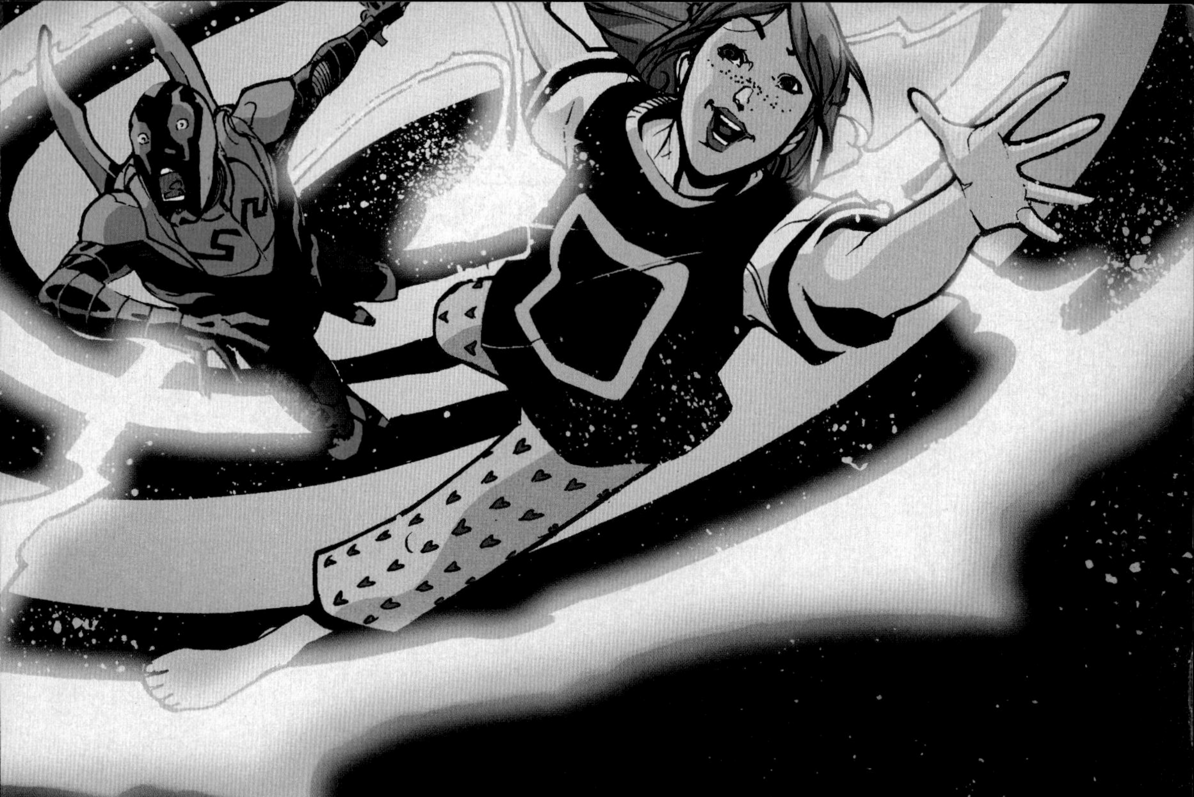

OUR STORY SO FAR...

When high school student Jaime Reyes stumbled upon an ancient scarab, it burrowed into his body, transforming Jaime into the armored Blue Beetle! But before Jaime had the time to fully process what had happened to him, he was recruited by Booster Gold to help in the Infinite Crisis — and thrust into the middle of space, where he teamed up with the likes of Batman, Green Lantern, Green Arrow and Black Lightning. With the unique abilities of the armor, Jaime was able to help in detecting the rogue Brother Eye satellite, which was threatening Earth.

Brother Eye was ultimately destroyed. However, Jaime's armor seemed to have a negative effect from being around Green Lantern, and so the scarab teleported Jaime away once the threat was over. He returned to Earth...

...only to discover an entire year had somehow passed.

With the help of his friends Paco and Brenda, Jaime readjusted to life in El Paso, Texas. But the fact that he was missing for a whole year proved to be difficult for Jaime's family — especially for his little sister, Milagro, who was frightened by her brother's new abilities.

Jaime did his best to try to control his new armor, but the scarab seemed to have a life of its own. At first Jaime believed the scarab was mystical in nature, but a mysterious man known only as the Peacemaker has told him that the scarab is actually extraterrestrial in origin — and that Jaime has a hunk of alien technology welded to his spine...

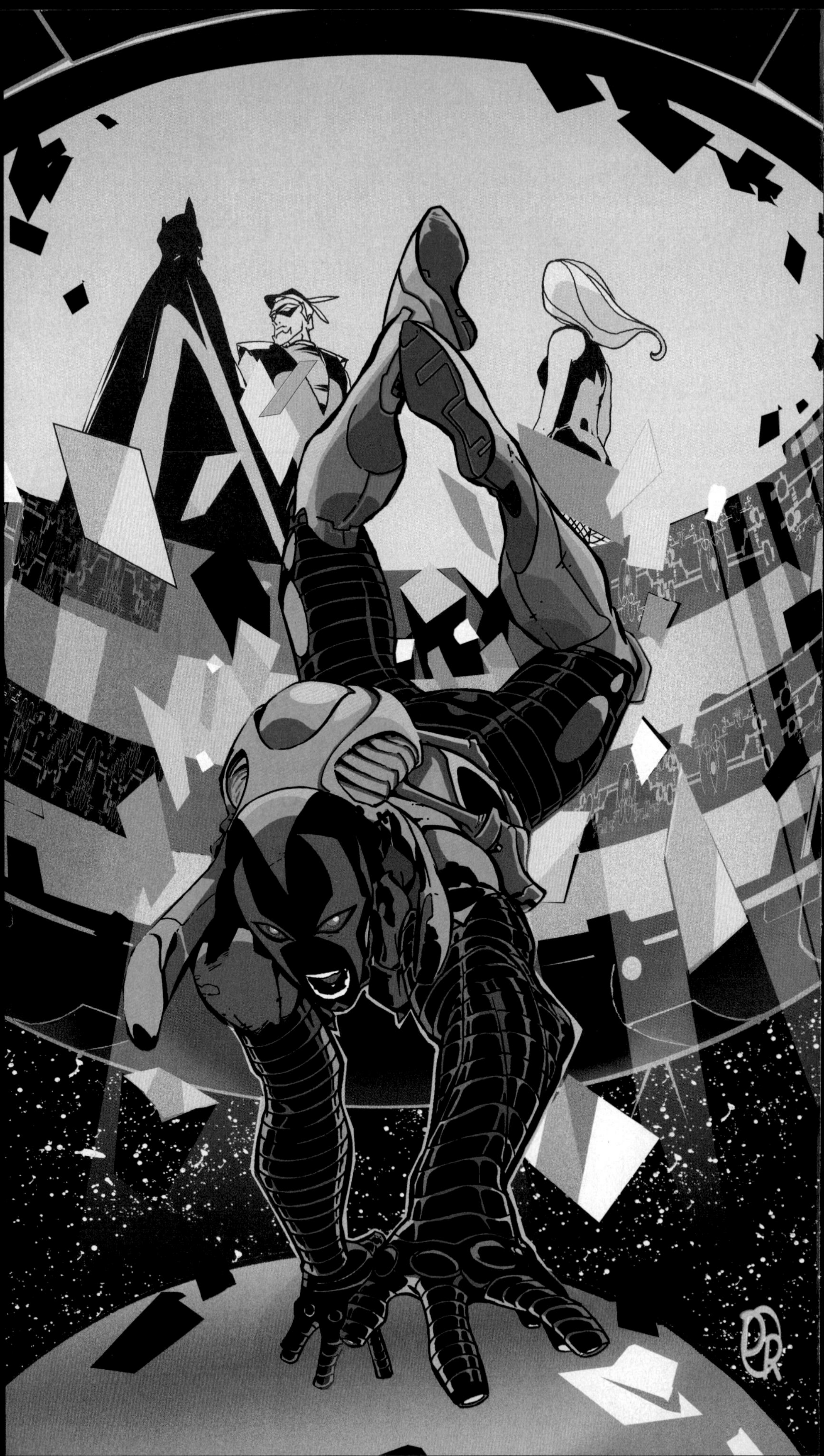

BLUE BEETLE #7 Written by John Rogers Cover by Duncan Rouleau Interior art by Cully Hamner

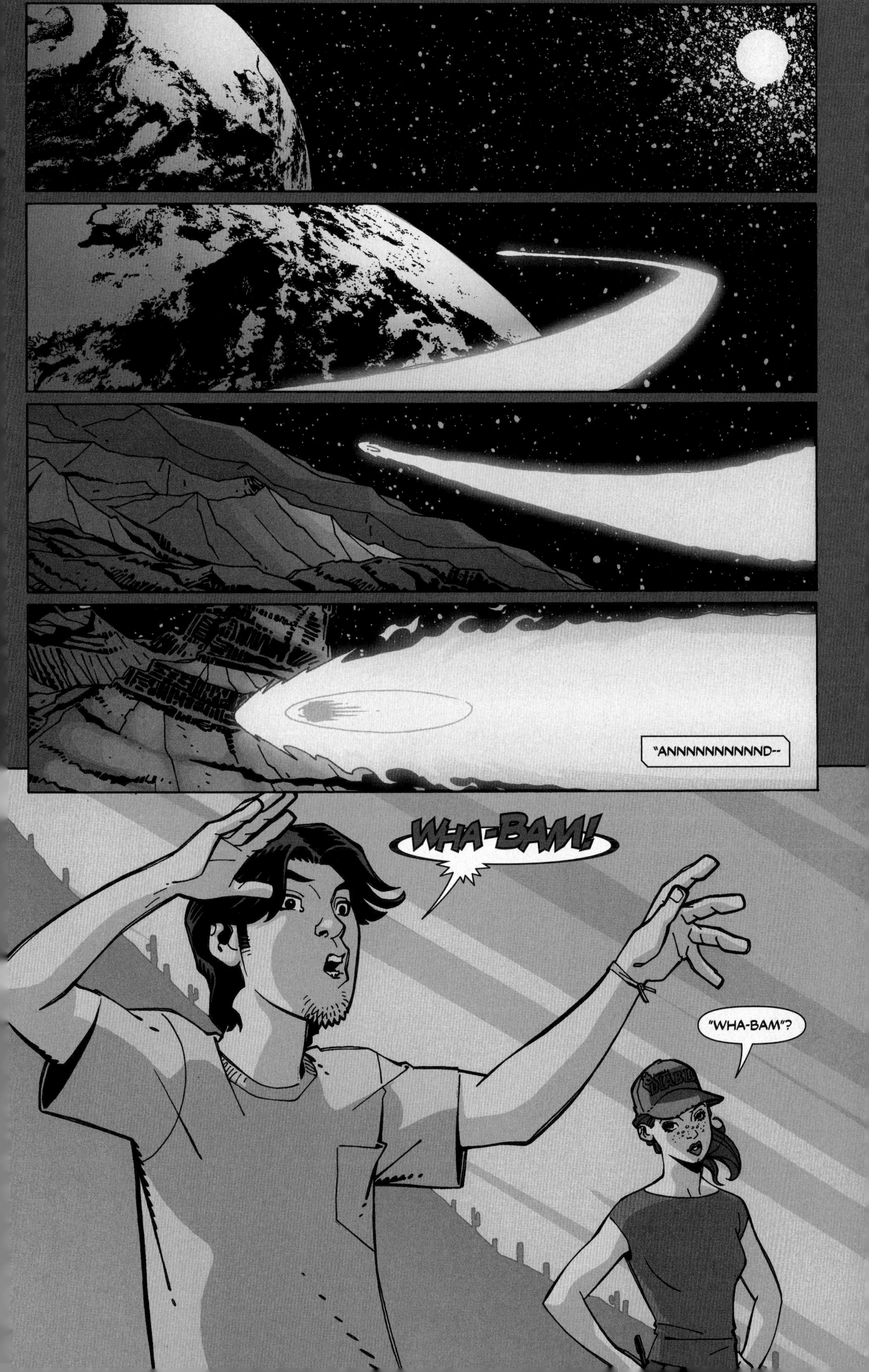
"ANNNNNNNNNND--
WHA-BAM!
"WHA-BAM"?

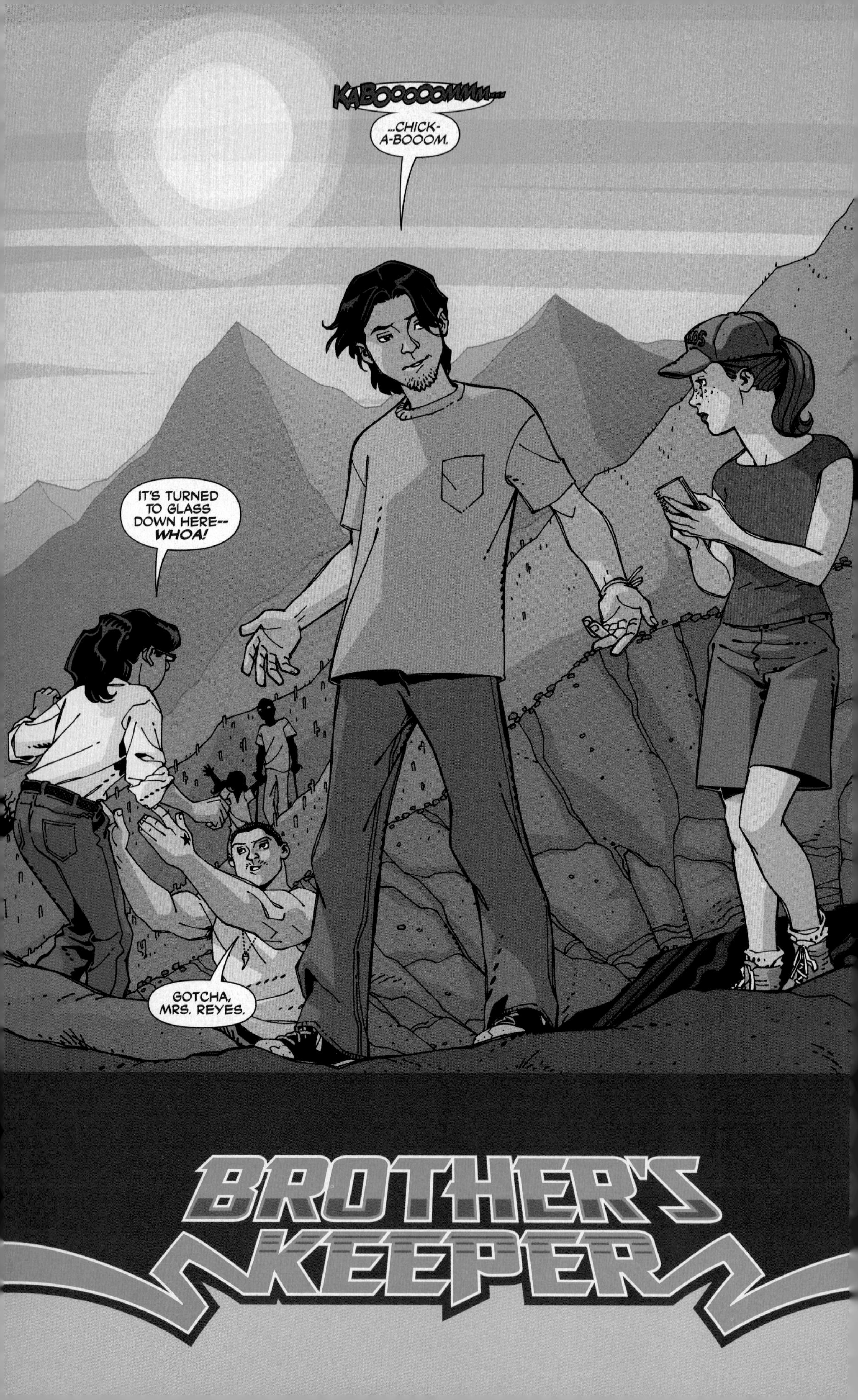
KABOOOOOOMMM...
...CHICK-A-BOOOM.
IT'S TURNED TO GLASS DOWN HERE-- WHOA!
GOTCHA, MRS. REYES.
BROTHER'S KEEPER

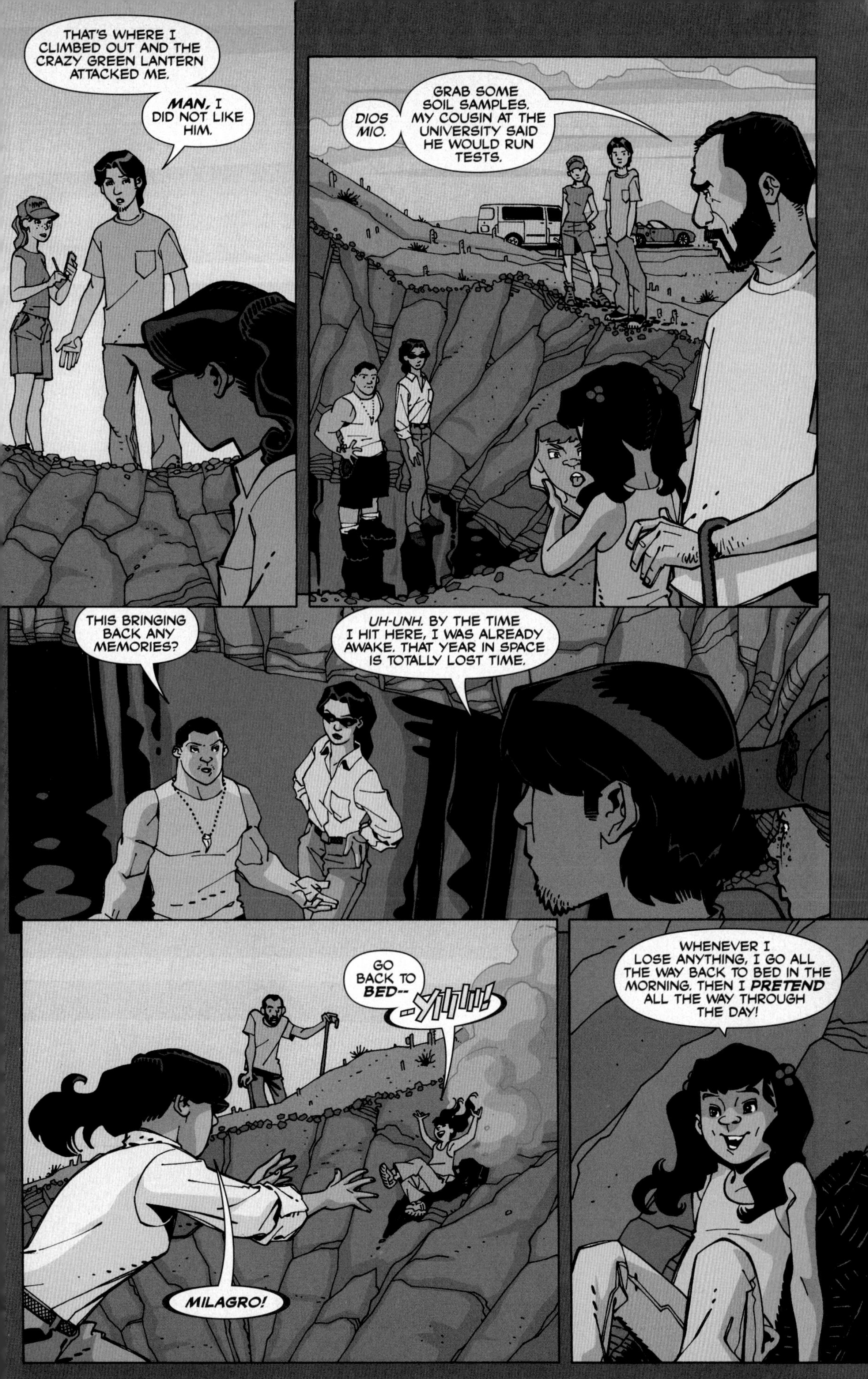
THAT'S WHERE I CLIMBED OUT AND THE CRAZY GREEN LANTERN ATTACKED ME.
MAN, I DID NOT LIKE HIM.
DIOS MIO.
GRAB SOME SOIL SAMPLES. MY COUSIN AT THE UNIVERSITY SAID HE WOULD RUN TESTS.
THIS BRINGING BACK ANY MEMORIES?
UH-UNH. BY THE TIME I HIT HERE, I WAS ALREADY AWAKE. THAT YEAR IN SPACE IS TOTALLY LOST TIME.
GO BACK TO BED--
-YIIIIII!
MILAGRO!
WHENEVER I LOSE ANYTHING, I GO ALL THE WAY BACK TO BED IN THE MORNING. THEN I PRETEND ALL THE WAY THROUGH THE DAY!

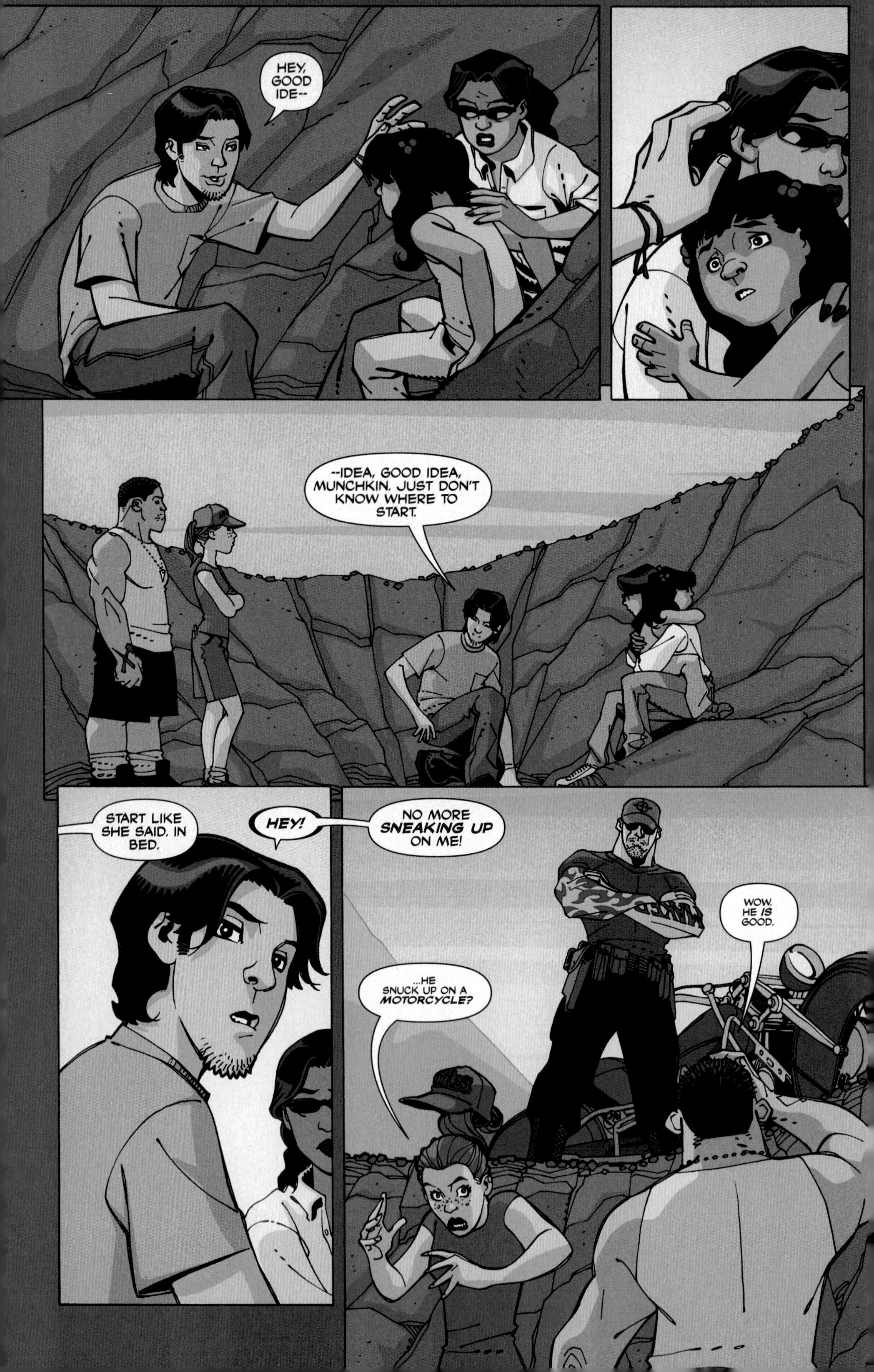
HEY, GOOD IDE--
--IDEA, GOOD IDEA, MUNCHKIN. JUST DON'T KNOW WHERE TO START.
START LIKE SHE SAID. IN BED.
HEY!
NO MORE SNEAKING UP ON ME!
WOW. HE IS GOOD.
...HE SNUCK UP ON A MOTORCYCLE?

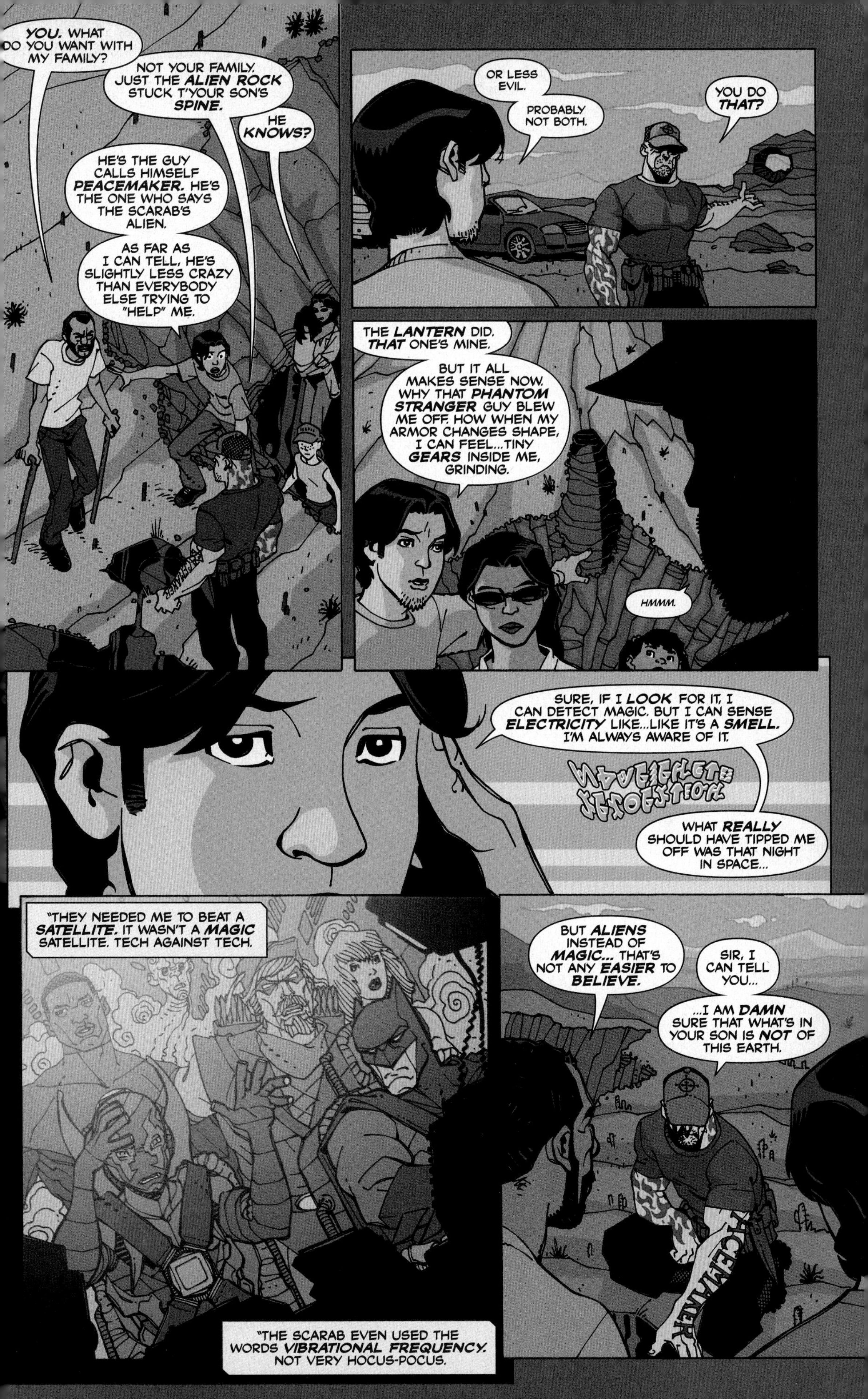
YOU. WHAT DO YOU WANT WITH MY FAMILY?
NOT YOUR FAMILY. JUST THE ALIEN ROCK STUCK T'YOUR SON'S SPINE.
HE KNOWS?
HE'S THE GUY CALLS HIMSELF PEACEMAKER. HE'S THE ONE WHO SAYS THE SCARAB'S ALIEN.
AS FAR AS I CAN TELL, HE'S SLIGHTLY LESS CRAZY THAN EVERYBODY ELSE TRYING TO "HELP" ME.
OR LESS EVIL.
PROBABLY NOT BOTH.
YOU DO THAT?
THE LANTERN DID. THAT ONE'S MINE.
BUT IT ALL MAKES SENSE NOW. WHY THAT PHANTOM STRANGER GUY BLEW ME OFF. HOW WHEN MY ARMOR CHANGES SHAPE, I CAN FEEL...TINY GEARS INSIDE ME, GRINDING.
HMMM.
SURE, IF I LOOK FOR IT, I CAN DETECT MAGIC. BUT I CAN SENSE ELECTRICITY LIKE...LIKE IT'S A SMELL. I'M ALWAYS AWARE OF IT.
WHAT REALLY SHOULD HAVE TIPPED ME OFF WAS THAT NIGHT IN SPACE...
"THEY NEEDED ME TO BEAT A SATELLITE. IT WASN'T A MAGIC SATELLITE. TECH AGAINST TECH.
"THE SCARAB EVEN USED THE WORDS VIBRATIONAL FREQUENCY. NOT VERY HOCUS-POCUS.
BUT ALIENS INSTEAD OF MAGIC... THAT'S NOT ANY EASIER TO BELIEVE.
SIR, I CAN TELL YOU...
...I AM DAMN SURE THAT WHAT'S IN YOUR SON IS NOT OF THIS EARTH.

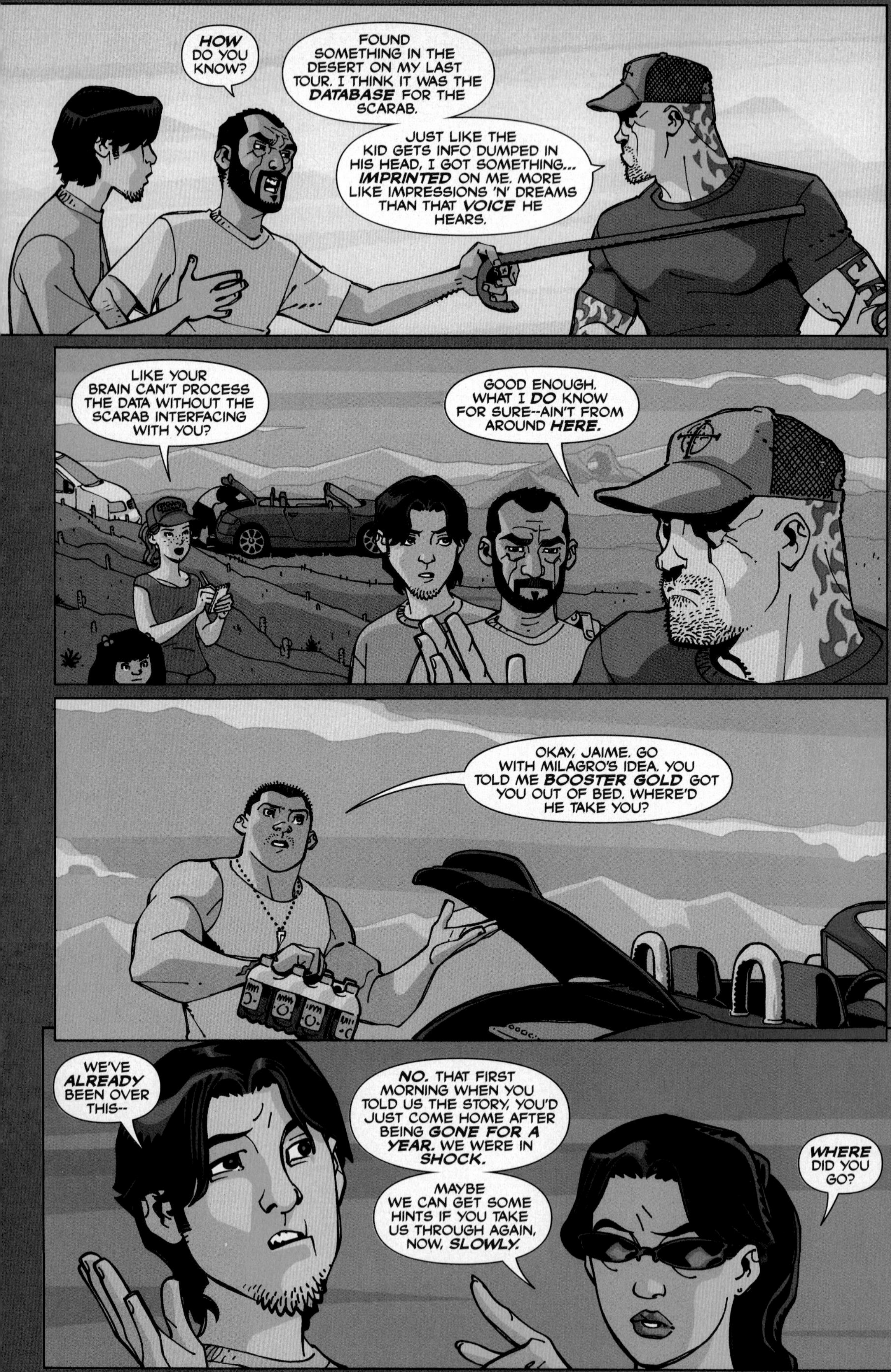

HOW DO YOU KNOW?
FOUND SOMETHING IN THE DESERT ON MY LAST TOUR. I THINK IT WAS THE DATABASE FOR THE SCARAB.
JUST LIKE THE KID GETS INFO DUMPED IN HIS HEAD, I GOT SOMETHING... IMPRINTED ON ME. MORE LIKE IMPRESSIONS 'N' DREAMS THAN THAT VOICE HE HEARS.
LIKE YOUR BRAIN CAN'T PROCESS THE DATA WITHOUT THE SCARAB INTERFACING WITH YOU?
GOOD ENOUGH. WHAT I DO KNOW FOR SURE--AIN'T FROM AROUND HERE.
OKAY, JAIME. GO WITH MILAGRO'S IDEA. YOU TOLD ME BOOSTER GOLD GOT YOU OUT OF BED. WHERE'D HE TAKE YOU?
WE'VE ALREADY BEEN OVER THIS--
NO. THAT FIRST MORNING WHEN YOU TOLD US THE STORY, YOU'D JUST COME HOME AFTER BEING GONE FOR A YEAR. WE WERE IN SHOCK.
MAYBE WE CAN GET SOME HINTS IF YOU TAKE US THROUGH AGAIN, NOW, SLOWLY.
WHERE DID YOU GO?

~CHHURRK~
I AM REALLY, REALLY SORRY I HURLED IN YOUR CAVE.

THE FLOORS HOSE CLEAN. I HAVE PEOPLE.

I THINK IT WAS THE *RIDE.* I SWEAR IT TOOK US THREE MONTHS TO GET HERE.

IT'S THE *ADRENALINE.* NOW, I KNOW THIS IS VERY FRIGHTENING, JAIME, TRY TO FOCUS.

YOU'LL BE LOOKING FOR THIS *SATELLITE.*

BeeP bEEP BOOP BEeP bE
EP BeeP BeeP BOOP bEEP bOOP BeeP bE

ACCESSING BROTHER EYE DATABASE.

AN EVIL, ALL-SEEING *ARTIFICIAL INTELLIGENCE*...

...WITH AN *ARMY* OF ROBOTS MANNED BY INNOCENT PEOPLE KIDNAPPED AGAINST THEIR WILL!?

WHAT PSYCHO-NUTJOB SUPERVILLAIN BUILT *THAT?*

DO ME A FAVOR, JAIME. DON'T TELL GREEN ARROW YOU SAID THAT.

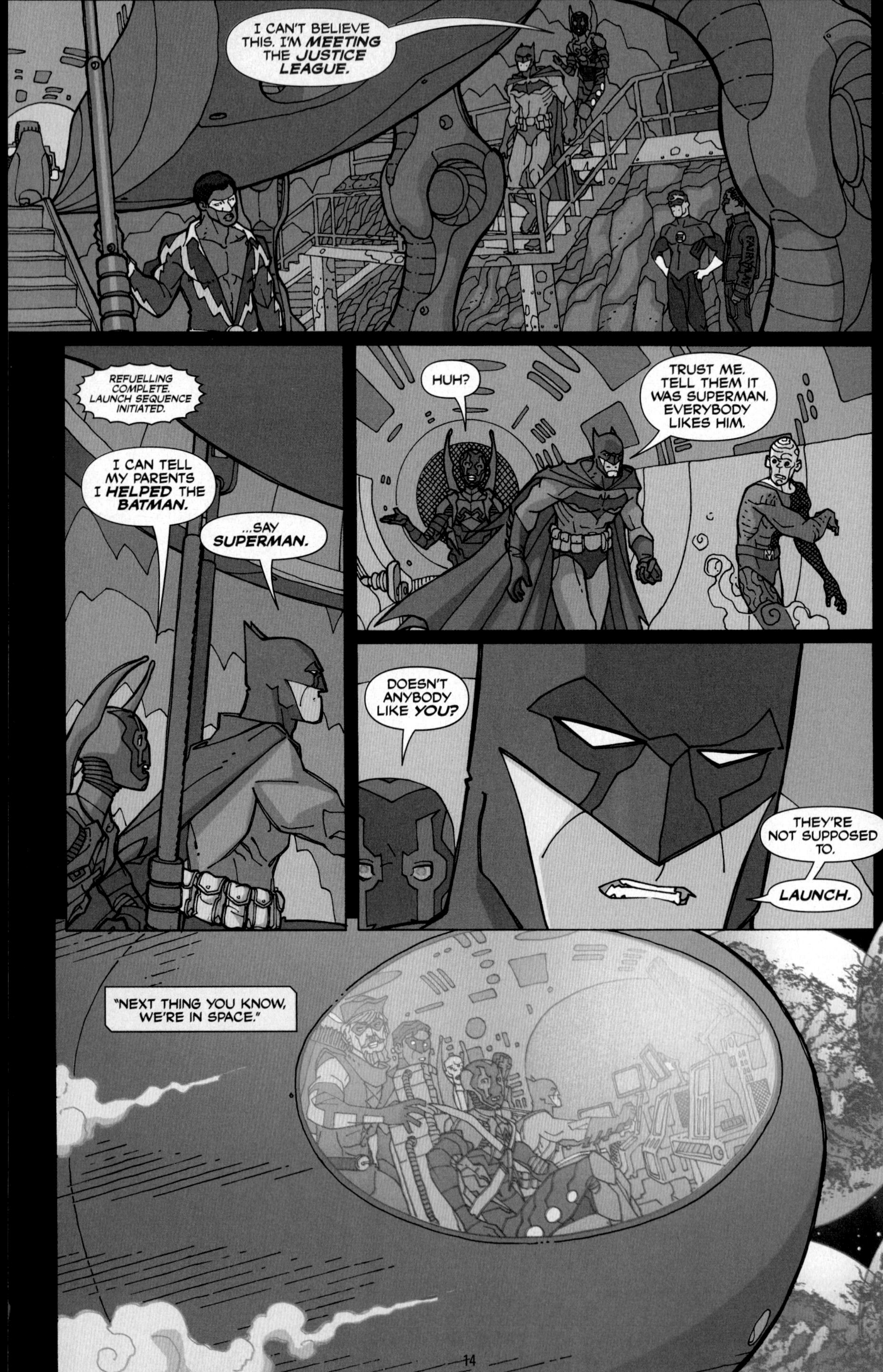

I CAN'T BELIEVE THIS. I'M MEETING THE JUSTICE LEAGUE.
REFUELLING COMPLETE. LAUNCH SEQUENCE INITIATED.
I CAN TELL MY PARENTS I HELPED THE BATMAN.
...SAY SUPERMAN.
HUH?
TRUST ME. TELL THEM IT WAS SUPERMAN. EVERYBODY LIKES HIM.
DOESN'T ANYBODY LIKE YOU?
THEY'RE NOT SUPPOSED TO.
LAUNCH.
"NEXT THING YOU KNOW, WE'RE IN SPACE."

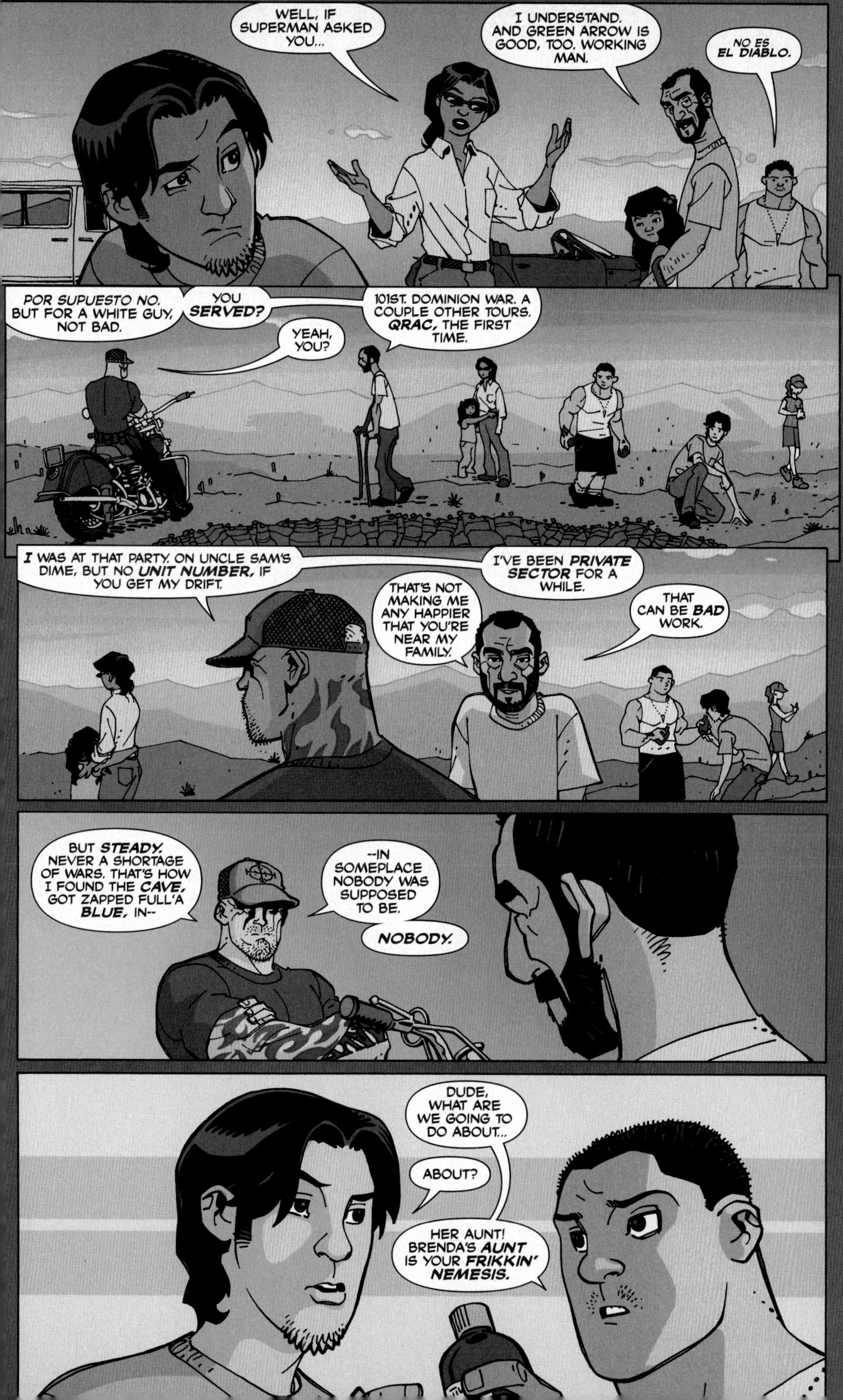
WELL, IF SUPERMAN ASKED YOU...
I UNDERSTAND. AND GREEN ARROW IS GOOD, TOO. WORKING MAN.
NO ES EL DIABLO.
POR SUPUESTO NO. BUT FOR A WHITE GUY, NOT BAD.
YOU SERVED?
101ST. DOMINION WAR. A COUPLE OTHER TOURS. QRAC, THE FIRST TIME.
YEAH, YOU?
I WAS AT THAT PARTY. ON UNCLE SAM'S DIME, BUT NO UNIT NUMBER, IF YOU GET MY DRIFT.
I'VE BEEN PRIVATE SECTOR FOR A WHILE.
THAT'S NOT MAKING ME ANY HAPPIER THAT YOU'RE NEAR MY FAMILY.
THAT CAN BE BAD WORK.
BUT STEADY. NEVER A SHORTAGE OF WARS. THAT'S HOW I FOUND THE CAVE, GOT ZAPPED FULL'A BLUE, IN--
--IN SOMEPLACE NOBODY WAS SUPPOSED TO BE.
NOBODY.
DUDE, WHAT ARE WE GOING TO DO ABOUT...
ABOUT?
HER AUNT! BRENDA'S AUNT IS YOUR FRIKKIN' NEMESIS.

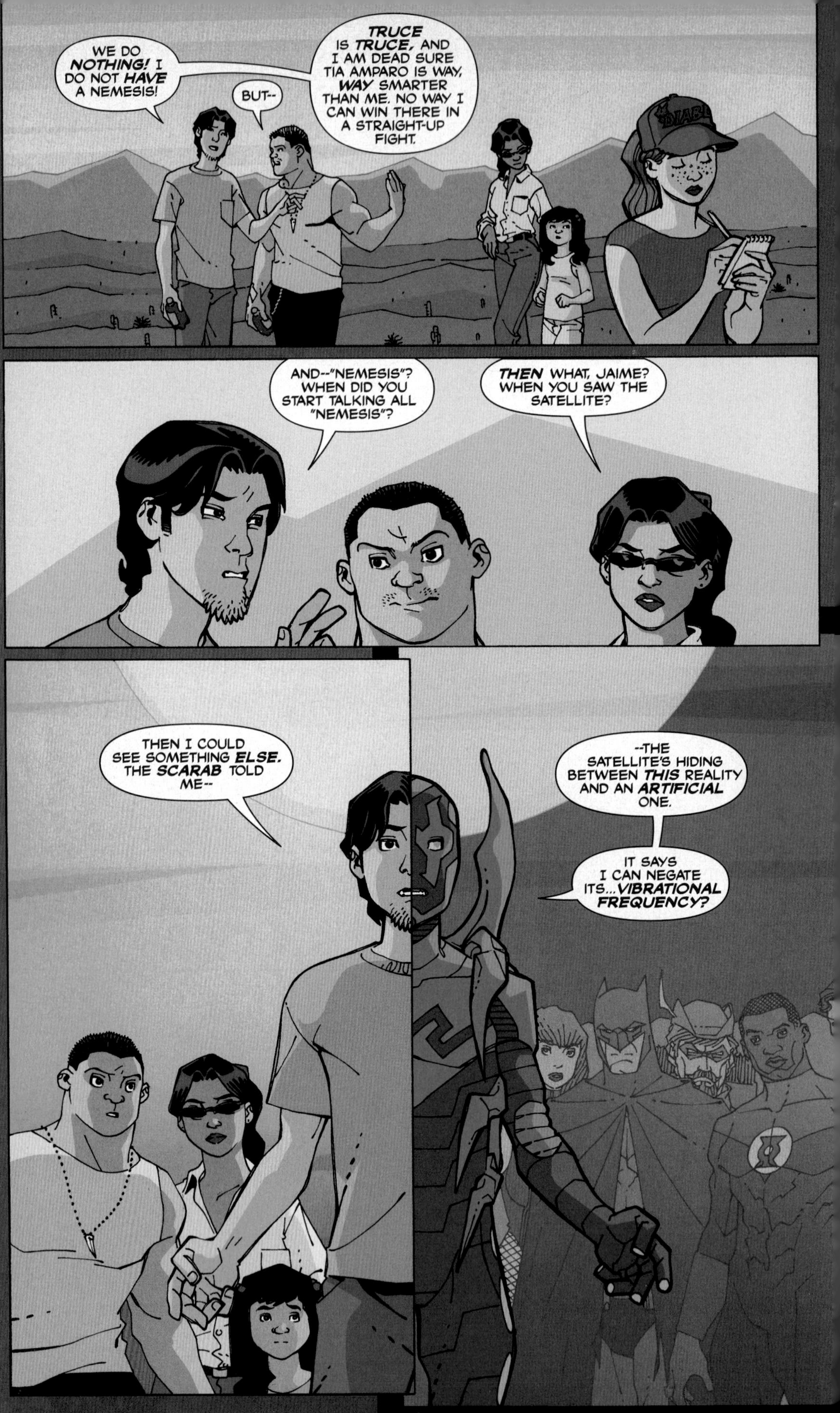
WE DO NOTHING! I DO NOT HAVE A NEMESIS!
BUT--
TRUCE IS TRUCE, AND I AM DEAD SURE TIA AMPARO IS WAY, WAY SMARTER THAN ME. NO WAY I CAN WIN THERE IN A STRAIGHT-UP FIGHT.
DIABL
AND--"NEMESIS"? WHEN DID YOU START TALKING ALL "NEMESIS"?
THEN WHAT, JAIME? WHEN YOU SAW THE SATELLITE?
THEN I COULD SEE SOMETHING ELSE. THE SCARAB TOLD ME--
--THE SATELLITE'S HIDING BETWEEN THIS REALITY AND AN ARTIFICIAL ONE.
IT SAYS I CAN NEGATE ITS...VIBRATIONAL FREQUENCY?

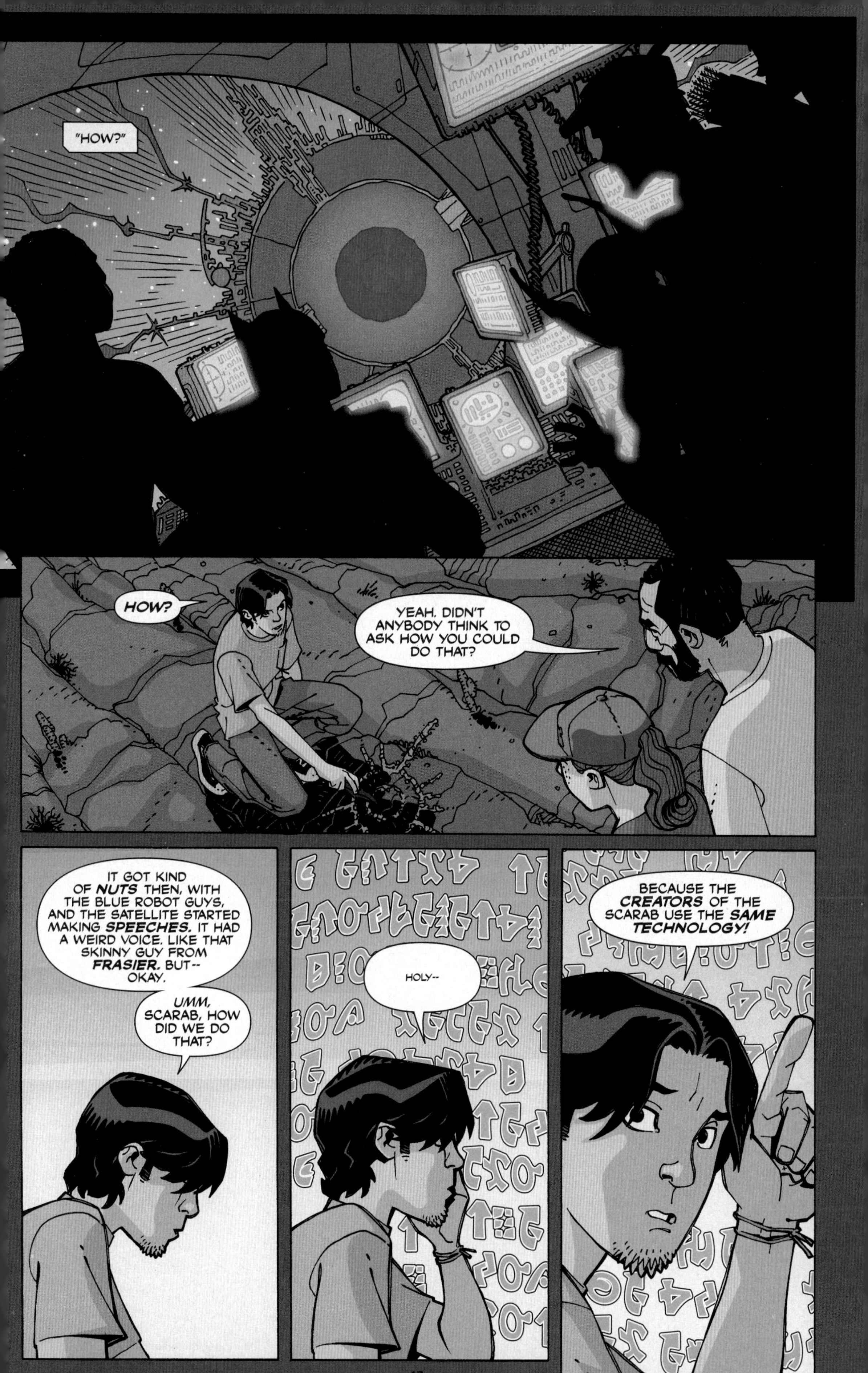
"HOW?"
HOW?
YEAH. DIDN'T ANYBODY THINK TO ASK HOW YOU COULD DO THAT?
IT GOT KIND OF NUTS THEN, WITH THE BLUE ROBOT GUYS, AND THE SATELLITE STARTED MAKING SPEECHES. IT HAD A WEIRD VOICE. LIKE THAT SKINNY GUY FROM FRASIER. BUT-- OKAY.
UMM, SCARAB, HOW DID WE DO THAT?
HOLY--
BECAUSE THE CREATORS OF THE SCARAB USE THE SAME TECHNOLOGY!

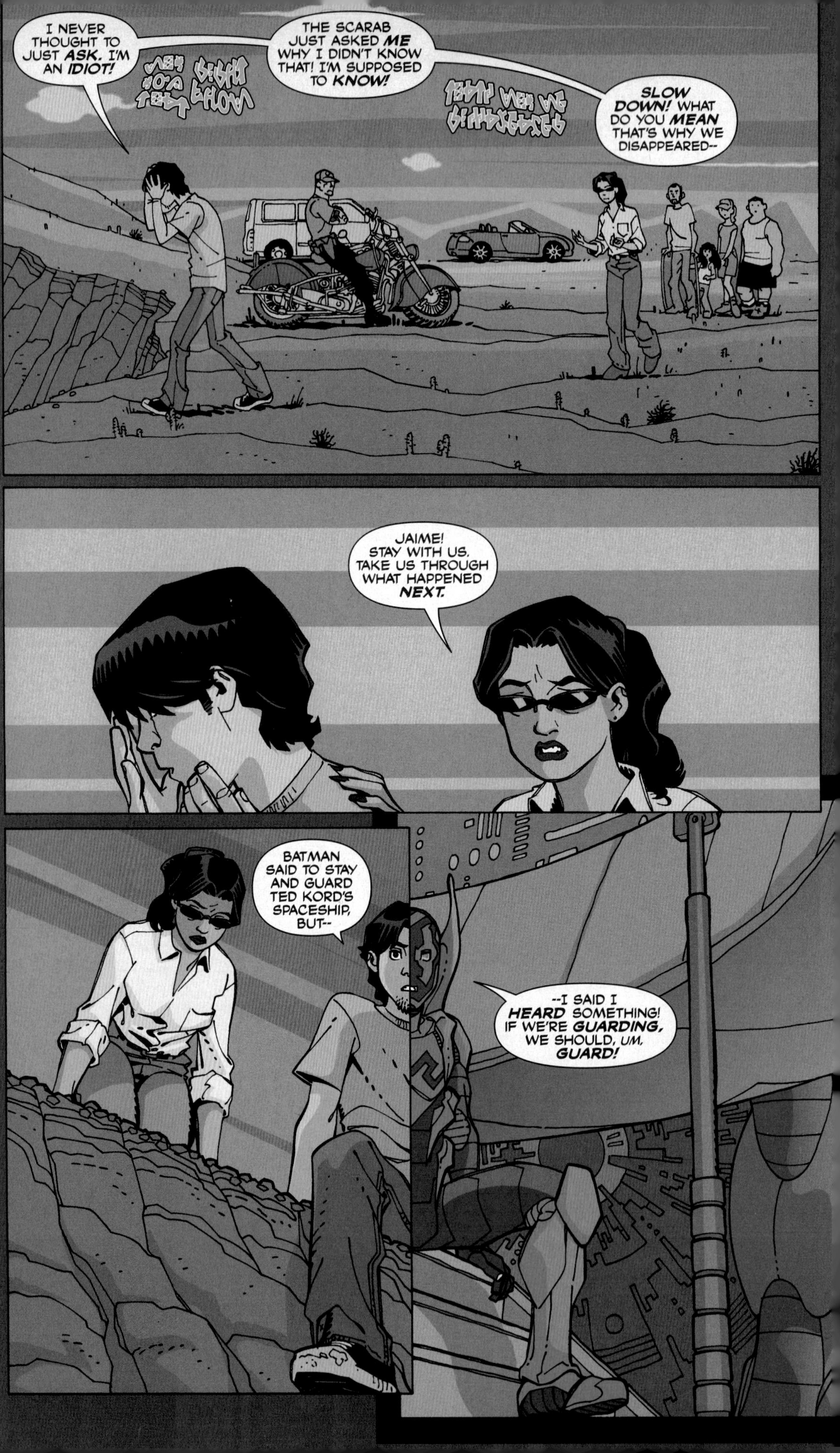

I NEVER THOUGHT TO JUST ASK. I'M AN IDIOT!
THE SCARAB JUST ASKED ME WHY I DIDN'T KNOW THAT! I'M SUPPOSED TO KNOW!
SLOW DOWN! WHAT DO YOU MEAN THAT'S WHY WE DISAPPEARED--
JAIME! STAY WITH US. TAKE US THROUGH WHAT HAPPENED NEXT.
BATMAN SAID TO STAY AND GUARD TED KORD'S SPACESHIP, BUT--
--I SAID I HEARD SOMETHING! IF WE'RE GUARDING, WE SHOULD, UM, GUARD!

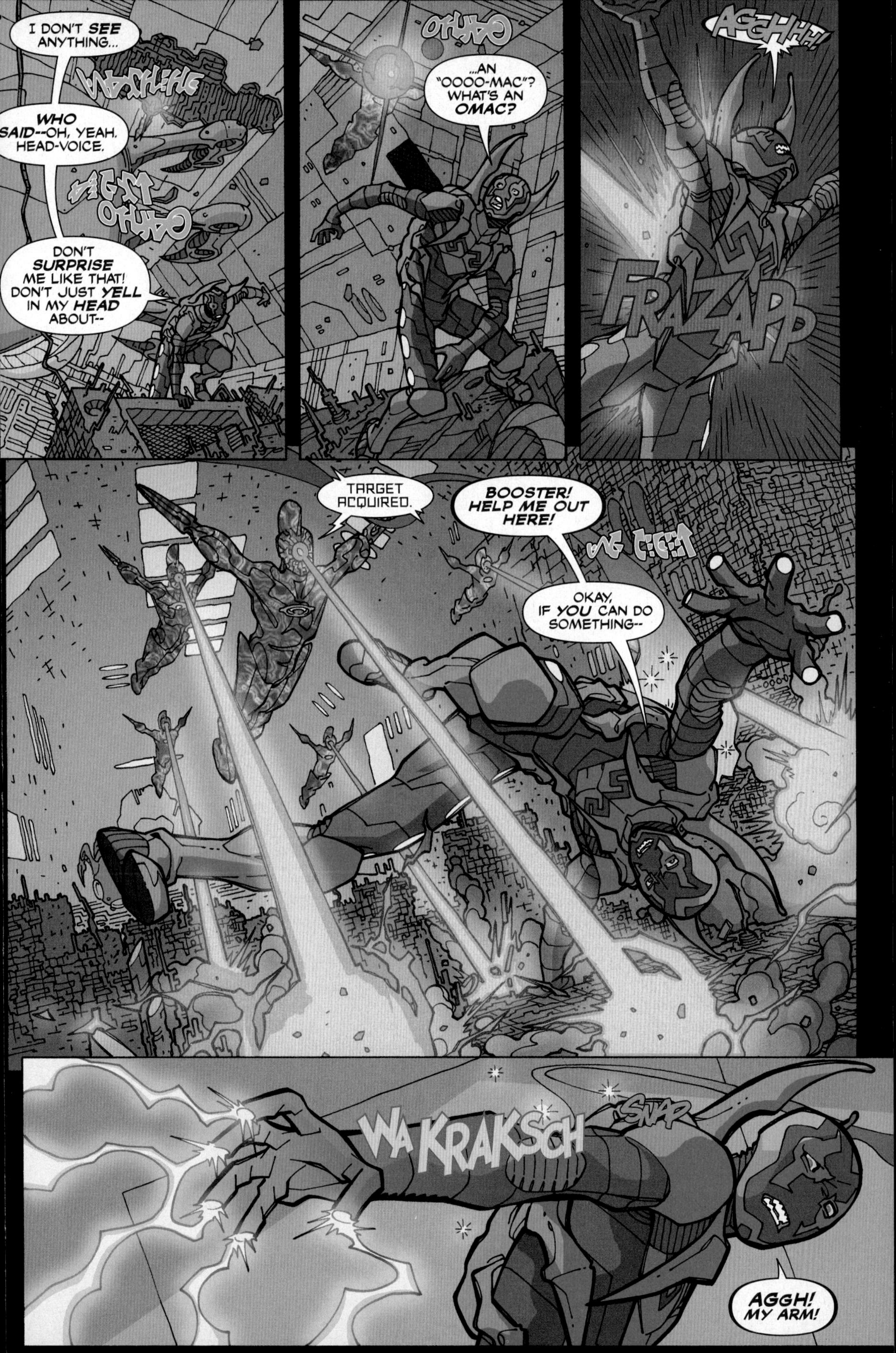
I DON'T SEE ANYTHING...
WHO SAID--OH, YEAH. HEAD-VOICE.
DON'T SURPRISE ME LIKE THAT! DON'T JUST YELL IN MY HEAD ABOUT--
...AN "OOOO-MAC"? WHAT'S AN OMAC?
AGGHH!
FRAZAPP
TARGET ACQUIRED.
BOOSTER! HELP ME OUT HERE!
OKAY, IF YOU CAN DO SOMETHING--
WAKRAKSCH
SNAP
AGGH! MY ARM!

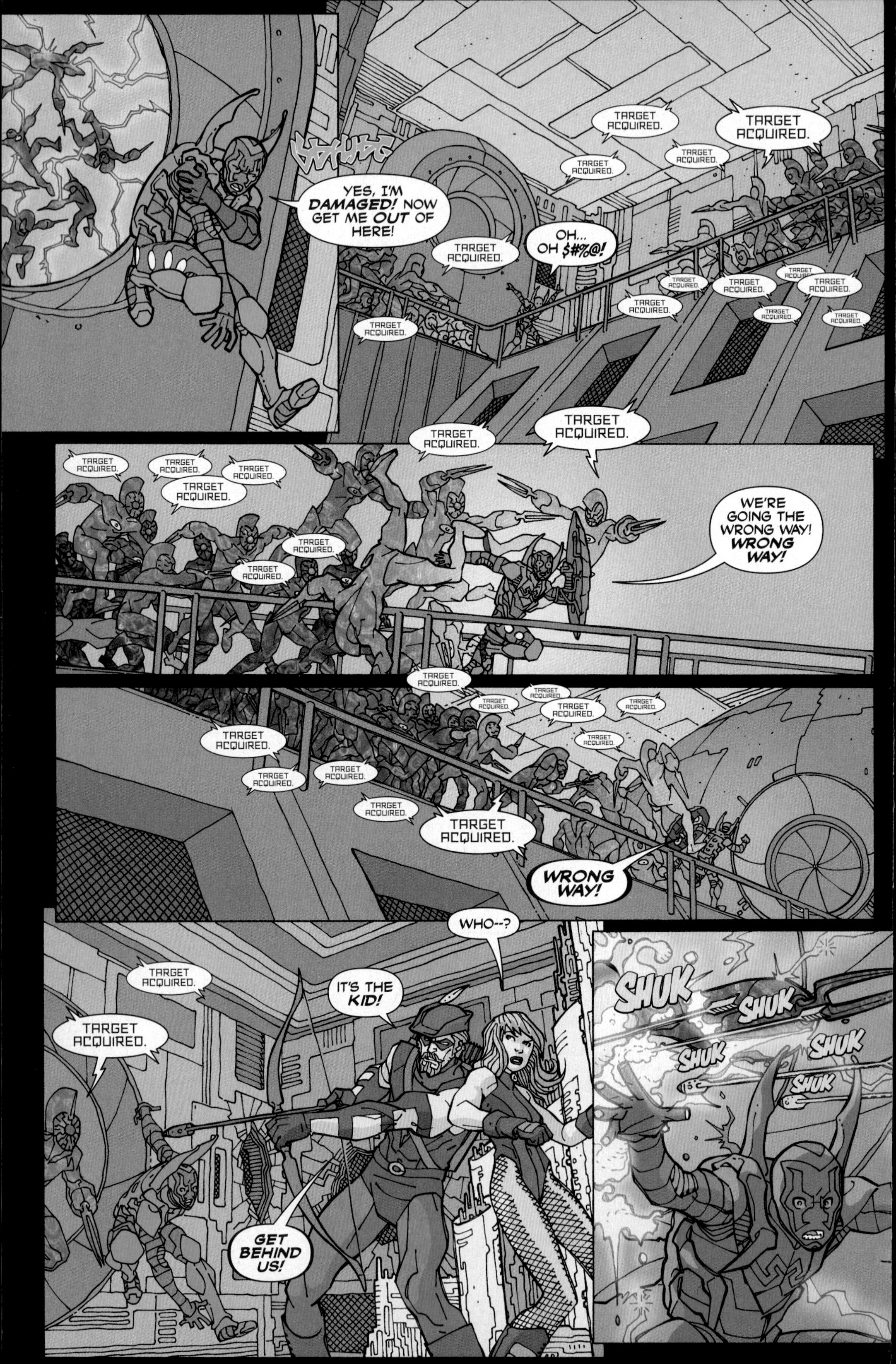
YES, I'M DAMAGED! NOW GET ME OUT OF HERE!
TARGET ACQUIRED.
TARGET ACQUIRED.
TARGET ACQUIRED.
TARGET ACQUIRED.
TARGET ACQUIRED.
OH... OH $#%@!
TARGET ACQUIRED.
TARGET ACQUIRED.
TARGET ACQUIRED.
TARGET ACQUIRED.
TARGET ACQUIRED.
TARGET ACQUIRED.
TARGET ACQUIRED.
TARGET ACQUIRED.
TARGET ACQUIRED.
TARGET ACQUIRED.
TARGET ACQUIRED.
TARGET ACQUIRED.
TARGET ACQUIRED.
TARGET ACQUIRED.
TARGET ACQUIRED.
WE'RE GOING THE WRONG WAY! WRONG WAY!
TARGET ACQUIRED.
TARGET ACQUIRED.
TARGET ACQUIRED.
TARGET ACQUIRED.
TARGET ACQUIRED.
TARGET ACQUIRED.
TARGET ACQUIRED.
TARGET ACQUIRED.
TARGET ACQUIRED.
TARGET ACQUIRED.
TARGET ACQUIRED.
TARGET ACQUIRED.
TARGET ACQUIRED.
WRONG WAY!
WHO--?
TARGET ACQUIRED.
TARGET ACQUIRED.
IT'S THE KID!
GET BEHIND US!
SHUK
SHUK
SHUK
SHUK
SHUK

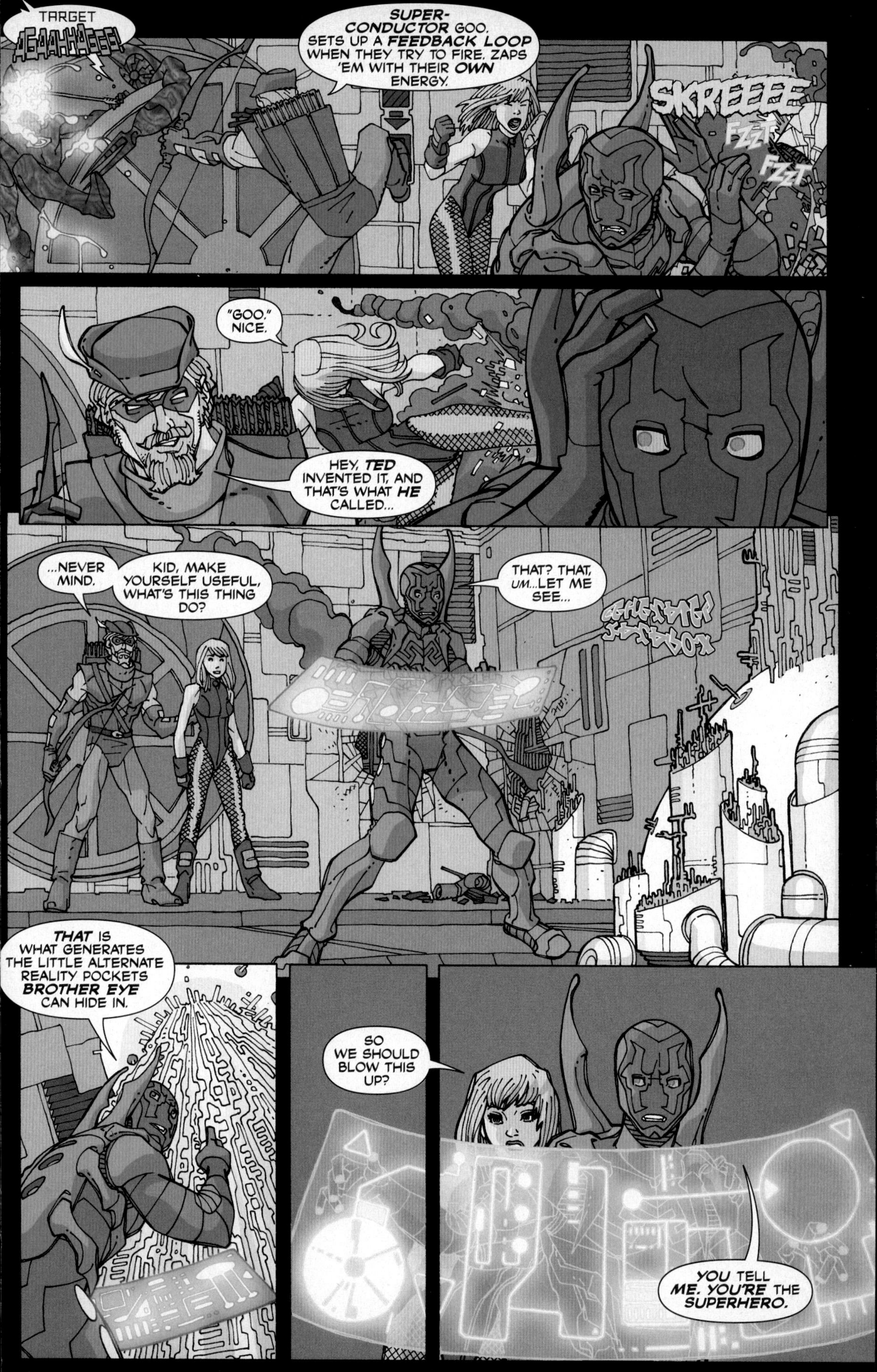
TARGET
AGAAHHAGGG!
SUPER-CONDUCTOR GOO. SETS UP A FEEDBACK LOOP WHEN THEY TRY TO FIRE. ZAPS 'EM WITH THEIR OWN ENERGY.
SKREEEEE
FZZT
FZZT
"GOO." NICE.
HEY, TED INVENTED IT, AND THAT'S WHAT HE CALLED...
...NEVER MIND.
KID, MAKE YOURSELF USEFUL, WHAT'S THIS THING DO?
THAT? THAT, UM...LET ME SEE...
THAT IS WHAT GENERATES THE LITTLE ALTERNATE REALITY POCKETS BROTHER EYE CAN HIDE IN.
SO WE SHOULD BLOW THIS UP?
YOU TELL ME. YOU'RE THE SUPERHERO.

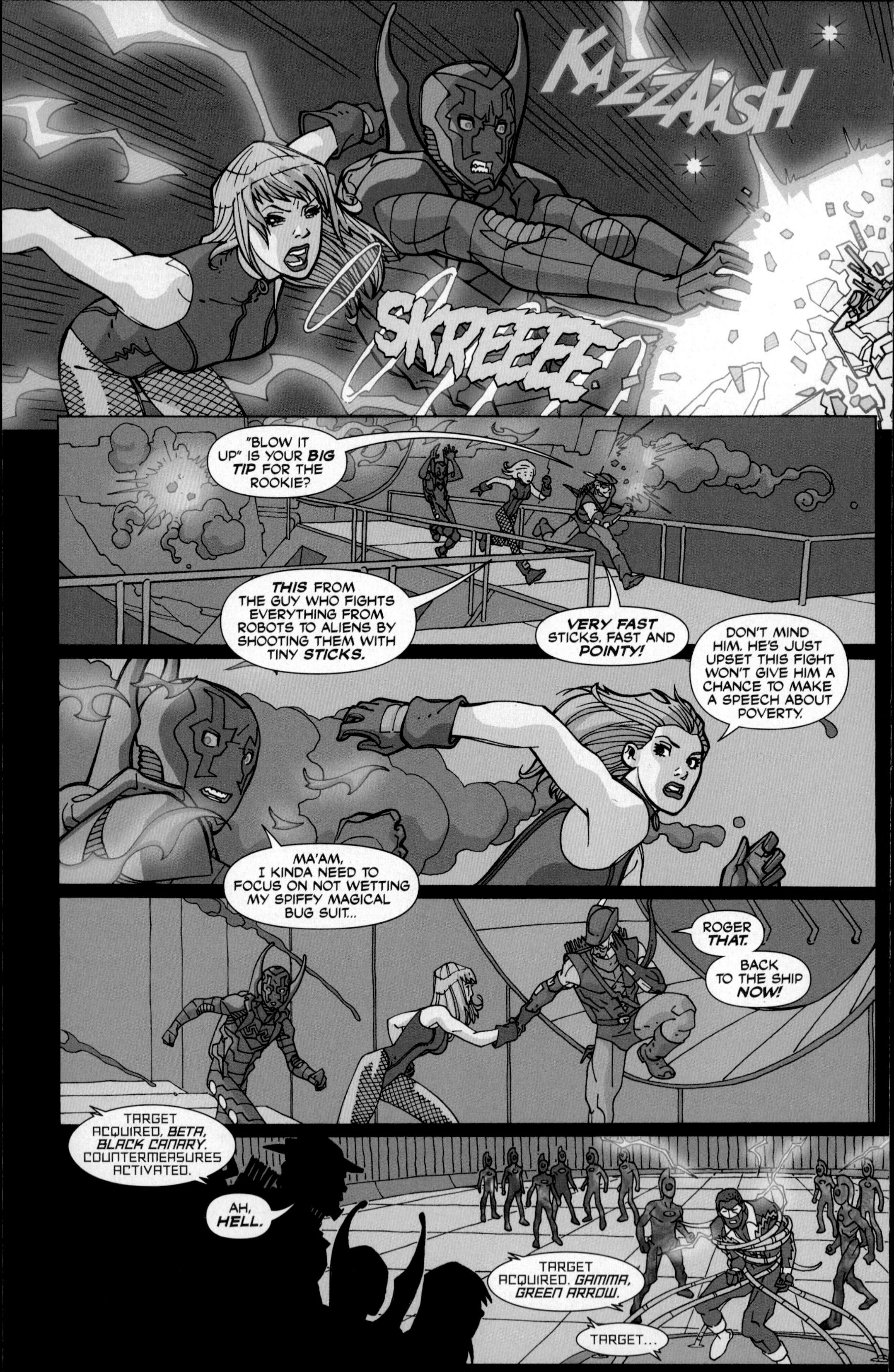
KAZZAASH
SKREEEEE
"BLOW IT UP" IS YOUR BIG TIP FOR THE ROOKIE?
THIS FROM THE GUY WHO FIGHTS EVERYTHING FROM ROBOTS TO ALIENS BY SHOOTING THEM WITH TINY STICKS.
VERY FAST STICKS. FAST AND POINTY!
DON'T MIND HIM. HE'S JUST UPSET THIS FIGHT WON'T GIVE HIM A CHANCE TO MAKE A SPEECH ABOUT POVERTY.
MA'AM, I KINDA NEED TO FOCUS ON NOT WETTING MY SPIFFY MAGICAL BUG SUIT...
ROGER THAT.
BACK TO THE SHIP NOW!
TARGET ACQUIRED, BETA, BLACK CANARY. COUNTERMEASURES ACTIVATED.
AH, HELL.
TARGET ACQUIRED. GAMMA, GREEN ARROW.
TARGET...

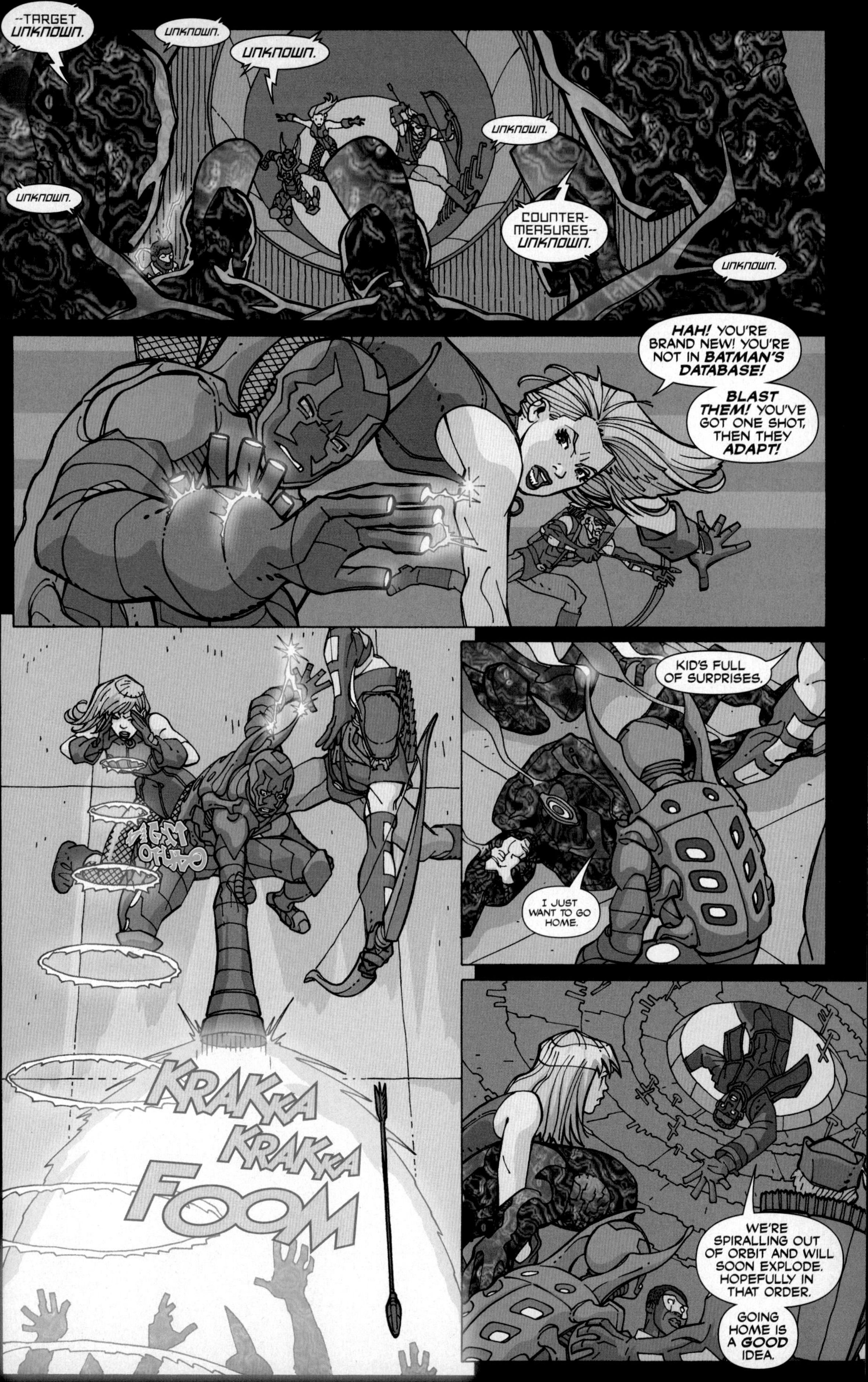
--TARGET UNKNOWN.
UNKNOWN.
UNKNOWN.
UNKNOWN.
UNKNOWN.
COUNTER-MEASURES--UNKNOWN.
UNKNOWN.
HAH! YOU'RE BRAND NEW! YOU'RE NOT IN BATMAN'S DATABASE!
BLAST THEM! YOU'VE GOT ONE SHOT, THEN THEY ADAPT!
KRAKKA KRAKKA FOOM
KID'S FULL OF SURPRISES.
I JUST WANT TO GO HOME.
WE'RE SPIRALLING OUT OF ORBIT AND WILL SOON EXPLODE. HOPEFULLY IN THAT ORDER.
GOING HOME IS A GOOD IDEA.

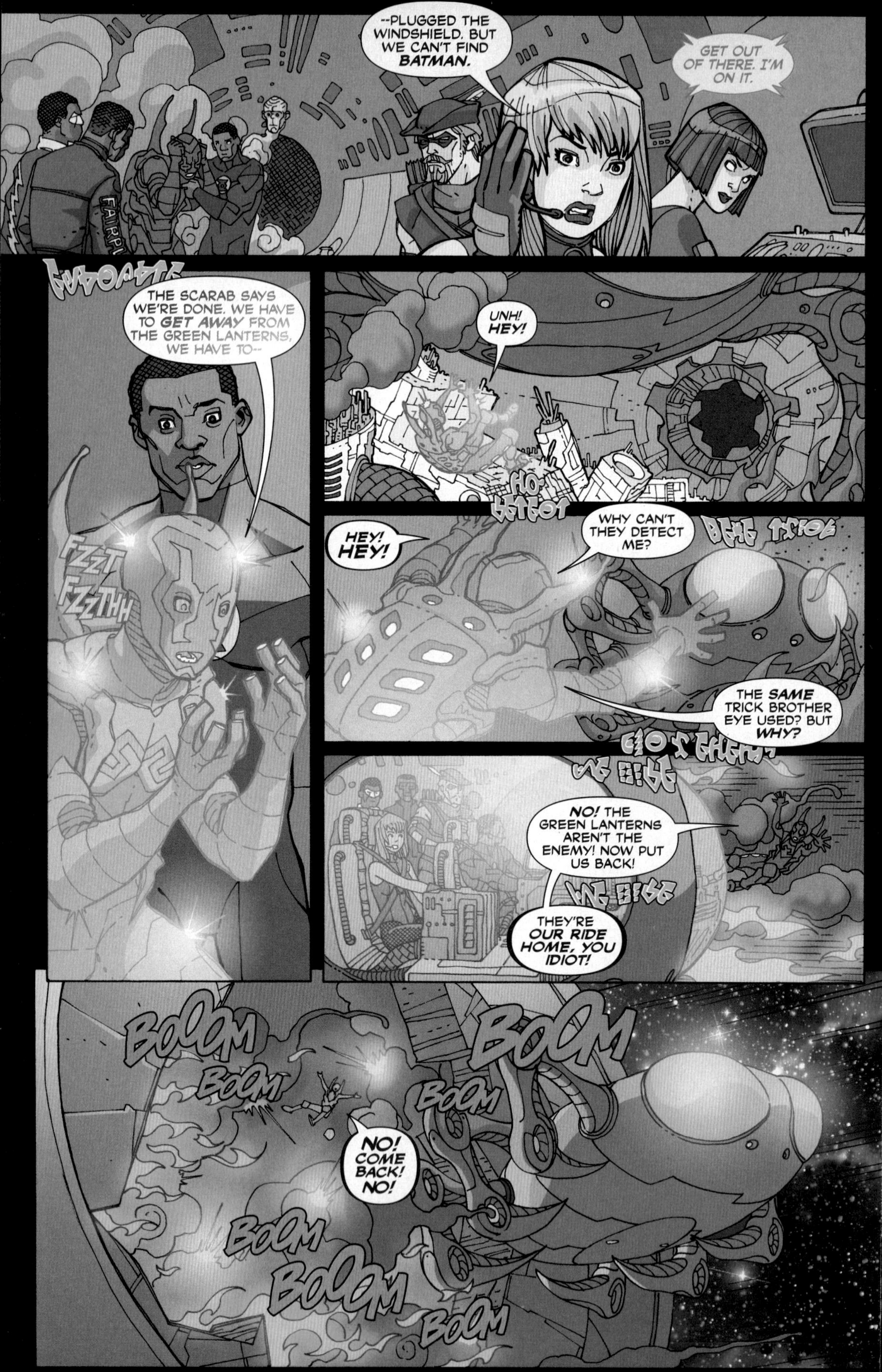
--PLUGGED THE WINDSHIELD. BUT WE CAN'T FIND BATMAN.
GET OUT OF THERE. I'M ON IT.
THE SCARAB SAYS WE'RE DONE. WE HAVE TO GET AWAY FROM THE GREEN LANTERNS, WE HAVE TO--
FZZT
FZZTHH
UNH! HEY!
HEY! HEY!
WHY CAN'T THEY DETECT ME?
THE SAME TRICK BROTHER EYE USED? BUT WHY?
NO! THE GREEN LANTERNS AREN'T THE ENEMY! NOW PUT US BACK!
THEY'RE OUR RIDE HOME, YOU IDIOT!
BOOM
BOOM
BOOM
BOOM
NO! COME BACK! NO!
BOOM
BOOM
BOOM

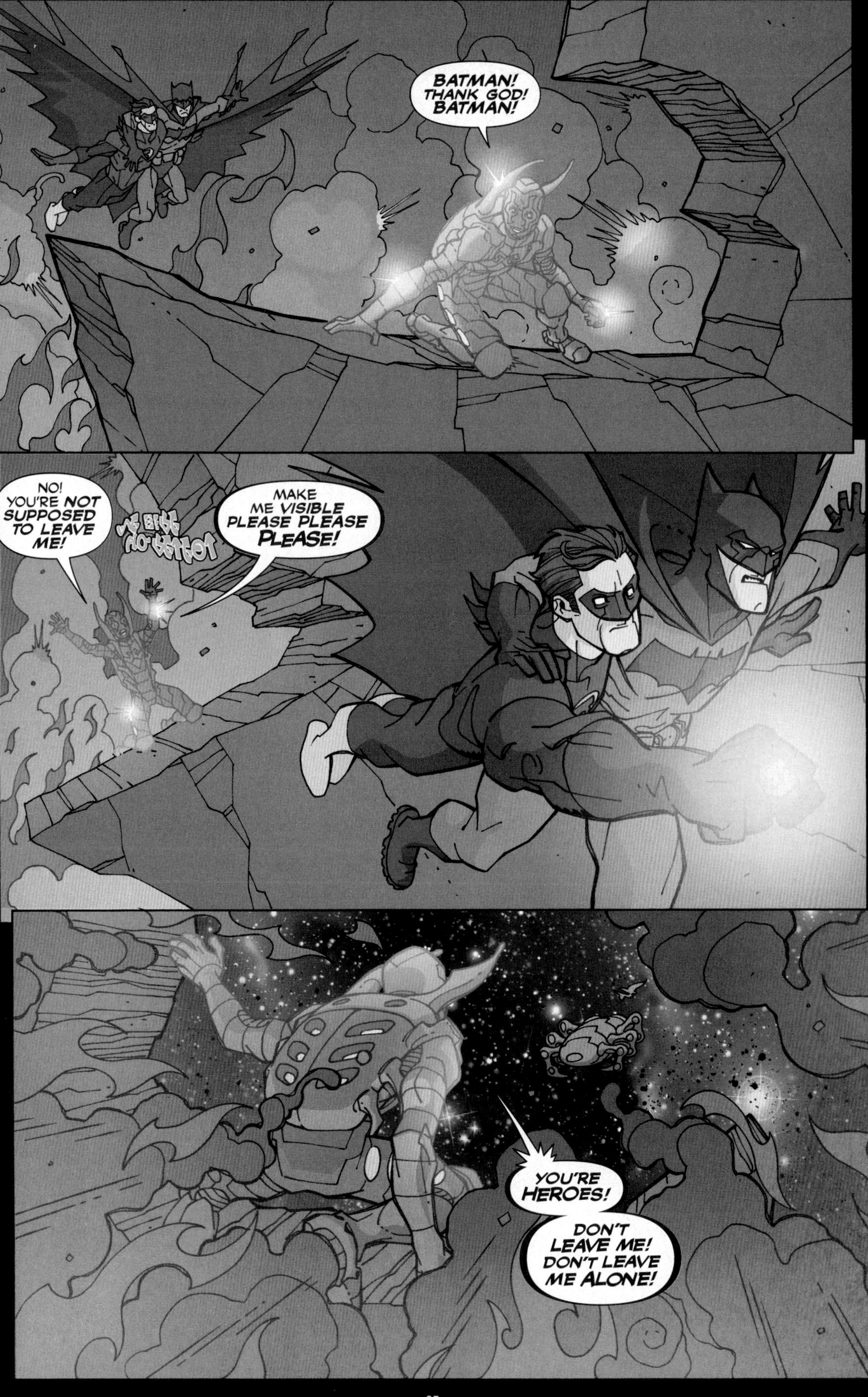
BATMAN! THANK GOD! BATMAN!
NO! YOU'RE NOT SUPPOSED TO LEAVE ME!
MAKE ME VISIBLE PLEASE PLEASE PLEASE!
YOU'RE HEROES!
DON'T LEAVE ME! DON'T LEAVE ME ALONE!

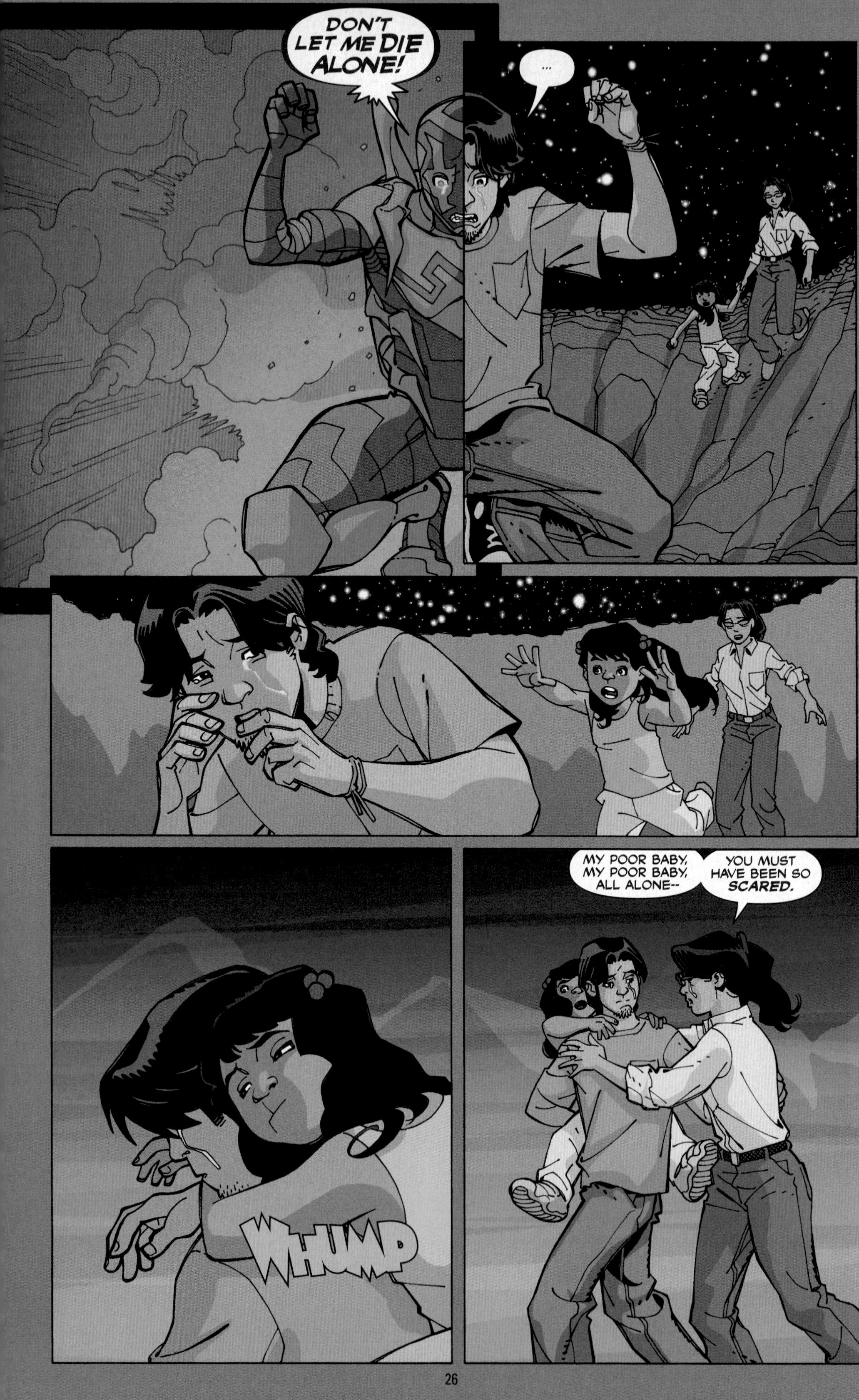
DON'T LET ME DIE ALONE!
...
MY POOR BABY, MY POOR BABY, ALL ALONE--
YOU MUST HAVE BEEN SO SCARED.
WHUMP

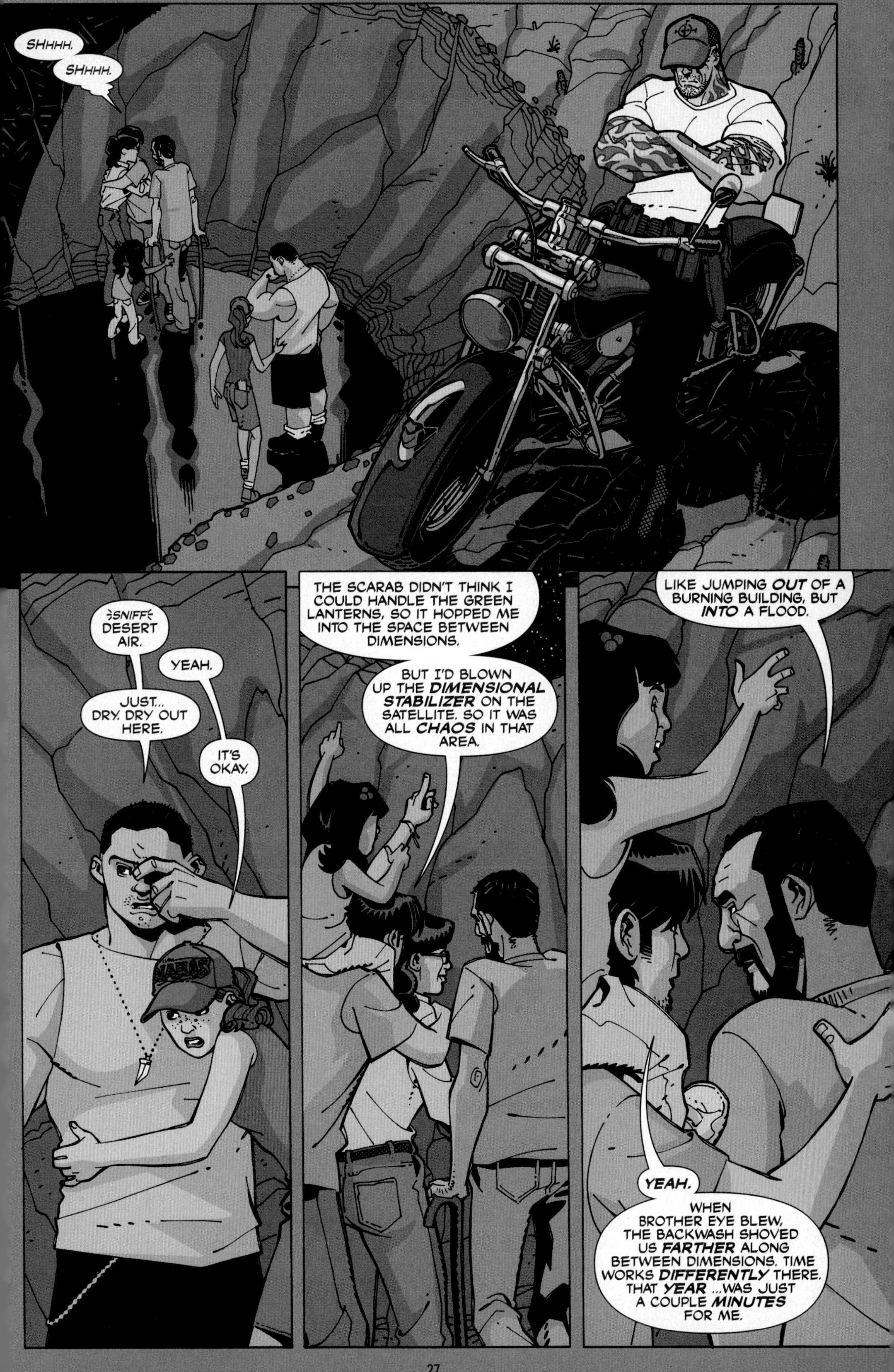
SHHHH.
SHHHH.
SNIFF
DESERT AIR.
YEAH.
JUST... DRY. DRY OUT HERE.
IT'S OKAY.
THE SCARAB DIDN'T THINK I COULD HANDLE THE GREEN LANTERNS, SO IT HOPPED ME INTO THE SPACE BETWEEN DIMENSIONS.
BUT I'D BLOWN UP THE *DIMENSIONAL STABILIZER* ON THE SATELLITE. SO IT WAS ALL *CHAOS* IN THAT AREA.
LIKE JUMPING *OUT* OF A BURNING BUILDING, BUT *INTO* A FLOOD.
YEAH.
WHEN BROTHER EYE BLEW, THE BACKWASH SHOVED US *FARTHER* ALONG BETWEEN DIMENSIONS. TIME WORKS *DIFFERENTLY* THERE. THAT *YEAR* ...WAS JUST A COUPLE *MINUTES* FOR ME.

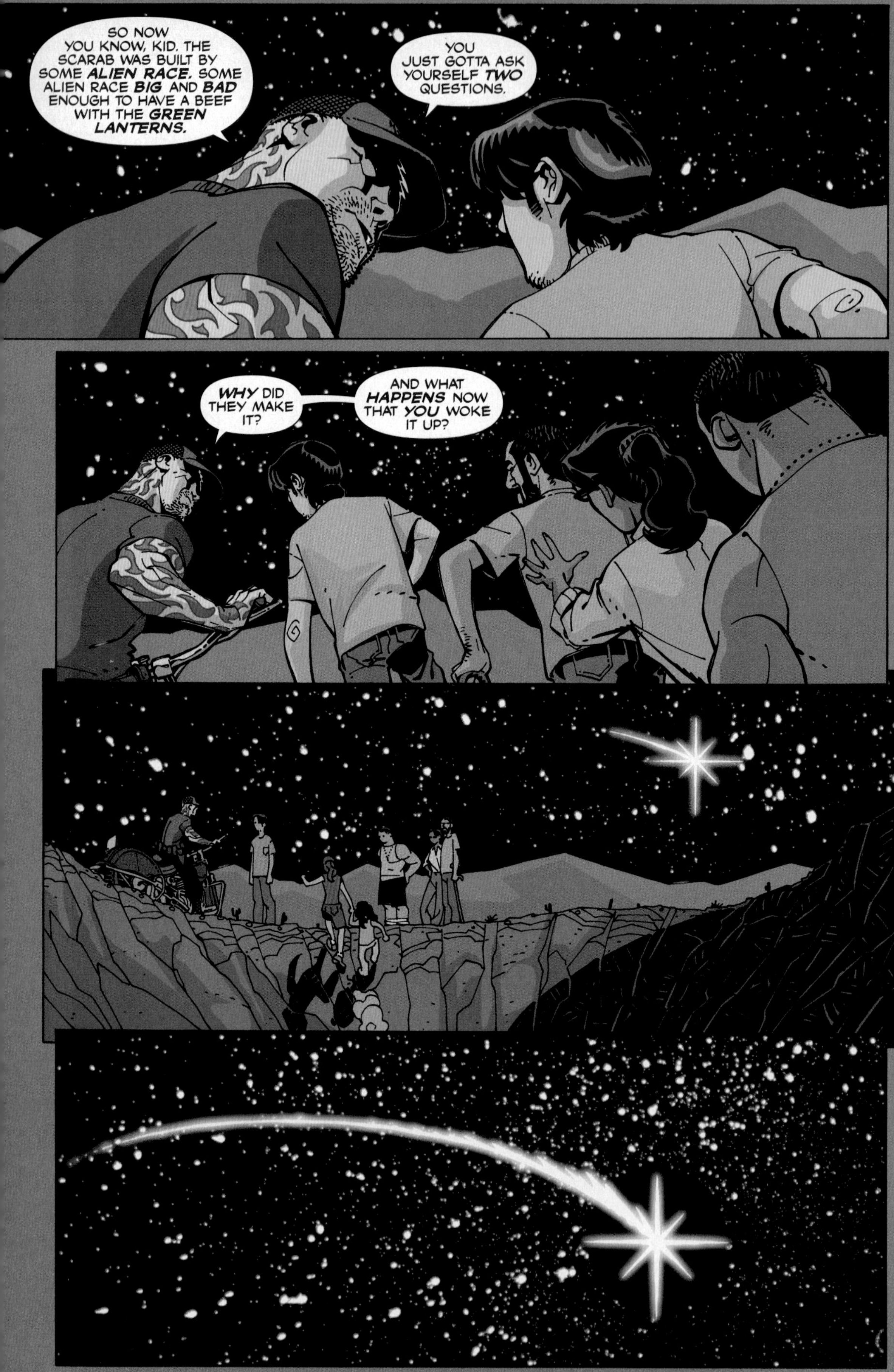
SO NOW YOU KNOW, KID. THE SCARAB WAS BUILT BY SOME ALIEN RACE. SOME ALIEN RACE BIG AND BAD ENOUGH TO HAVE A BEEF WITH THE GREEN LANTERNS.
YOU JUST GOTTA ASK YOURSELF TWO QUESTIONS.
WHY DID THEY MAKE IT?
AND WHAT HAPPENS NOW THAT YOU WOKE IT UP?

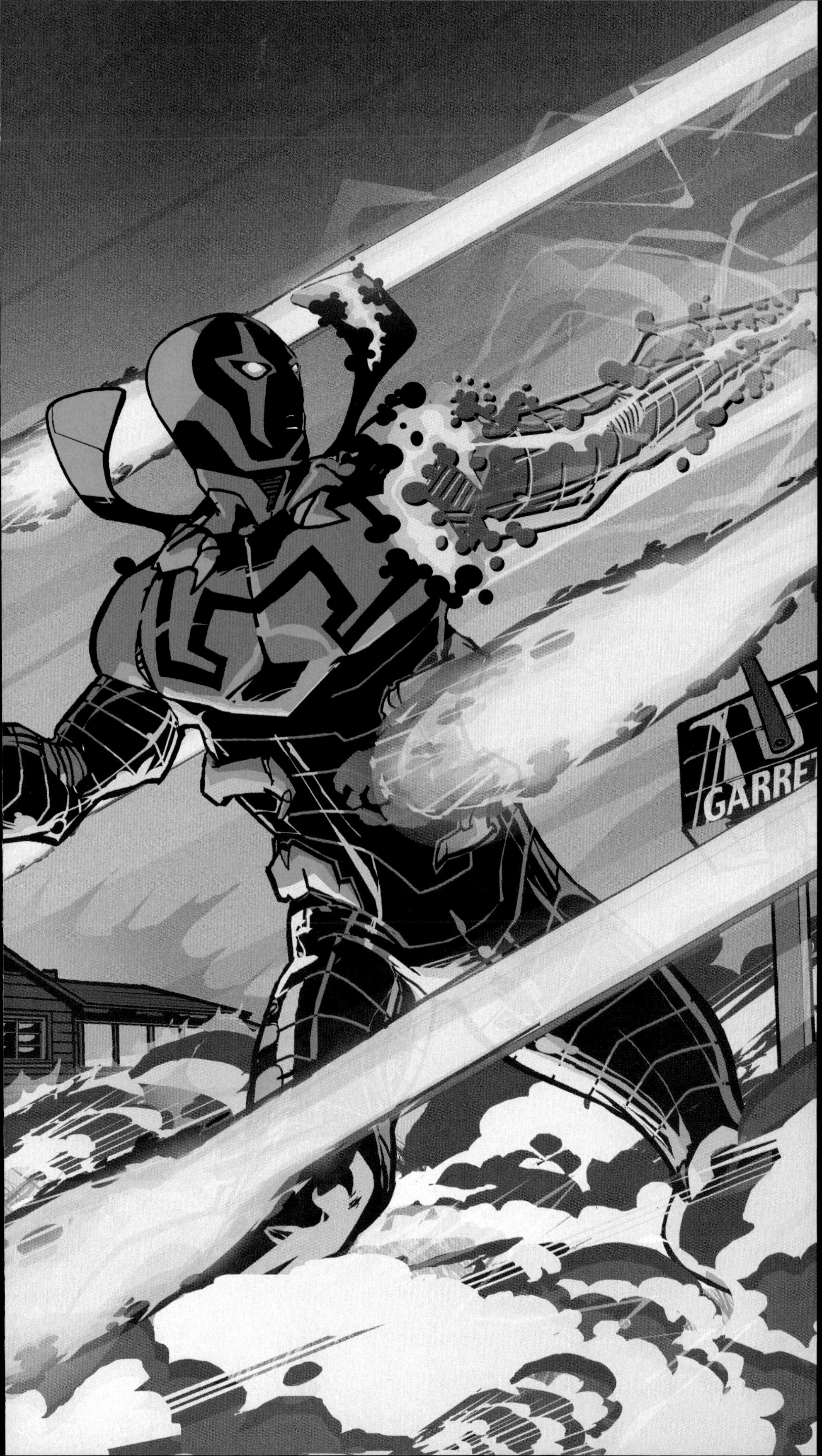

BLUE BEETLE #8 Written by Keith Giffen & John Rogers Cover by Duncan Rouleau Interior art by Cully Hamner and Casey Jones

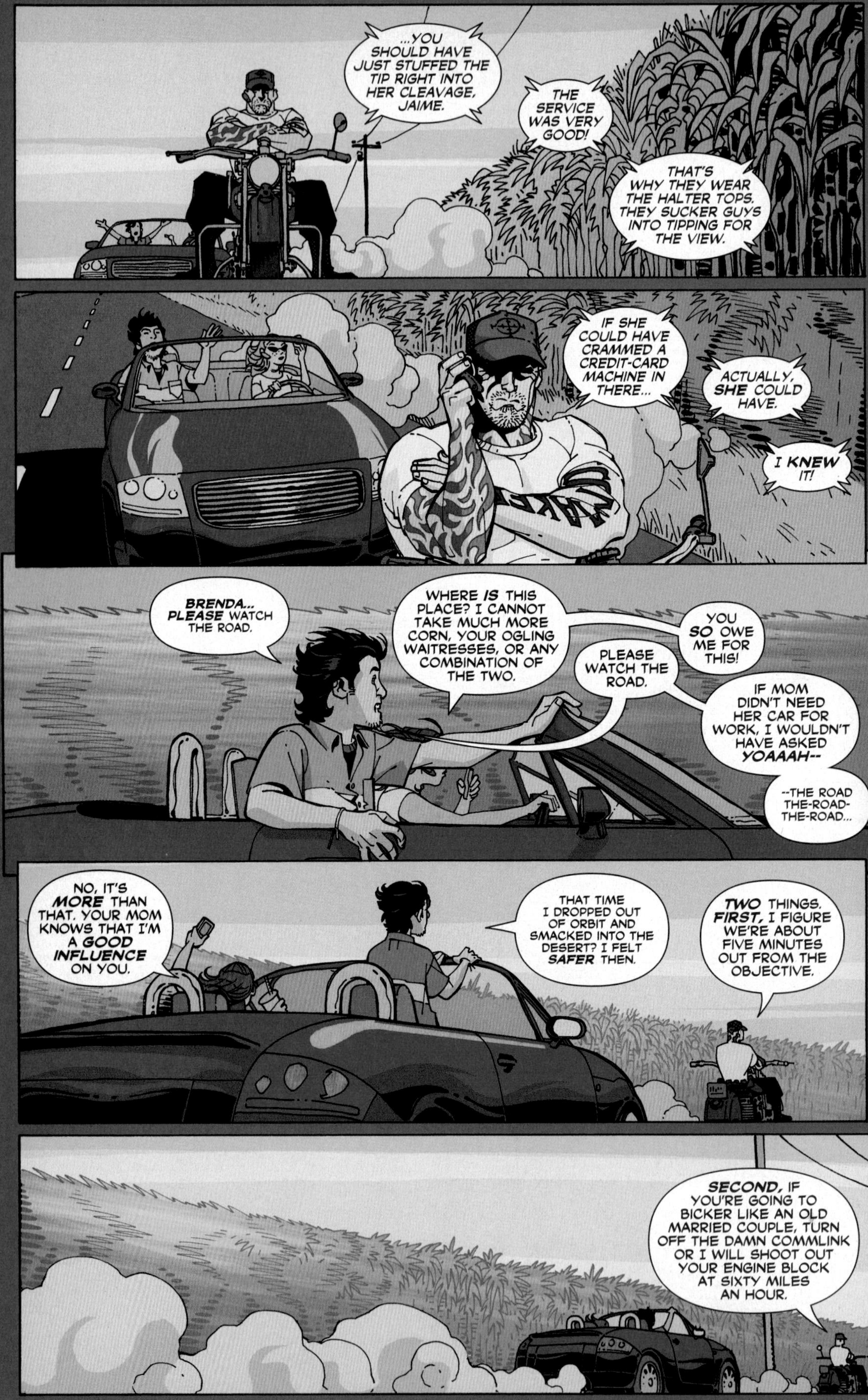
...YOU SHOULD HAVE JUST STUFFED THE TIP RIGHT INTO HER CLEAVAGE, JAIME.
THE SERVICE WAS VERY GOOD!
THAT'S WHY THEY WEAR THE HALTER TOPS. THEY SUCKER GUYS INTO TIPPING FOR THE VIEW.
IF SHE COULD HAVE CRAMMED A CREDIT-CARD MACHINE IN THERE...
ACTUALLY, SHE COULD HAVE.
I KNEW IT!
BRENDA... PLEASE WATCH THE ROAD.
WHERE IS THIS PLACE? I CANNOT TAKE MUCH MORE CORN, YOUR OGLING WAITRESSES, OR ANY COMBINATION OF THE TWO.
YOU SO OWE ME FOR THIS!
PLEASE WATCH THE ROAD.
IF MOM DIDN'T NEED HER CAR FOR WORK, I WOULDN'T HAVE ASKED YOAAAH--
--THE ROAD THE-ROAD-THE-ROAD...
NO, IT'S MORE THAN THAT. YOUR MOM KNOWS THAT I'M A GOOD INFLUENCE ON YOU.
THAT TIME I DROPPED OUT OF ORBIT AND SMACKED INTO THE DESERT? I FELT SAFER THEN.
TWO THINGS. FIRST, I FIGURE WE'RE ABOUT FIVE MINUTES OUT FROM THE OBJECTIVE.
SECOND, IF YOU'RE GOING TO BICKER LIKE AN OLD MARRIED COUPLE, TURN OFF THE DAMN COMMLINK OR I WILL SHOOT OUT YOUR ENGINE BLOCK AT SIXTY MILES AN HOUR.

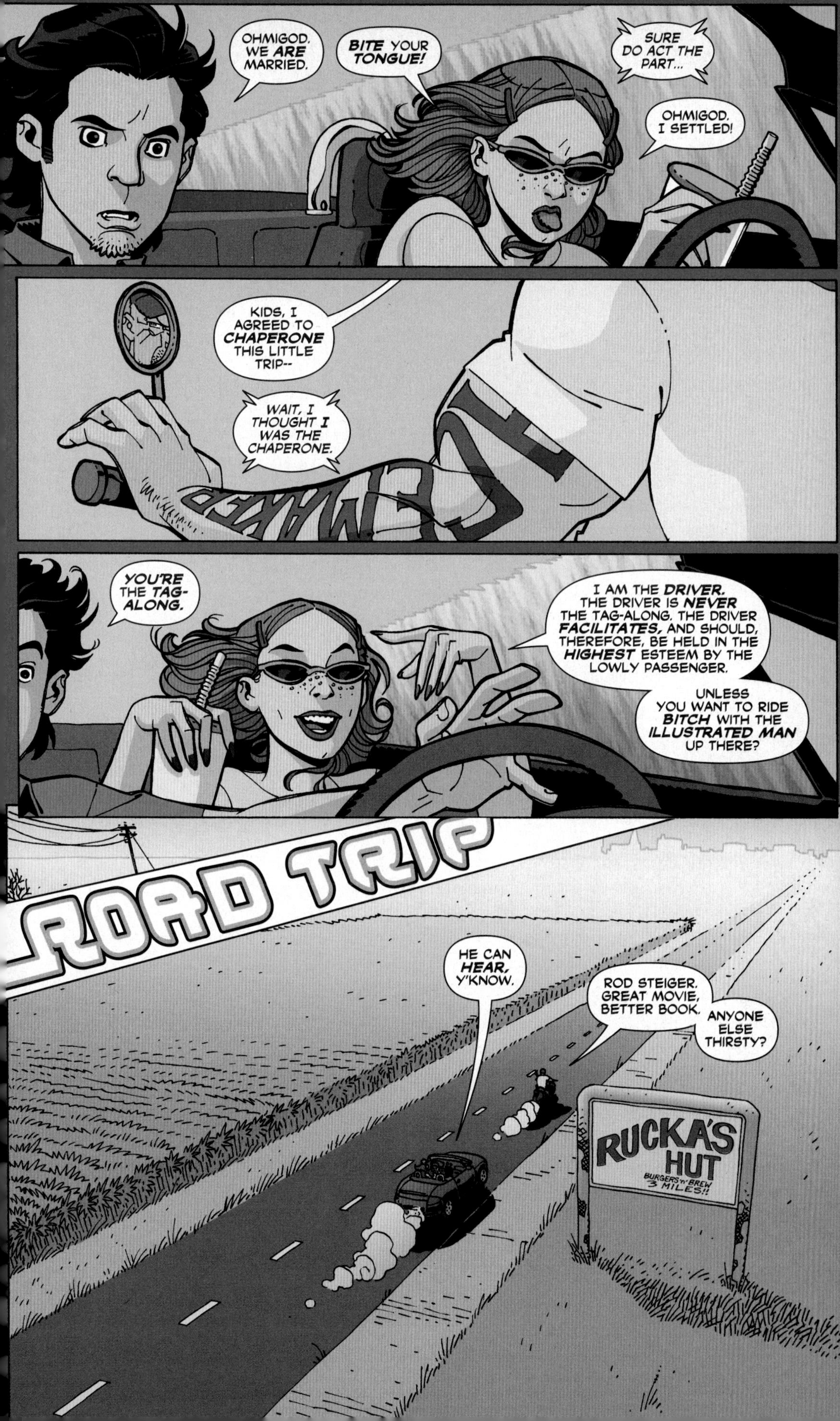
OHMIGOD. WE ARE MARRIED.
BITE YOUR TONGUE!
SURE DO ACT THE PART...
OHMIGOD. I SETTLED!
KIDS, I AGREED TO CHAPERONE THIS LITTLE TRIP--
WAIT, I THOUGHT I WAS THE CHAPERONE.
YOU'RE THE TAG-ALONG.
I AM THE DRIVER. THE DRIVER IS NEVER THE TAG-ALONG. THE DRIVER FACILITATES, AND SHOULD, THEREFORE, BE HELD IN THE HIGHEST ESTEEM BY THE LOWLY PASSENGER.
UNLESS YOU WANT TO RIDE BITCH WITH THE ILLUSTRATED MAN UP THERE?
ROAD TRIP
HE CAN HEAR, Y'KNOW.
ROD STEIGER. GREAT MOVIE, BETTER BOOK.
ANYONE ELSE THIRSTY?
RUCKA'S HUT
BURGERS 'N' BREW 3 MILES!!

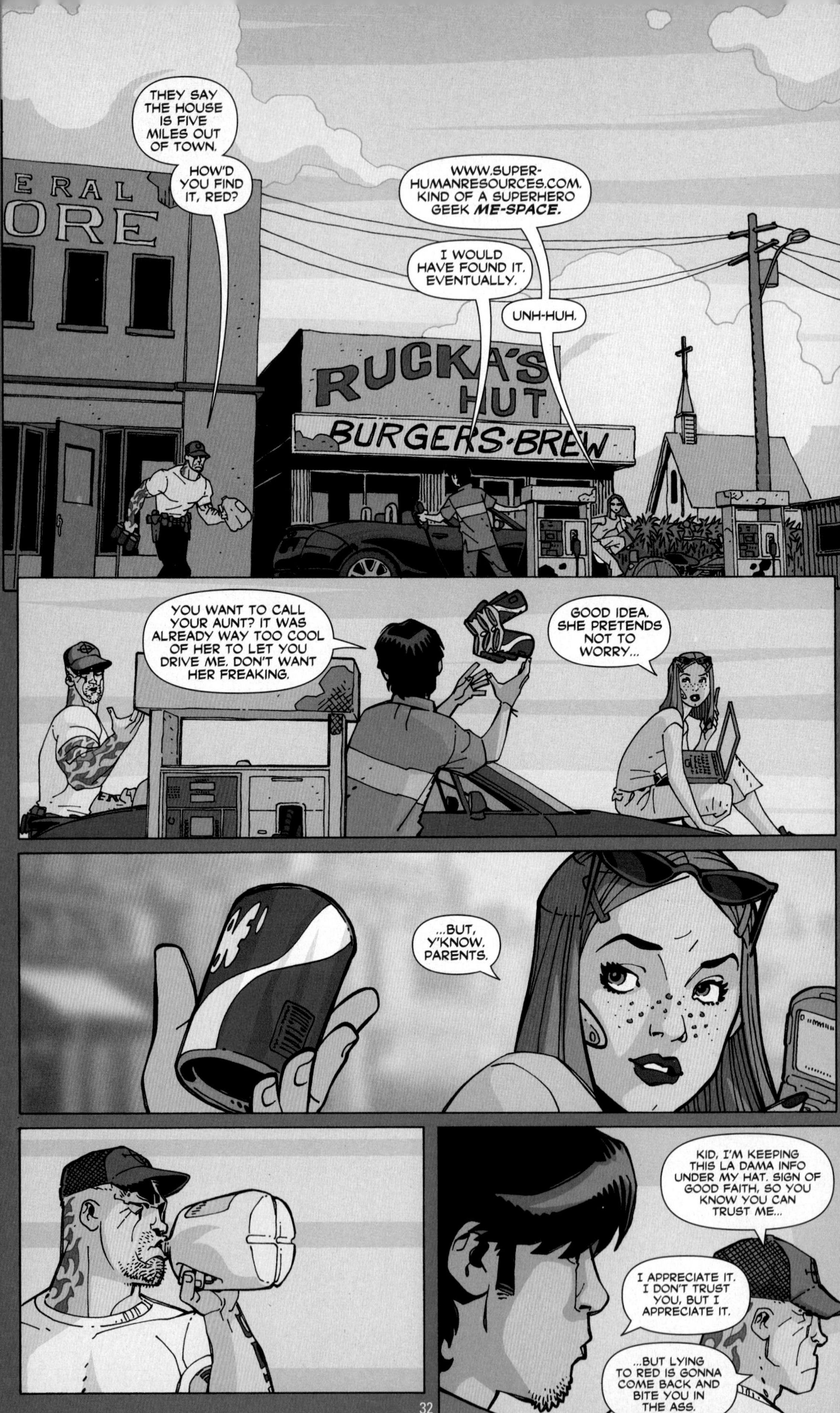
THEY SAY THE HOUSE IS FIVE MILES OUT OF TOWN.
HOW'D YOU FIND IT, RED?
WWW.SUPER-HUMANRESOURCES.COM. KIND OF A SUPERHERO GEEK ME-SPACE.
I WOULD HAVE FOUND IT. EVENTUALLY.
UNH-HUH.
ERAL
ORE
RUCKA'S HUT
BURGERS·BREW
YOU WANT TO CALL YOUR AUNT? IT WAS ALREADY WAY TOO COOL OF HER TO LET YOU DRIVE ME. DON'T WANT HER FREAKING.
GOOD IDEA. SHE PRETENDS NOT TO WORRY...
...BUT, Y'KNOW. PARENTS.
KID, I'M KEEPING THIS LA DAMA INFO UNDER MY HAT. SIGN OF GOOD FAITH, SO YOU KNOW YOU CAN TRUST ME...
I APPRECIATE IT. I DON'T TRUST YOU, BUT I APPRECIATE IT.
...BUT LYING TO RED IS GONNA COME BACK AND BITE YOU IN THE ASS.

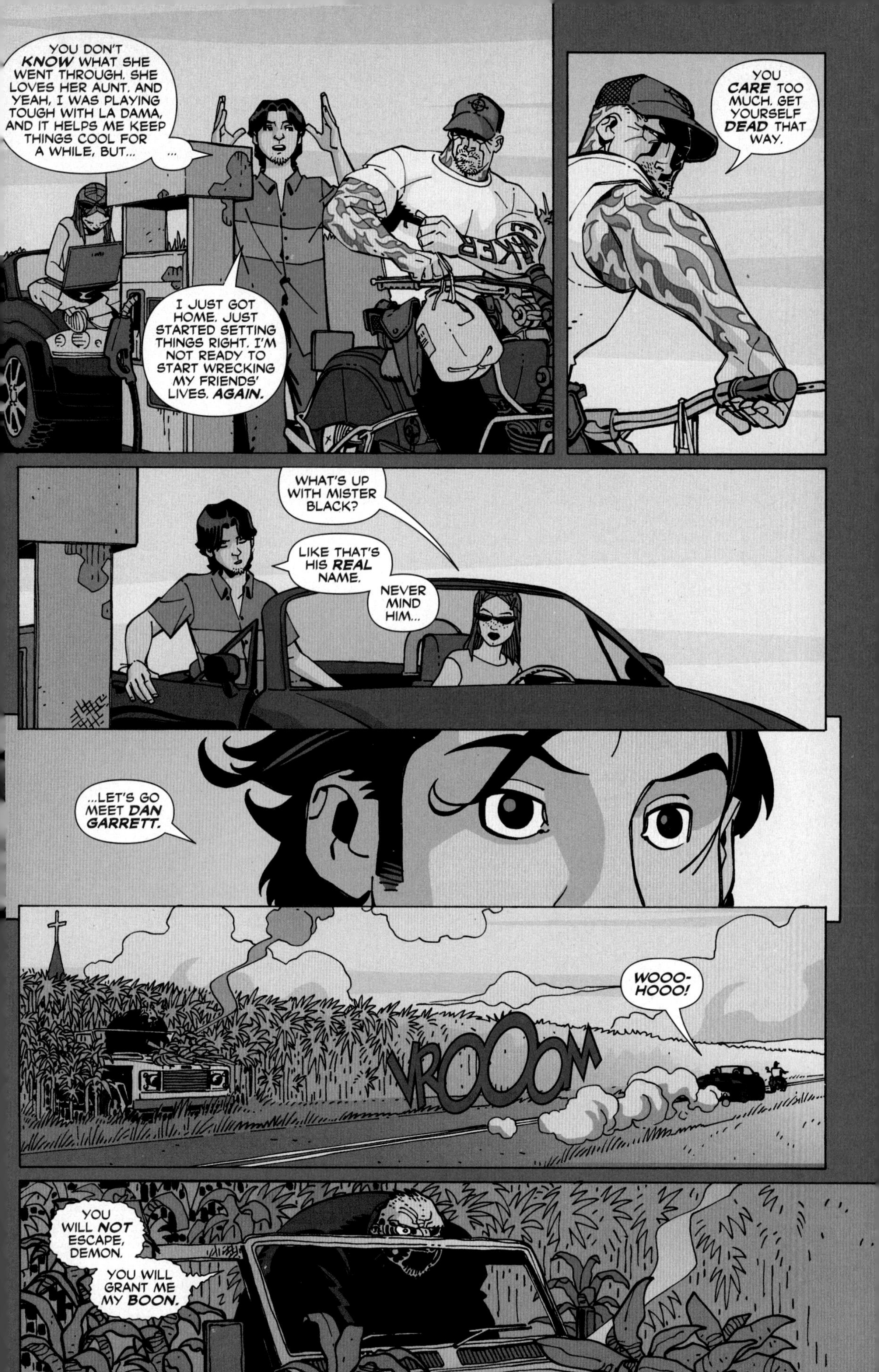

YOU DON'T KNOW WHAT SHE WENT THROUGH. SHE LOVES HER AUNT. AND YEAH, I WAS PLAYING TOUGH WITH LA DAMA, AND IT HELPS ME KEEP THINGS COOL FOR A WHILE, BUT...
...
I JUST GOT HOME. JUST STARTED SETTING THINGS RIGHT. I'M NOT READY TO START WRECKING MY FRIENDS' LIVES. AGAIN.
YOU CARE TOO MUCH. GET YOURSELF DEAD THAT WAY.
WHAT'S UP WITH MISTER BLACK?
LIKE THAT'S HIS REAL NAME.
NEVER MIND HIM...
...LET'S GO MEET DAN GARRETT.
WOOO-HOOO!
VROOOOM
YOU WILL NOT ESCAPE, DEMON.
YOU WILL GRANT ME MY BOON.

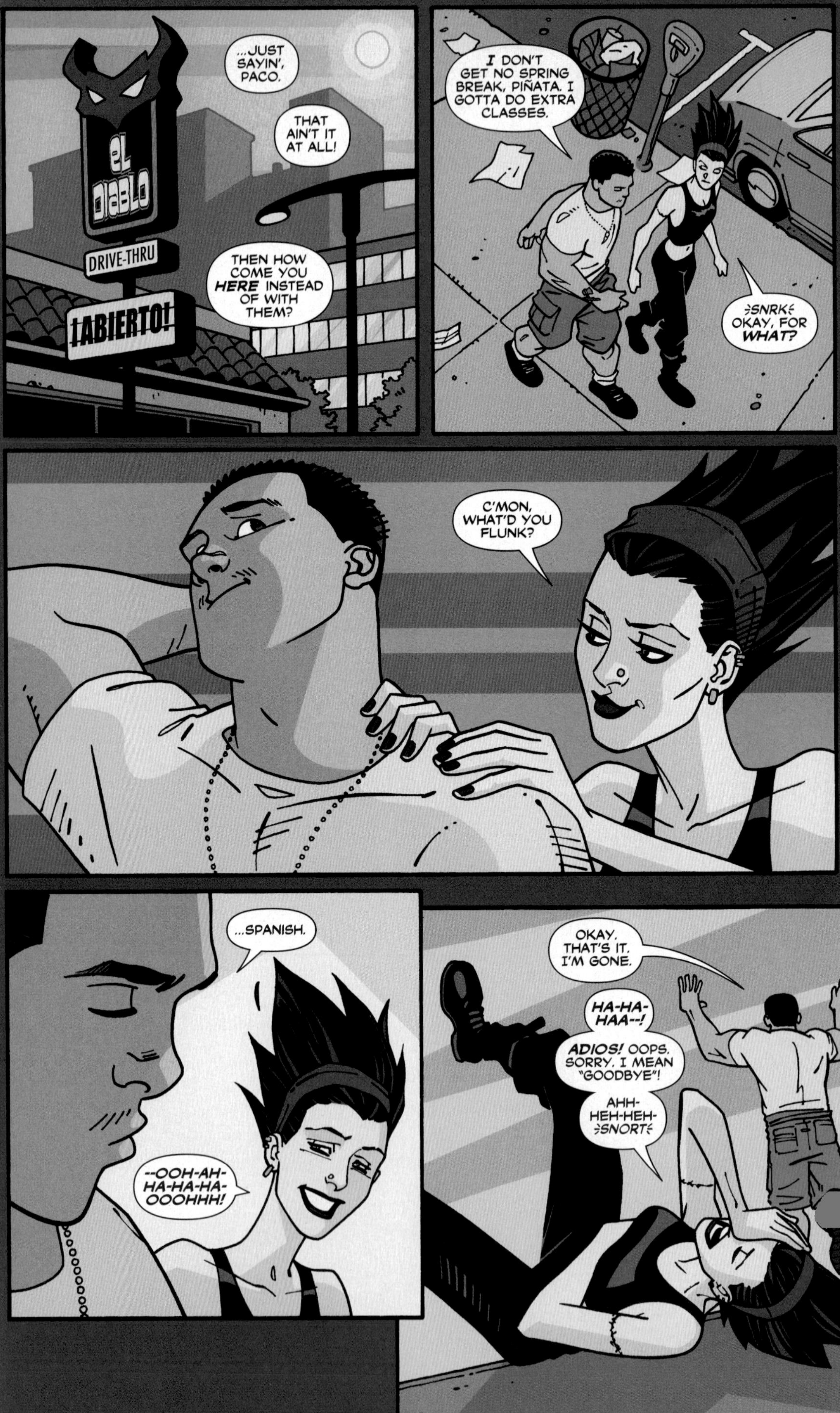

EL DIABLO
DRIVE-THRU
¡ABIERTO!
...JUST SAYIN', PACO.
THAT AIN'T IT AT ALL!
THEN HOW COME YOU HERE INSTEAD OF WITH THEM?
I DON'T GET NO SPRING BREAK, PIÑATA. I GOTTA DO EXTRA CLASSES.
SNRK OKAY, FOR WHAT?
C'MON, WHAT'D YOU FLUNK?
...SPANISH.
--OOH-AH-HA-HA-HA-OOOHHH!
OKAY. THAT'S IT. I'M GONE.
HA-HA-HAA--!
ADIOS! OOPS. SORRY. I MEAN "GOODBYE"!
AHH-HEH-HEH-SNORT

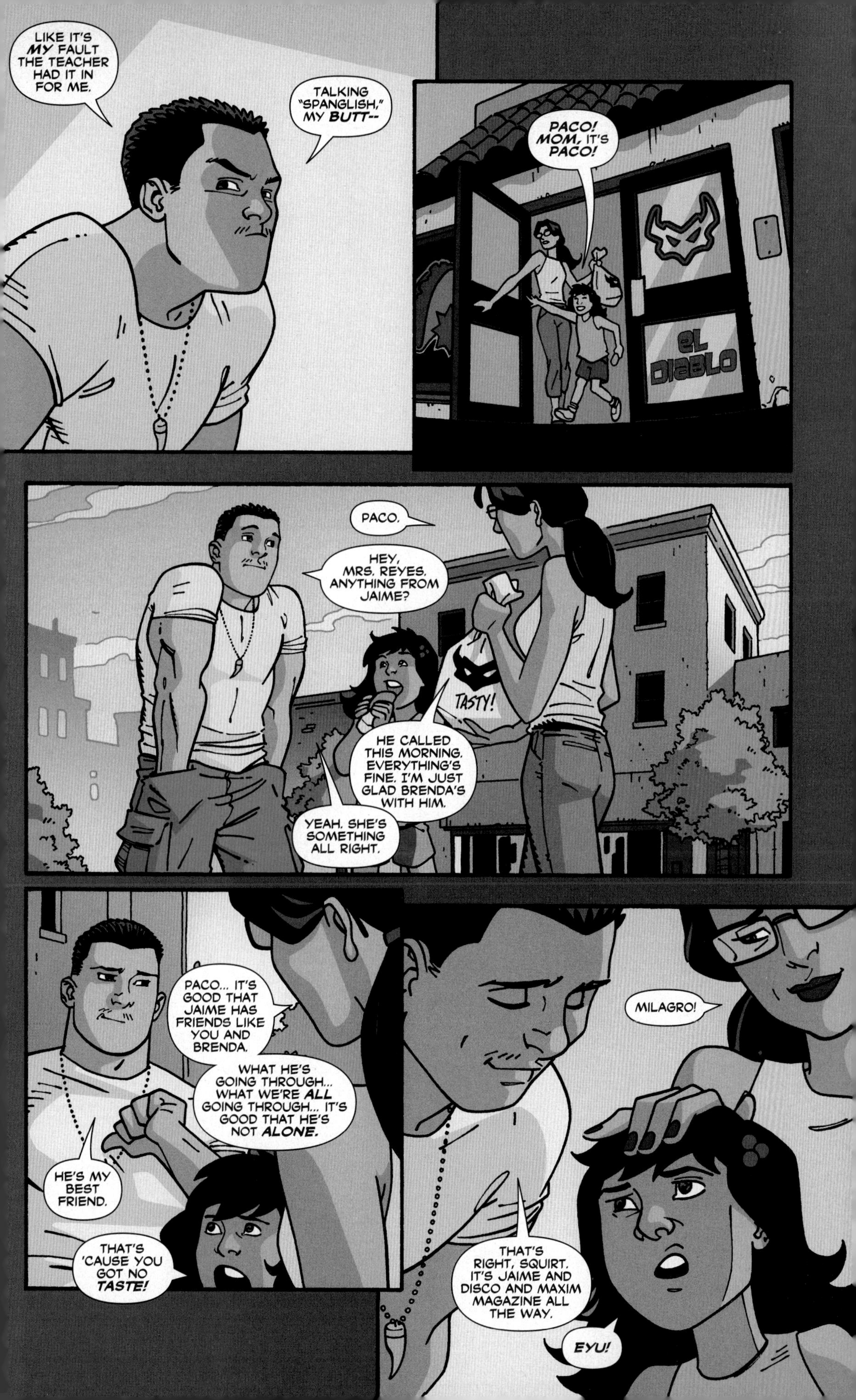
LIKE IT'S MY FAULT THE TEACHER HAD IT IN FOR ME.
TALKING "SPANGLISH," MY BUTT--
PACO! MOM, IT'S PACO!
EL DIABLO
PACO.
HEY, MRS. REYES. ANYTHING FROM JAIME?
TASTY!
HE CALLED THIS MORNING. EVERYTHING'S FINE. I'M JUST GLAD BRENDA'S WITH HIM.
YEAH. SHE'S SOMETHING ALL RIGHT.
PACO... IT'S GOOD THAT JAIME HAS FRIENDS LIKE YOU AND BRENDA.
WHAT HE'S GOING THROUGH... WHAT WE'RE ALL GOING THROUGH... IT'S GOOD THAT HE'S NOT ALONE.
HE'S MY BEST FRIEND.
THAT'S 'CAUSE YOU GOT NO TASTE!
MILAGRO!
THAT'S RIGHT, SQUIRT. IT'S JAIME AND DISCO AND MAXIM MAGAZINE ALL THE WAY.
EYU!

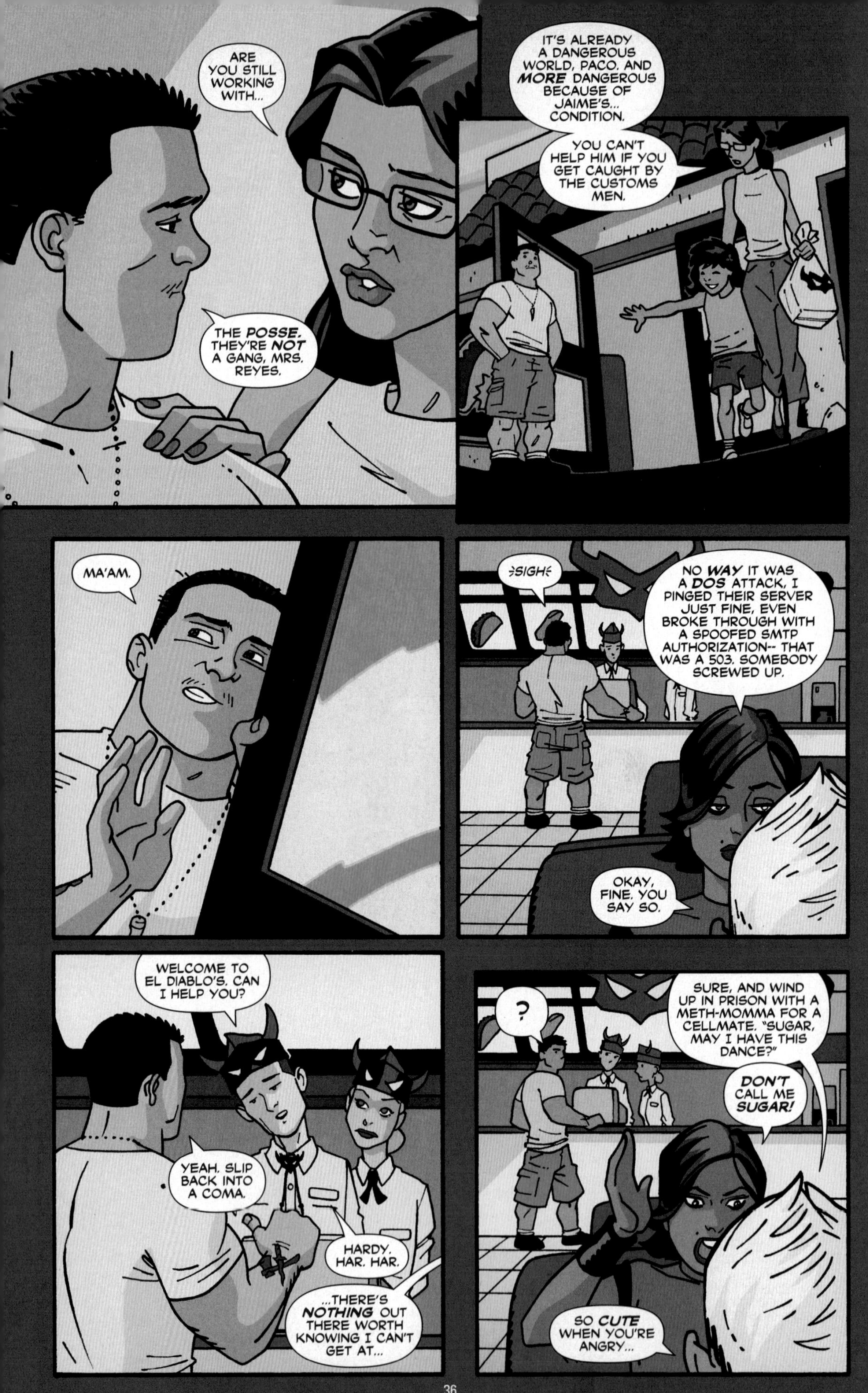
ARE YOU STILL WORKING WITH...
THE POSSE. THEY'RE NOT A GANG, MRS. REYES.
IT'S ALREADY A DANGEROUS WORLD, PACO. AND MORE DANGEROUS BECAUSE OF JAIME'S... CONDITION.
YOU CAN'T HELP HIM IF YOU GET CAUGHT BY THE CUSTOMS MEN.
MA'AM.
SIGH
NO WAY IT WAS A DOS ATTACK, I PINGED THEIR SERVER JUST FINE, EVEN BROKE THROUGH WITH A SPOOFED SMTP AUTHORIZATION-- THAT WAS A 503. SOMEBODY SCREWED UP.
OKAY, FINE. YOU SAY SO.
WELCOME TO EL DIABLO'S. CAN I HELP YOU?
YEAH. SLIP BACK INTO A COMA.
HARDY. HAR. HAR.
...THERE'S NOTHING OUT THERE WORTH KNOWING I CAN'T GET AT...
?
SURE, AND WIND UP IN PRISON WITH A METH-MOMMA FOR A CELLMATE. "SUGAR, MAY I HAVE THIS DANCE?"
DON'T CALL ME SUGAR!
SO CUTE WHEN YOU'RE ANGRY...

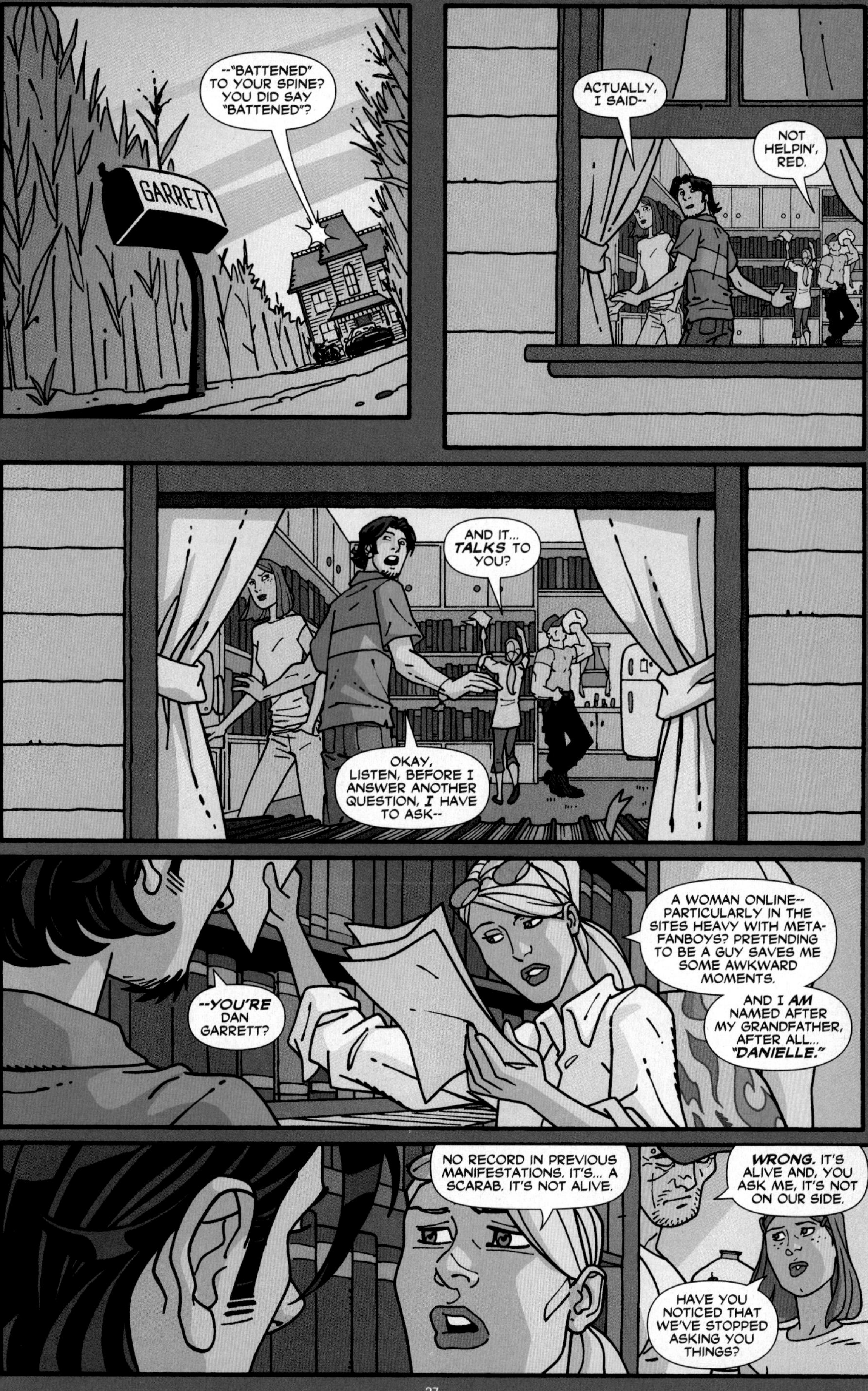
--"BATTENED" TO YOUR SPINE? YOU DID SAY "BATTENED"?
GARRETT
ACTUALLY, I SAID--
NOT HELPIN', RED.
AND IT... *TALKS* TO YOU?
OKAY, LISTEN, BEFORE I ANSWER ANOTHER QUESTION, *I* HAVE TO ASK--
--YOU'RE DAN GARRETT?
A WOMAN ONLINE-- PARTICULARLY IN THE SITES HEAVY WITH META-FANBOYS? PRETENDING TO BE A GUY SAVES ME SOME AWKWARD MOMENTS.
AND I *AM* NAMED AFTER MY GRANDFATHER, AFTER ALL... *"DANIELLE."*
NO RECORD IN PREVIOUS MANIFESTATIONS. IT'S... A SCARAB. IT'S NOT ALIVE.
WRONG. IT'S ALIVE AND, YOU ASK ME, IT'S NOT ON OUR SIDE.
HAVE YOU NOTICED THAT WE'VE STOPPED ASKING YOU THINGS?

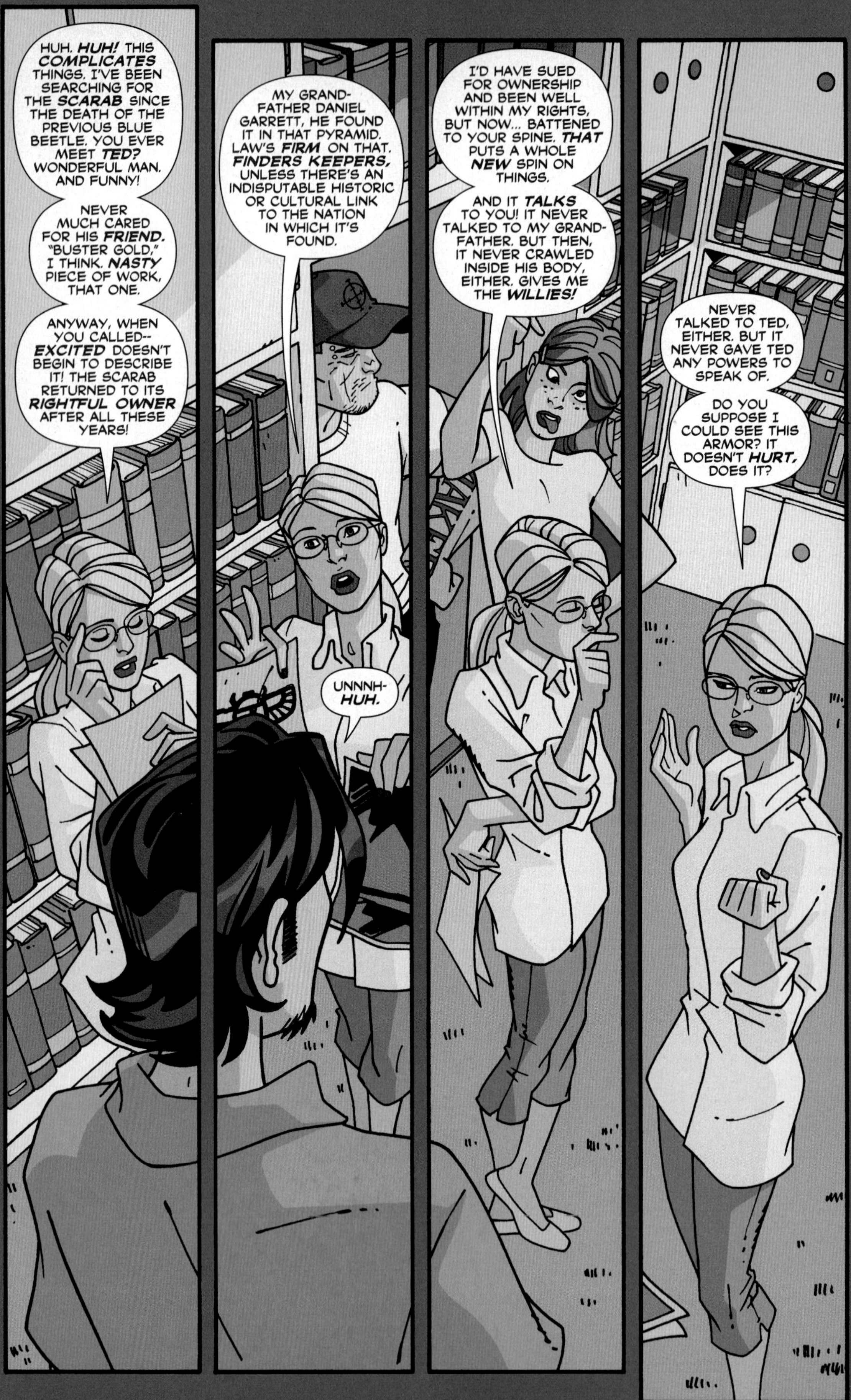
HUH. HUH! THIS COMPLICATES THINGS. I'VE BEEN SEARCHING FOR THE SCARAB SINCE THE DEATH OF THE PREVIOUS BLUE BEETLE. YOU EVER MEET TED? WONDERFUL MAN. AND FUNNY!
NEVER MUCH CARED FOR HIS FRIEND. "BUSTER GOLD," I THINK. NASTY PIECE OF WORK, THAT ONE.
ANYWAY, WHEN YOU CALLED-- EXCITED DOESN'T BEGIN TO DESCRIBE IT! THE SCARAB RETURNED TO ITS RIGHTFUL OWNER AFTER ALL THESE YEARS!
MY GRAND-FATHER DANIEL GARRETT, HE FOUND IT IN THAT PYRAMID. LAW'S FIRM ON THAT. FINDERS KEEPERS, UNLESS THERE'S AN INDISPUTABLE HISTORIC OR CULTURAL LINK TO THE NATION IN WHICH IT'S FOUND.
UNNNH-HUH.
I'D HAVE SUED FOR OWNERSHIP AND BEEN WELL WITHIN MY RIGHTS, BUT NOW... BATTENED TO YOUR SPINE, THAT PUTS A WHOLE NEW SPIN ON THINGS.
AND IT TALKS TO YOU! IT NEVER TALKED TO MY GRAND-FATHER. BUT THEN, IT NEVER CRAWLED INSIDE HIS BODY, EITHER. GIVES ME THE WILLIES!
NEVER TALKED TO TED, EITHER. BUT IT NEVER GAVE TED ANY POWERS TO SPEAK OF.
DO YOU SUPPOSE I COULD SEE THIS ARMOR? IT DOESN'T HURT, DOES IT?

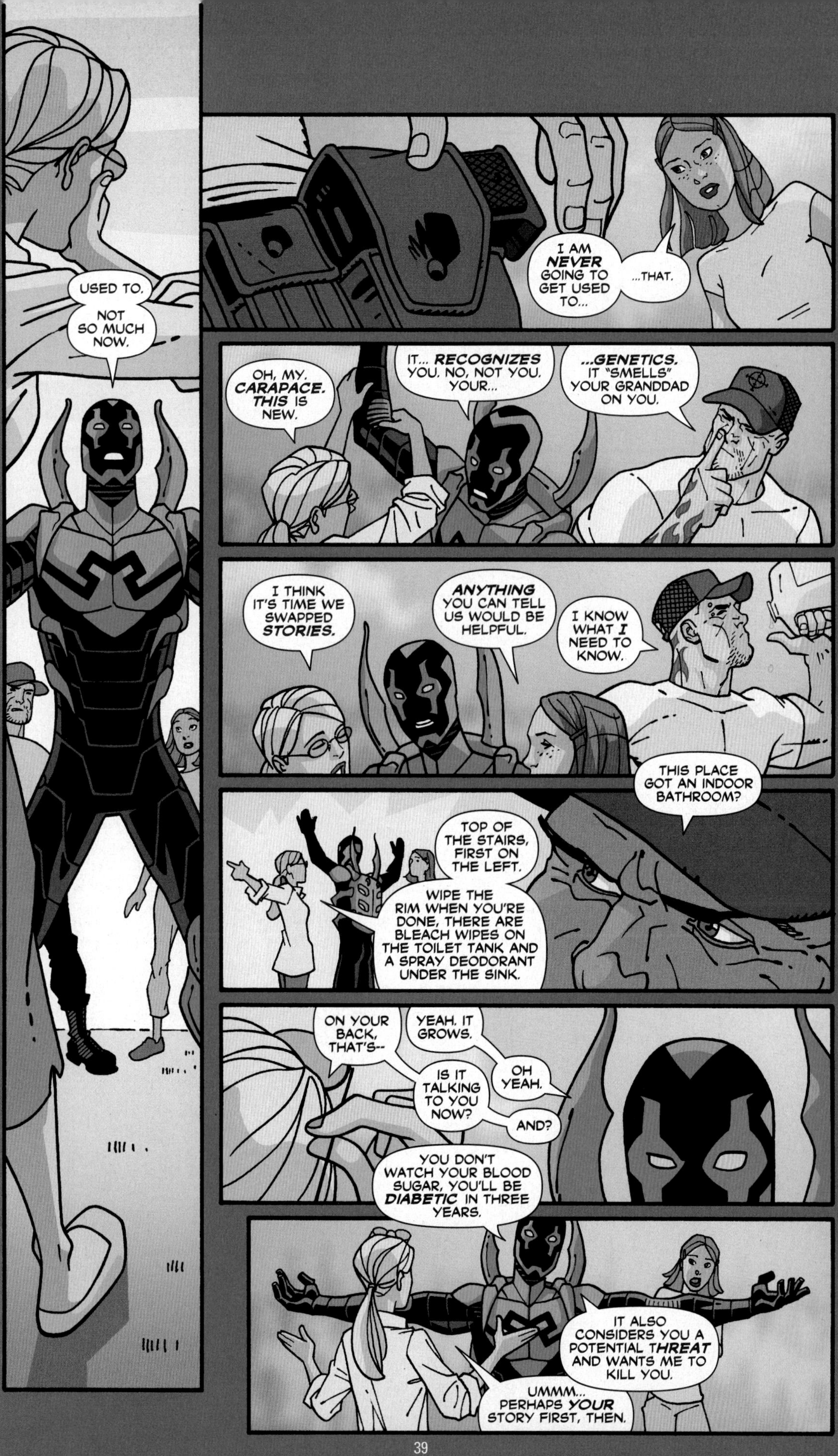
USED TO. NOT SO MUCH NOW.
I AM NEVER GOING TO GET USED TO...
...THAT.
OH, MY. CARAPACE. THIS IS NEW.
IT... RECOGNIZES YOU. NO, NOT YOU. YOUR...
...GENETICS. IT "SMELLS" YOUR GRANDDAD ON YOU.
I THINK IT'S TIME WE SWAPPED STORIES.
ANYTHING YOU CAN TELL US WOULD BE HELPFUL.
I KNOW WHAT I NEED TO KNOW.
THIS PLACE GOT AN INDOOR BATHROOM?
TOP OF THE STAIRS, FIRST ON THE LEFT.
WIPE THE RIM WHEN YOU'RE DONE. THERE ARE BLEACH WIPES ON THE TOILET TANK AND A SPRAY DEODORANT UNDER THE SINK.
ON YOUR BACK, THAT'S--
YEAH. IT GROWS.
IS IT TALKING TO YOU NOW?
OH YEAH.
AND?
YOU DON'T WATCH YOUR BLOOD SUGAR, YOU'LL BE DIABETIC IN THREE YEARS.
IT ALSO CONSIDERS YOU A POTENTIAL THREAT AND WANTS ME TO KILL YOU.
UMMM... PERHAPS YOUR STORY FIRST, THEN.

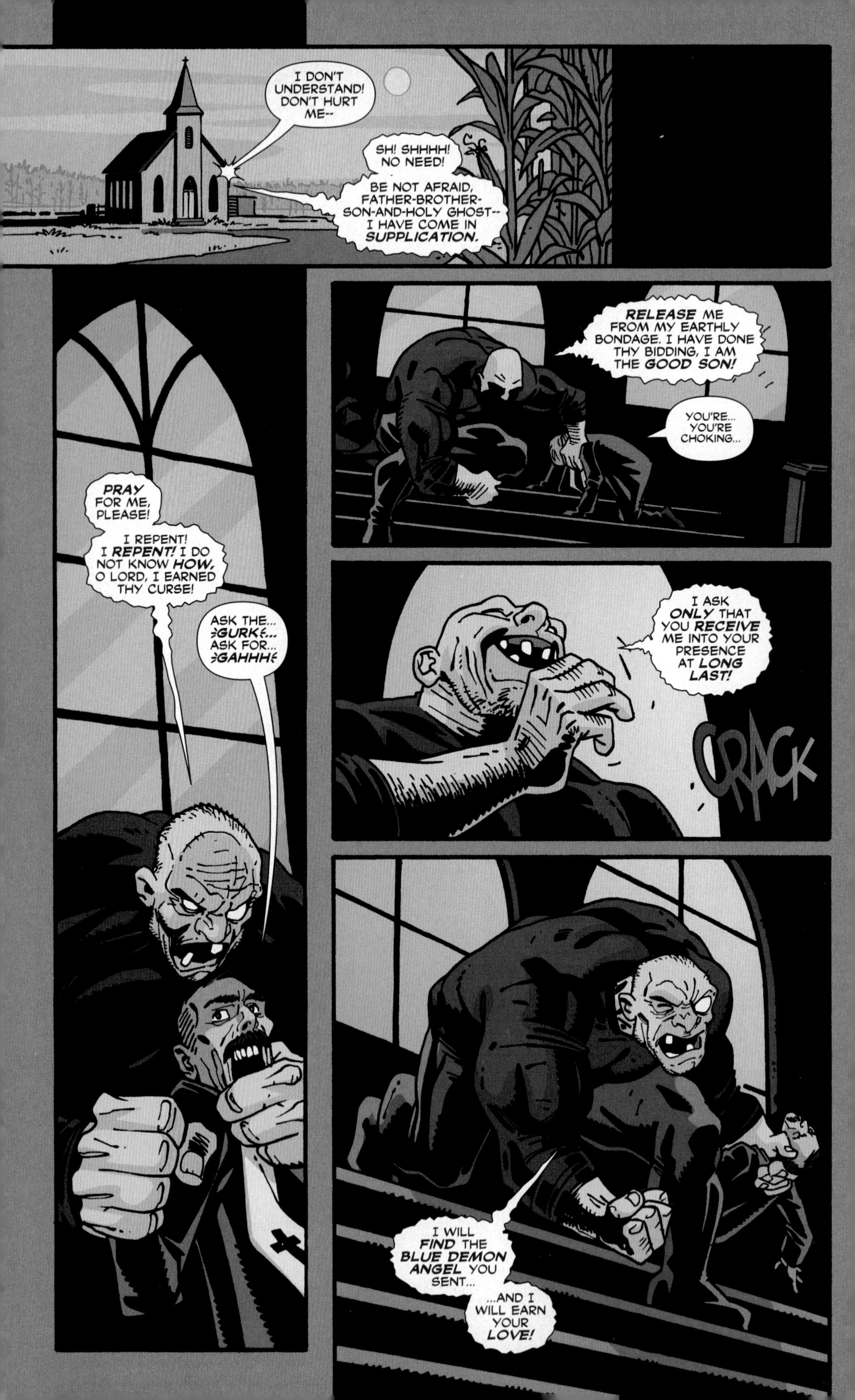

I DON'T UNDERSTAND! DON'T HURT ME--
SH! SHHHH! NO NEED!
BE NOT AFRAID, FATHER-BROTHER-SON-AND-HOLY GHOST--I HAVE COME IN SUPPLICATION.
PRAY FOR ME, PLEASE!
I REPENT! I REPENT! I DO NOT KNOW HOW, O LORD, I EARNED THY CURSE!
ASK THE... GURK... ASK FOR... GAHHH
RELEASE ME FROM MY EARTHLY BONDAGE. I HAVE DONE THY BIDDING, I AM THE GOOD SON!
YOU'RE... YOU'RE CHOKING...
I ASK ONLY THAT YOU RECEIVE ME INTO YOUR PRESENCE AT LONG LAST!
CRACK
I WILL FIND THE BLUE DEMON ANGEL YOU SENT...
...AND I WILL EARN YOUR LOVE!

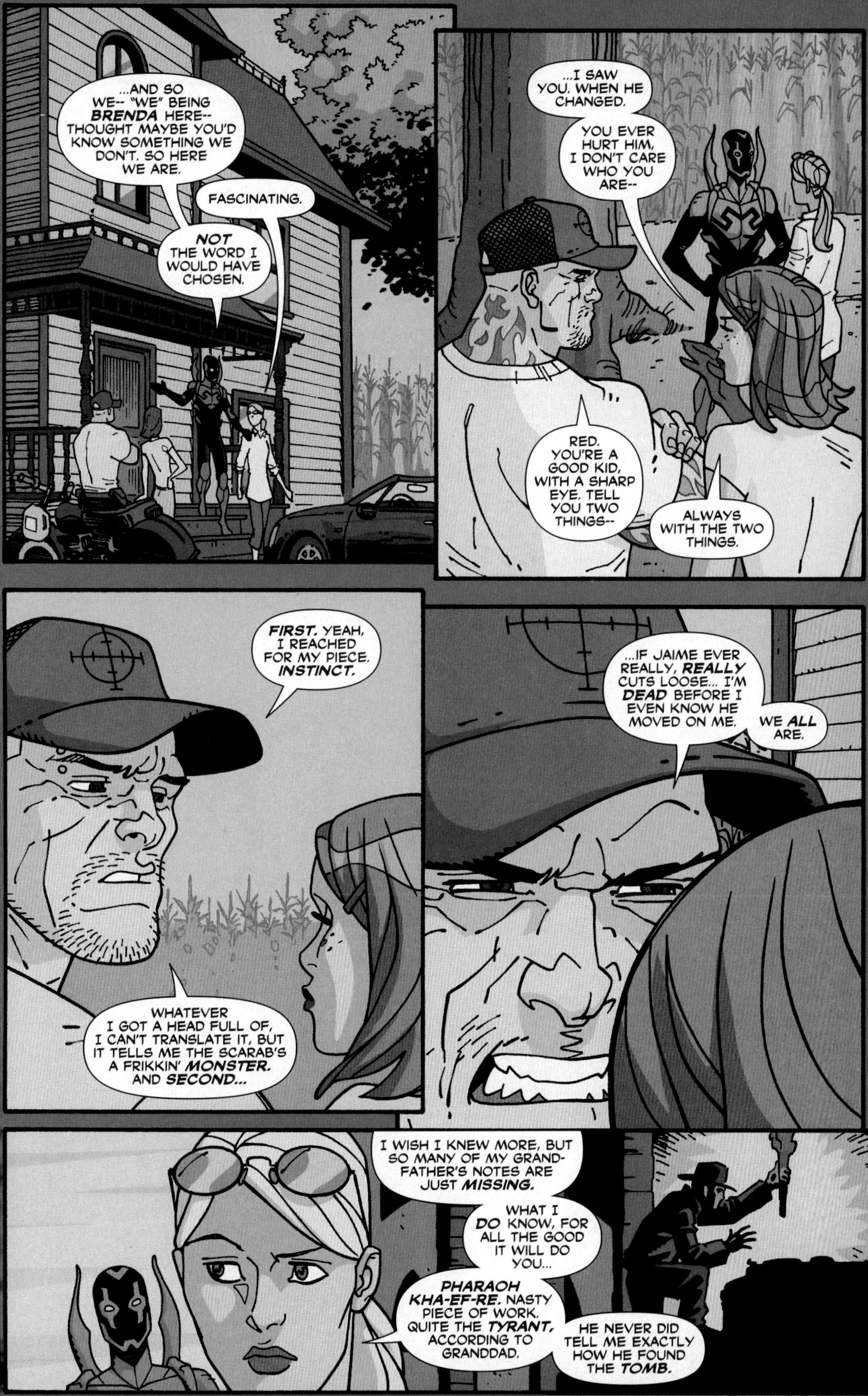
...AND SO WE-- "WE" BEING BRENDA HERE-- THOUGHT MAYBE YOU'D KNOW SOMETHING WE DON'T. SO HERE WE ARE.
FASCINATING.
NOT THE WORD I WOULD HAVE CHOSEN.
...I SAW YOU, WHEN HE CHANGED.
YOU EVER HURT HIM, I DON'T CARE WHO YOU ARE--
RED. YOU'RE A GOOD KID, WITH A SHARP EYE. TELL YOU TWO THINGS--
ALWAYS WITH THE TWO THINGS.
FIRST. YEAH, I REACHED FOR MY PIECE. INSTINCT.
WHATEVER I GOT A HEAD FULL OF, I CAN'T TRANSLATE IT, BUT IT TELLS ME THE SCARAB'S A FRIKKIN' MONSTER. AND SECOND...
...IF JAIME EVER REALLY, REALLY CUTS LOOSE... I'M DEAD BEFORE I EVEN KNOW HE MOVED ON ME.
WE ALL ARE.
I WISH I KNEW MORE, BUT SO MANY OF MY GRAND-FATHER'S NOTES ARE JUST MISSING.
WHAT I DO KNOW, FOR ALL THE GOOD IT WILL DO YOU...
PHARAOH KHA-EF-RE. NASTY PIECE OF WORK. QUITE THE TYRANT, ACCORDING TO GRANDDAD.
HE NEVER DID TELL ME EXACTLY HOW HE FOUND THE TOMB.

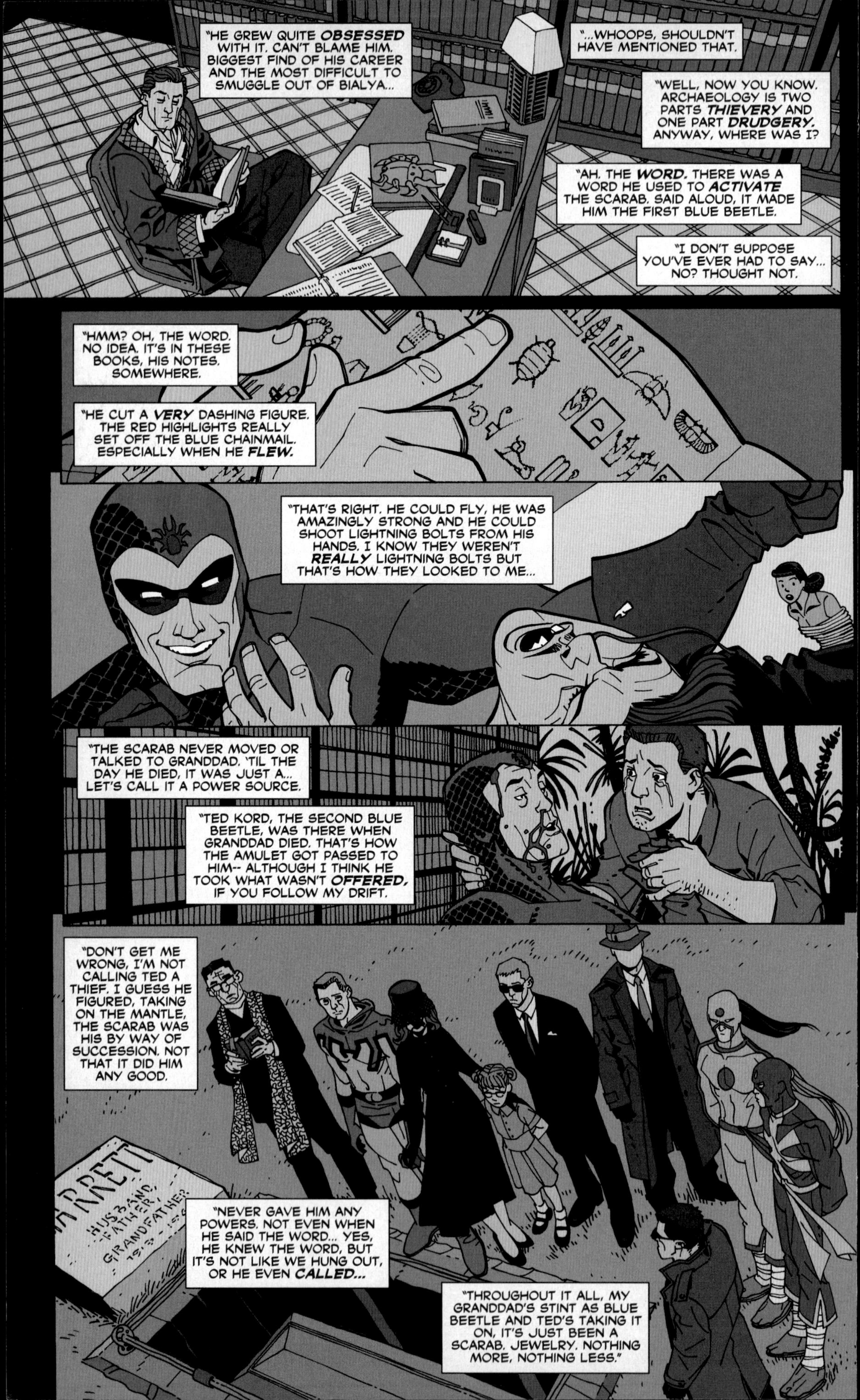
"HE GREW QUITE OBSESSED WITH IT. CAN'T BLAME HIM. BIGGEST FIND OF HIS CAREER AND THE MOST DIFFICULT TO SMUGGLE OUT OF BIALYA...
"...WHOOPS, SHOULDN'T HAVE MENTIONED THAT.
"WELL, NOW YOU KNOW. ARCHAEOLOGY IS TWO PARTS THIEVERY AND ONE PART DRUDGERY. ANYWAY, WHERE WAS I?
"AH. THE WORD. THERE WAS A WORD HE USED TO ACTIVATE THE SCARAB. SAID ALOUD, IT MADE HIM THE FIRST BLUE BEETLE.
"I DON'T SUPPOSE YOU'VE EVER HAD TO SAY... NO? THOUGHT NOT.
"HMM? OH, THE WORD. NO IDEA. IT'S IN THESE BOOKS, HIS NOTES. SOMEWHERE.
"HE CUT A VERY DASHING FIGURE. THE RED HIGHLIGHTS REALLY SET OFF THE BLUE CHAINMAIL. ESPECIALLY WHEN HE FLEW.
"THAT'S RIGHT. HE COULD FLY, HE WAS AMAZINGLY STRONG AND HE COULD SHOOT LIGHTNING BOLTS FROM HIS HANDS. I KNOW THEY WEREN'T REALLY LIGHTNING BOLTS BUT THAT'S HOW THEY LOOKED TO ME...
"THE SCARAB NEVER MOVED OR TALKED TO GRANDDAD. 'TIL THE DAY HE DIED, IT WAS JUST A... LET'S CALL IT A POWER SOURCE.
"TED KORD, THE SECOND BLUE BEETLE, WAS THERE WHEN GRANDDAD DIED. THAT'S HOW THE AMULET GOT PASSED TO HIM-- ALTHOUGH I THINK HE TOOK WHAT WASN'T OFFERED, IF YOU FOLLOW MY DRIFT.
"DON'T GET ME WRONG, I'M NOT CALLING TED A THIEF. I GUESS HE FIGURED, TAKING ON THE MANTLE, THE SCARAB WAS HIS BY WAY OF SUCCESSION. NOT THAT IT DID HIM ANY GOOD.
HUSBAND FATHER GRANDFATHER
"NEVER GAVE HIM ANY POWERS. NOT EVEN WHEN HE SAID THE WORD... YES, HE KNEW THE WORD, BUT IT'S NOT LIKE WE HUNG OUT, OR HE EVEN CALLED...
"THROUGHOUT IT ALL, MY GRANDDAD'S STINT AS BLUE BEETLE AND TED'S TAKING IT ON, IT'S JUST BEEN A SCARAB. JEWELRY. NOTHING MORE, NOTHING LESS."

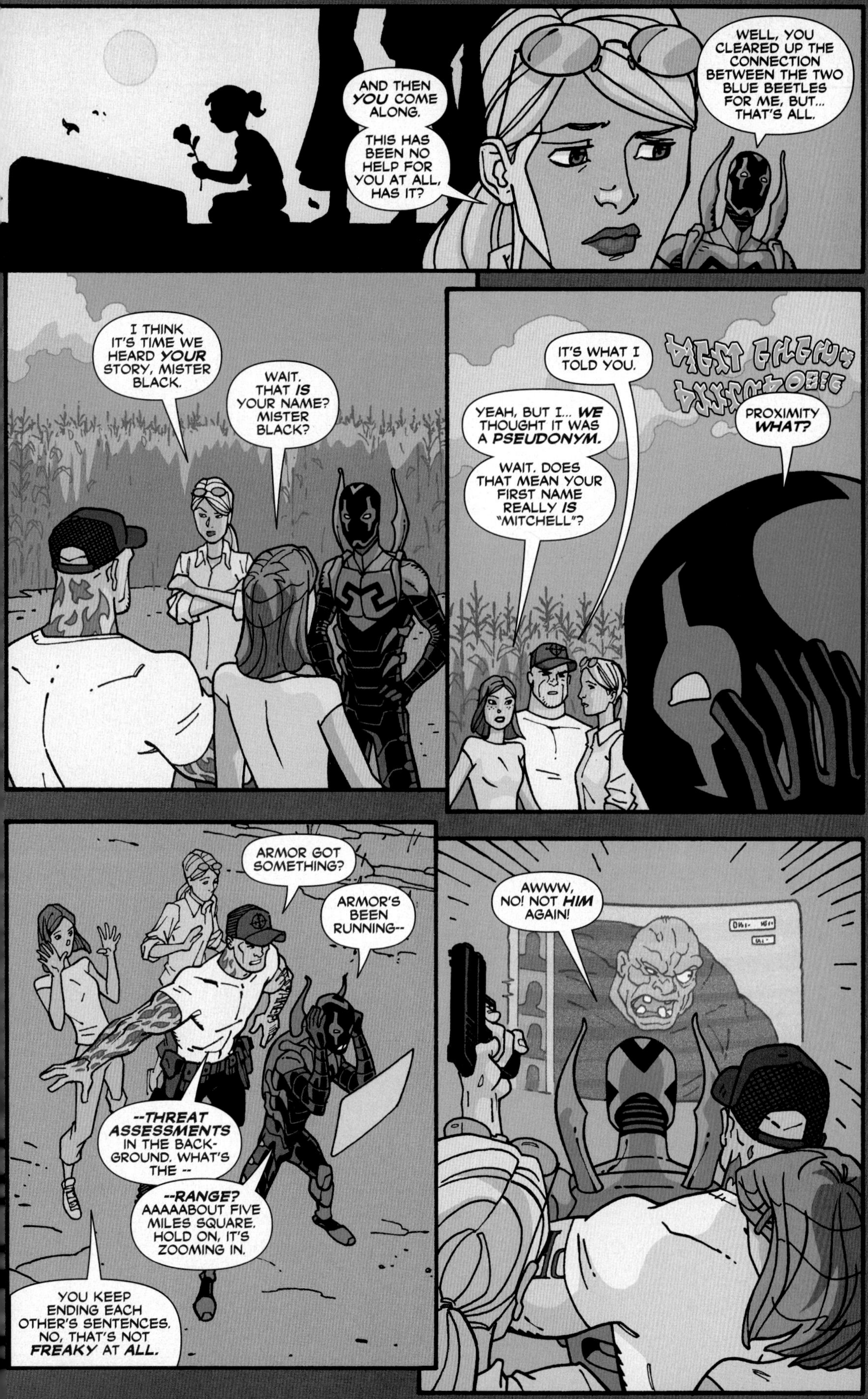
AND THEN *YOU* COME ALONG.
THIS HAS BEEN NO HELP FOR YOU AT ALL, HAS IT?
WELL, YOU CLEARED UP THE CONNECTION BETWEEN THE TWO BLUE BEETLES FOR ME, BUT... THAT'S ALL.
I THINK IT'S TIME WE HEARD *YOUR* STORY, MISTER BLACK.
WAIT. THAT *IS* YOUR NAME? MISTER BLACK?
IT'S WHAT I TOLD YOU.
YEAH, BUT I... *WE* THOUGHT IT WAS A *PSEUDONYM.*
WAIT. DOES THAT MEAN YOUR FIRST NAME REALLY *IS* "MITCHELL"?
PROXIMITY *WHAT?*
ARMOR GOT SOMETHING?
ARMOR'S BEEN RUNNING--
--THREAT ASSESSMENTS IN THE BACK-GROUND. WHAT'S THE --
--RANGE? AAAAABOUT FIVE MILES SQUARE. HOLD ON, IT'S ZOOMING IN.
YOU KEEP ENDING EACH OTHER'S SENTENCES. NO, THAT'S NOT *FREAKY* AT *ALL.*
AWWW, NO! NOT *HIM* AGAIN!

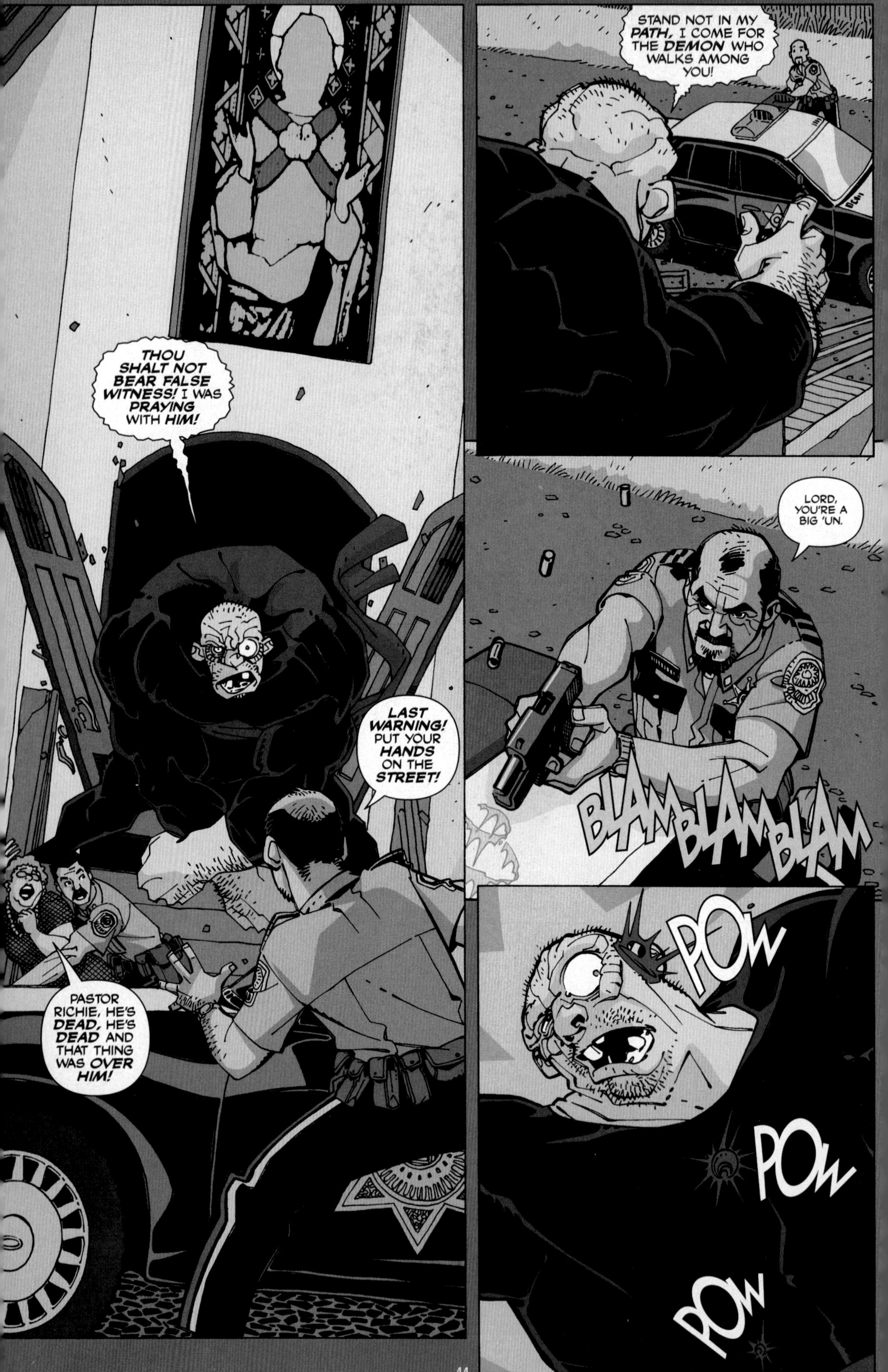
THOU SHALT NOT BEAR FALSE WITNESS! I WAS PRAYING WITH HIM!
LAST WARNING! PUT YOUR HANDS ON THE STREET!
PASTOR RICHIE, HE'S DEAD, HE'S DEAD AND THAT THING WAS OVER HIM!
STAND NOT IN MY PATH, I COME FOR THE DEMON WHO WALKS AMONG YOU!
LORD, YOU'RE A BIG 'UN.
BLAM BLAM BLAM
POW
POW
POW

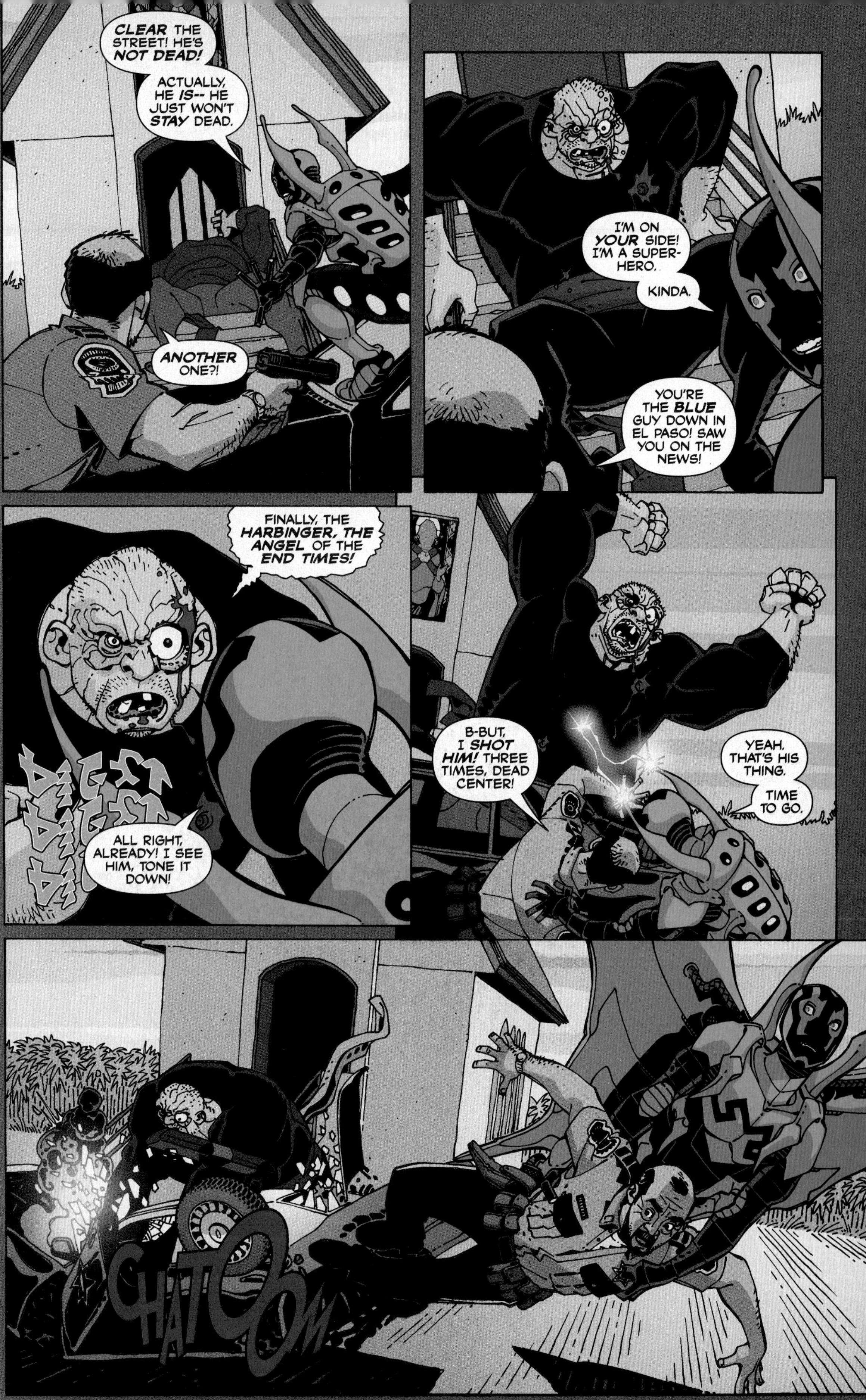

CLEAR THE STREET! HE'S NOT DEAD!
ACTUALLY, HE IS-- HE JUST WON'T STAY DEAD.
ANOTHER ONE?!
I'M ON YOUR SIDE! I'M A SUPER-HERO.
KINDA.
YOU'RE THE BLUE GUY DOWN IN EL PASO! SAW YOU ON THE NEWS!
FINALLY, THE HARBINGER, THE ANGEL OF THE END TIMES!
ALL RIGHT, ALREADY! I SEE HIM, TONE IT DOWN!
B-BUT, I SHOT HIM! THREE TIMES, DEAD CENTER!
YEAH, THAT'S HIS THING.
TIME TO GO.
CHATOOM

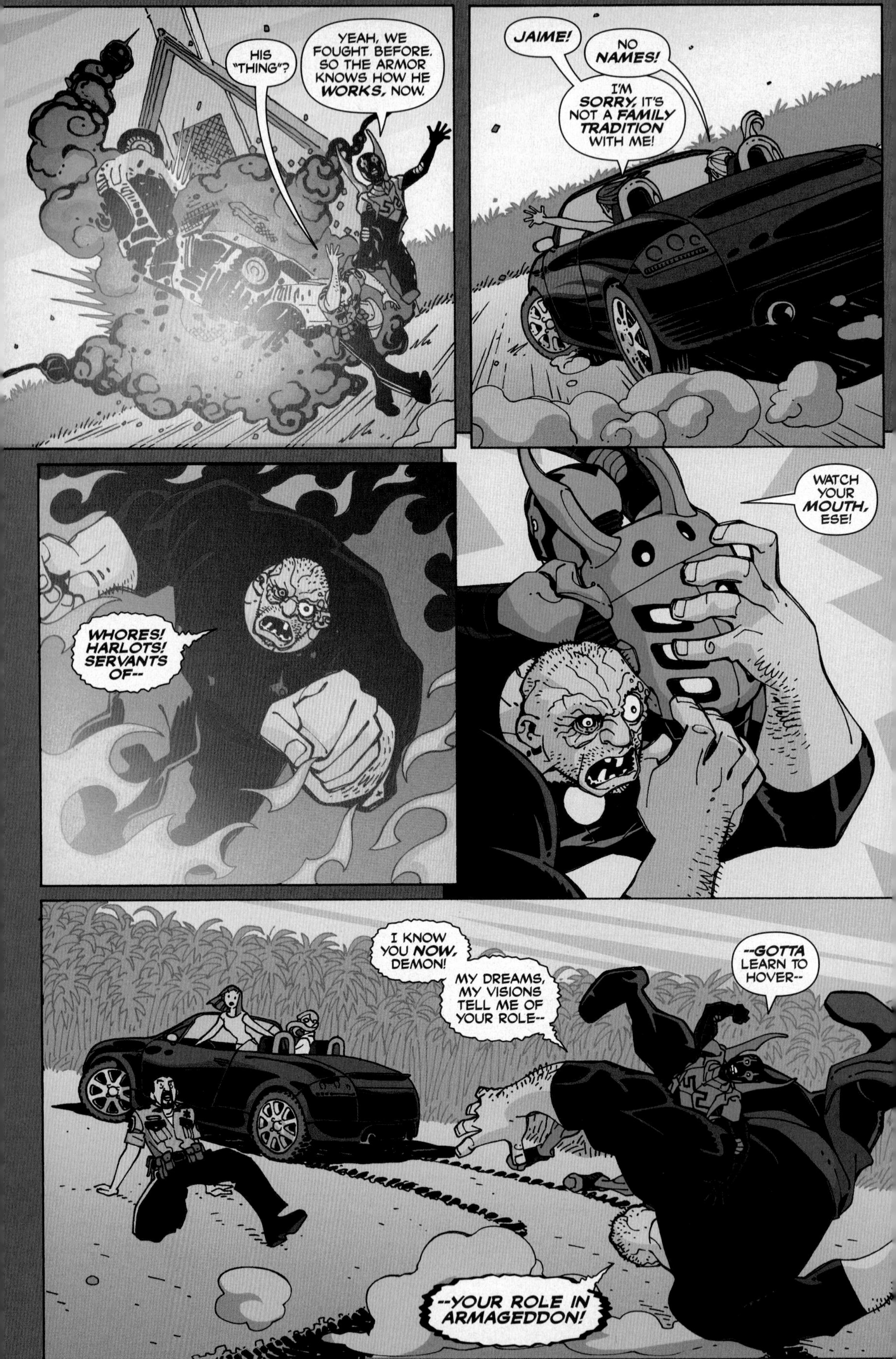
YEAH, WE FOUGHT BEFORE. SO THE ARMOR KNOWS HOW HE WORKS, NOW.
HIS "THING"?
JAIME!
NO NAMES!
I'M SORRY, IT'S NOT A FAMILY TRADITION WITH ME!
WHORES! HARLOTS! SERVANTS OF--
WATCH YOUR MOUTH, ESE!
I KNOW YOU NOW, DEMON!
MY DREAMS, MY VISIONS TELL ME OF YOUR ROLE--
--GOTTA LEARN TO HOVER--
--YOUR ROLE IN ARMAGEDDON!

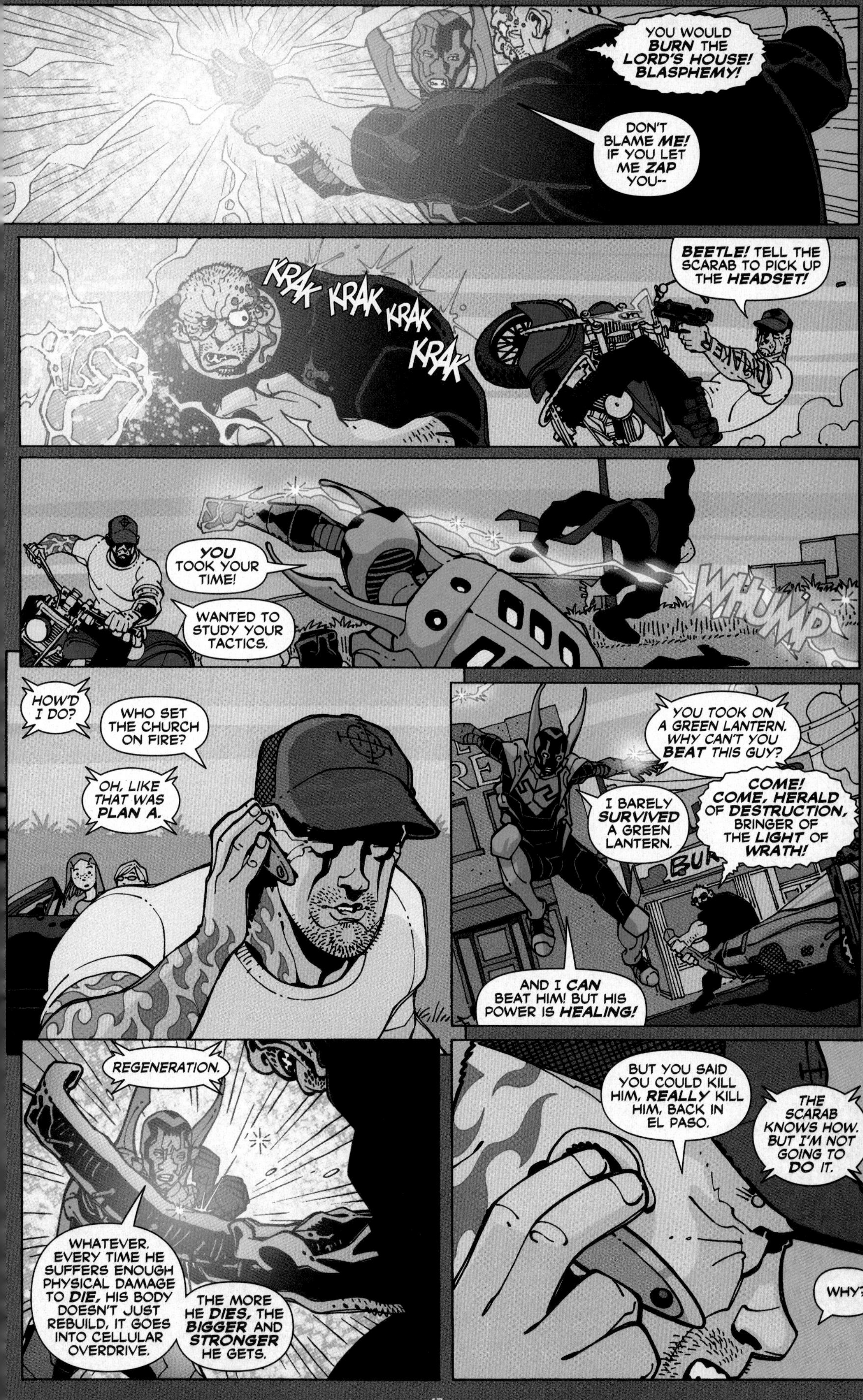
YOU WOULD BURN THE LORD'S HOUSE! BLASPHEMY!
DON'T BLAME ME! IF YOU LET ME ZAP YOU--
KRAK KRAK KRAK KRAK
BEETLE! TELL THE SCARAB TO PICK UP THE HEADSET!
YOU TOOK YOUR TIME!
WANTED TO STUDY YOUR TACTICS.
WHUMP
HOW'D I DO?
WHO SET THE CHURCH ON FIRE?
OH, LIKE THAT WAS PLAN A.
YOU TOOK ON A GREEN LANTERN. WHY CAN'T YOU BEAT THIS GUY?
I BARELY SURVIVED A GREEN LANTERN.
COME! COME, HERALD OF DESTRUCTION, BRINGER OF THE LIGHT OF WRATH!
AND I CAN BEAT HIM! BUT HIS POWER IS HEALING!
REGENERATION.
WHATEVER. EVERY TIME HE SUFFERS ENOUGH PHYSICAL DAMAGE TO DIE, HIS BODY DOESN'T JUST REBUILD, IT GOES INTO CELLULAR OVERDRIVE.
THE MORE HE DIES, THE BIGGER AND STRONGER HE GETS.
BUT YOU SAID YOU COULD KILL HIM, REALLY KILL HIM, BACK IN EL PASO.
THE SCARAB KNOWS HOW. BUT I'M NOT GOING TO DO IT.
WHY?

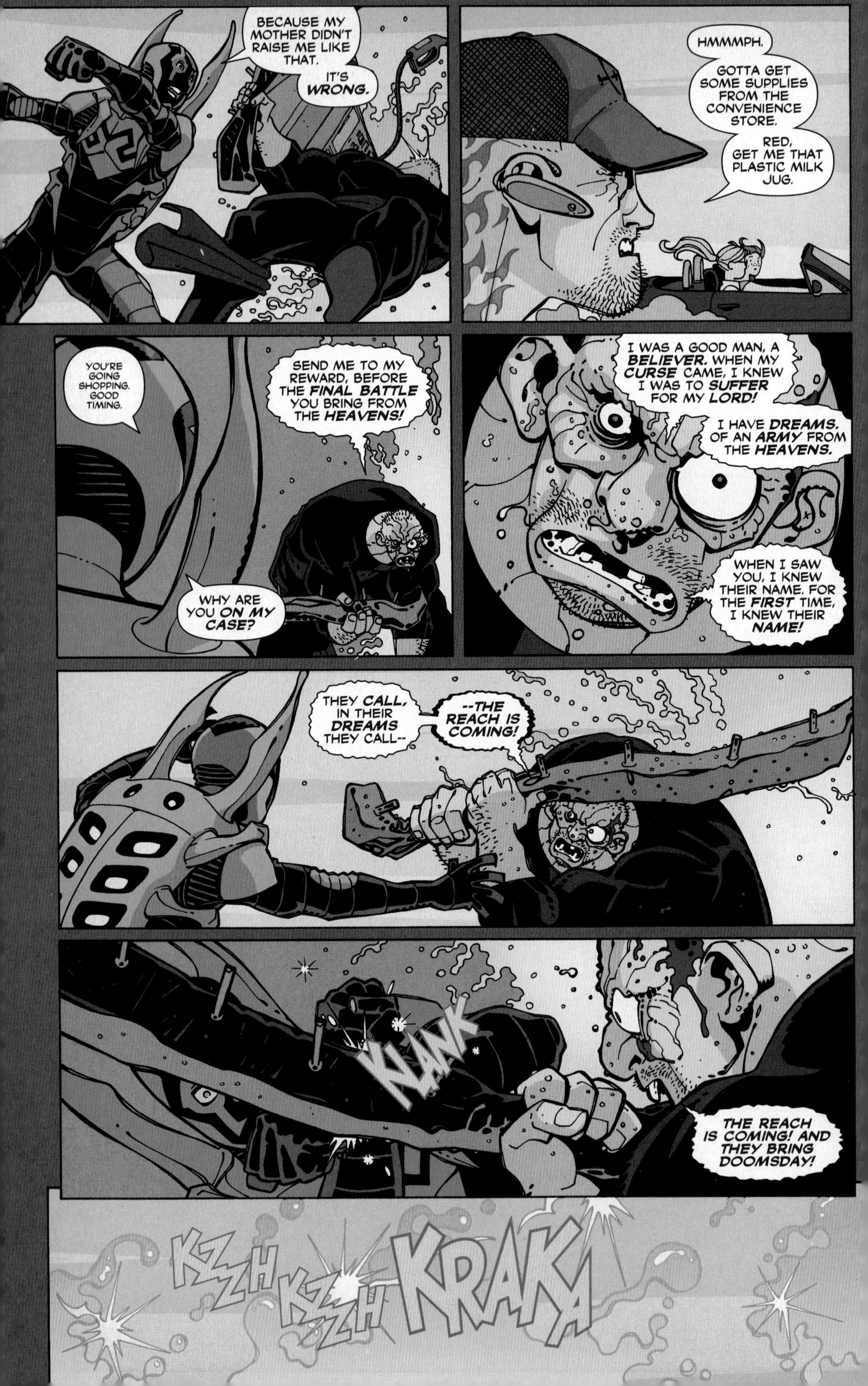
BECAUSE MY MOTHER DIDN'T RAISE ME LIKE THAT.
IT'S WRONG.
HMMMPH.
GOTTA GET SOME SUPPLIES FROM THE CONVENIENCE STORE.
RED, GET ME THAT PLASTIC MILK JUG.
YOU'RE GOING SHOPPING. GOOD TIMING.
SEND ME TO MY REWARD, BEFORE THE FINAL BATTLE YOU BRING FROM THE HEAVENS!
WHY ARE YOU ON MY CASE?
I WAS A GOOD MAN, A BELIEVER. WHEN MY CURSE CAME, I KNEW I WAS TO SUFFER FOR MY LORD!
I HAVE DREAMS. OF AN ARMY FROM THE HEAVENS.
WHEN I SAW YOU, I KNEW THEIR NAME. FOR THE FIRST TIME, I KNEW THEIR NAME!
THEY CALL, IN THEIR DREAMS THEY CALL--
--THE REACH IS COMING!
KLANK
THE REACH IS COMING! AND THEY BRING DOOMSDAY!
KZZH KZZH KRAKA

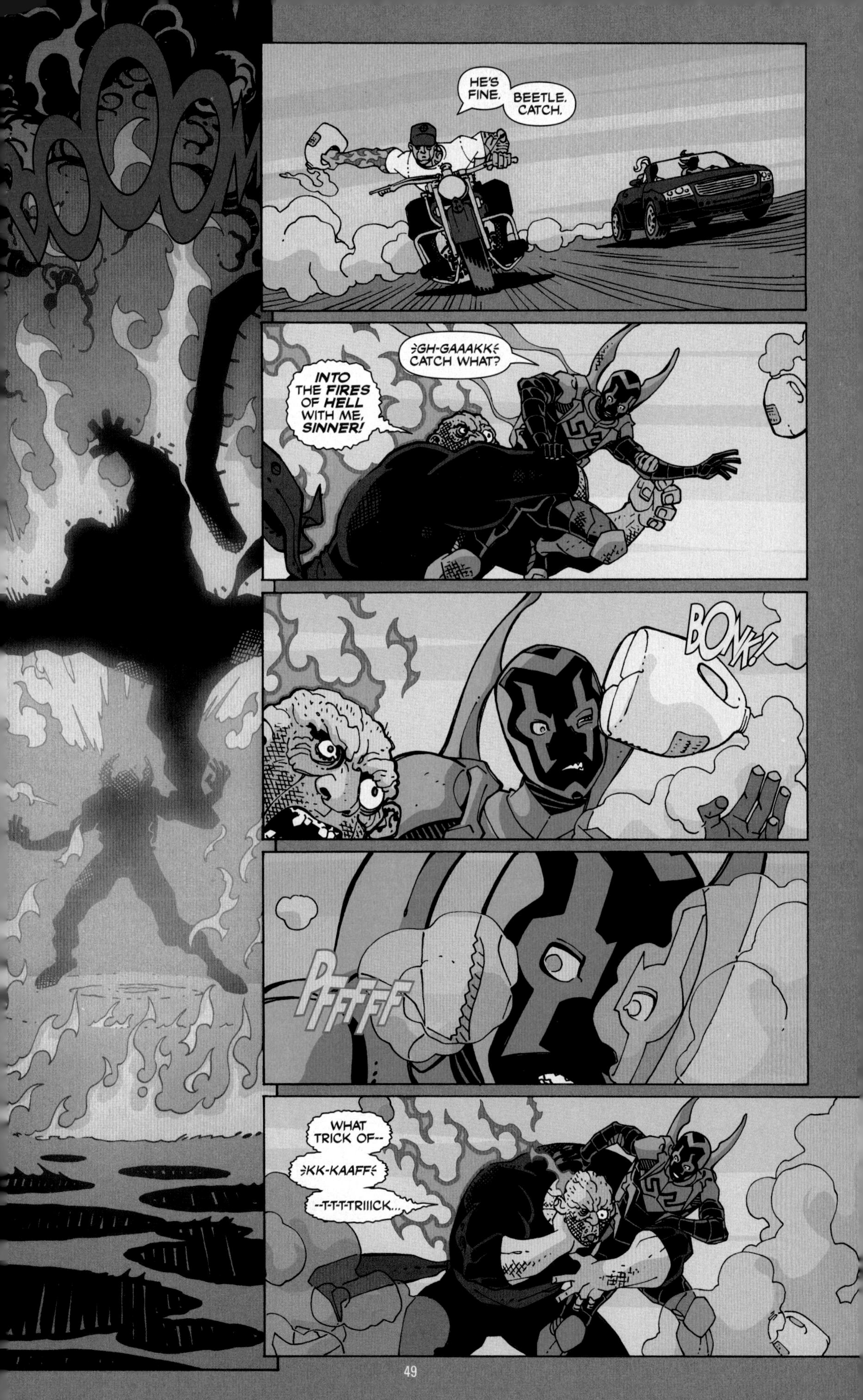
BOOOOM
HE'S FINE.
BEETLE. CATCH.
INTO THE FIRES OF HELL WITH ME, SINNER!
GH-GAAAKK CATCH WHAT?
BONK!
PFFFFF
WHAT TRICK OF--
KK-KAAFF
--T-T-T-TRIIICK...

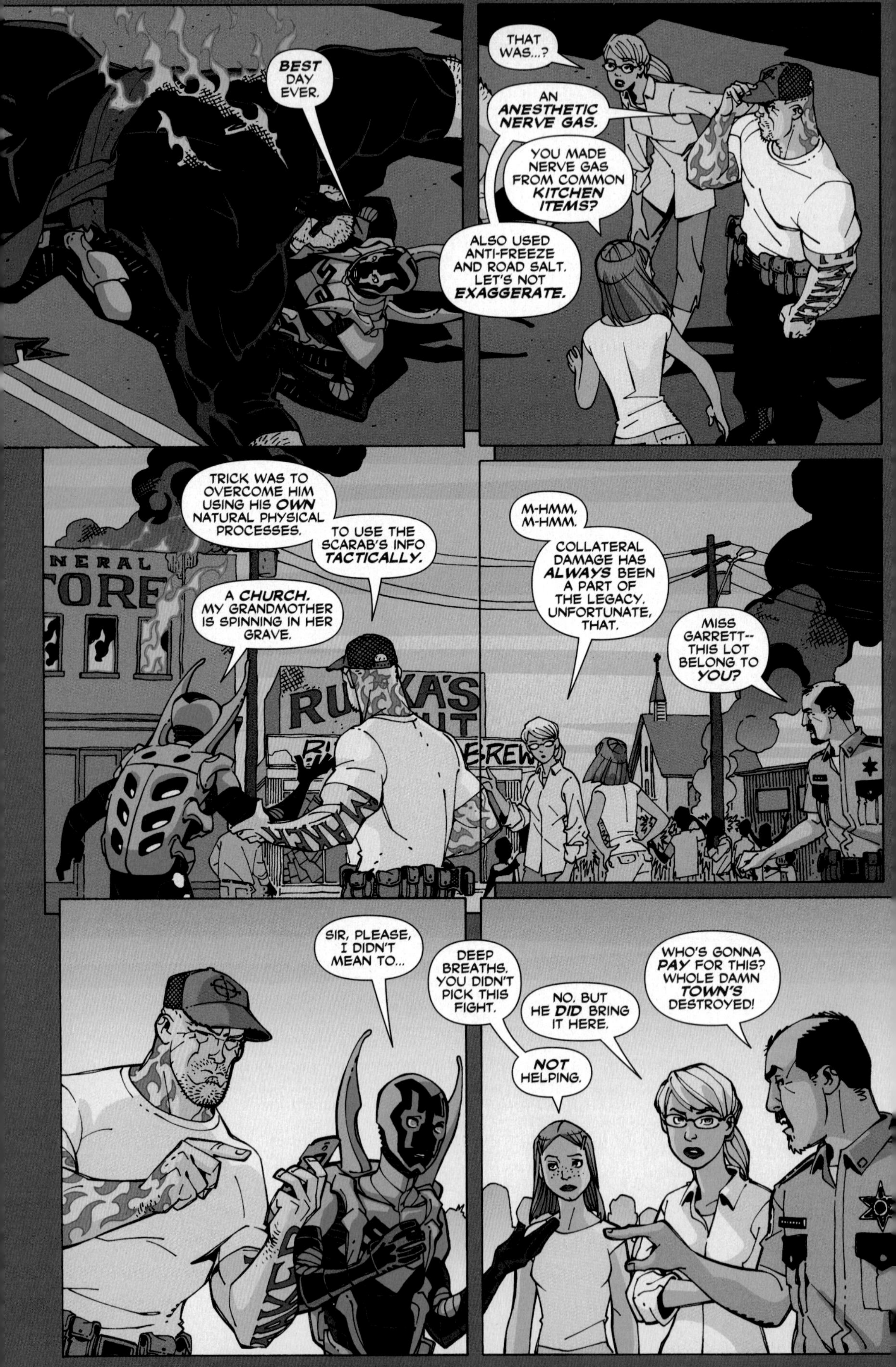
BEST DAY EVER.
THAT WAS...?
AN ANESTHETIC NERVE GAS.
YOU MADE NERVE GAS FROM COMMON KITCHEN ITEMS?
ALSO USED ANTI-FREEZE AND ROAD SALT. LET'S NOT EXAGGERATE.
TRICK WAS TO OVERCOME HIM USING HIS OWN NATURAL PHYSICAL PROCESSES.
TO USE THE SCARAB'S INFO TACTICALLY.
A CHURCH. MY GRANDMOTHER IS SPINNING IN HER GRAVE.
M-HMM, M-HMM.
COLLATERAL DAMAGE HAS ALWAYS BEEN A PART OF THE LEGACY. UNFORTUNATE, THAT.
MISS GARRETT-- THIS LOT BELONG TO YOU?
SIR, PLEASE, I DIDN'T MEAN TO...
DEEP BREATHS. YOU DIDN'T PICK THIS FIGHT.
NO, BUT HE DID BRING IT HERE.
NOT HELPING.
WHO'S GONNA PAY FOR THIS? WHOLE DAMN TOWN'S DESTROYED!

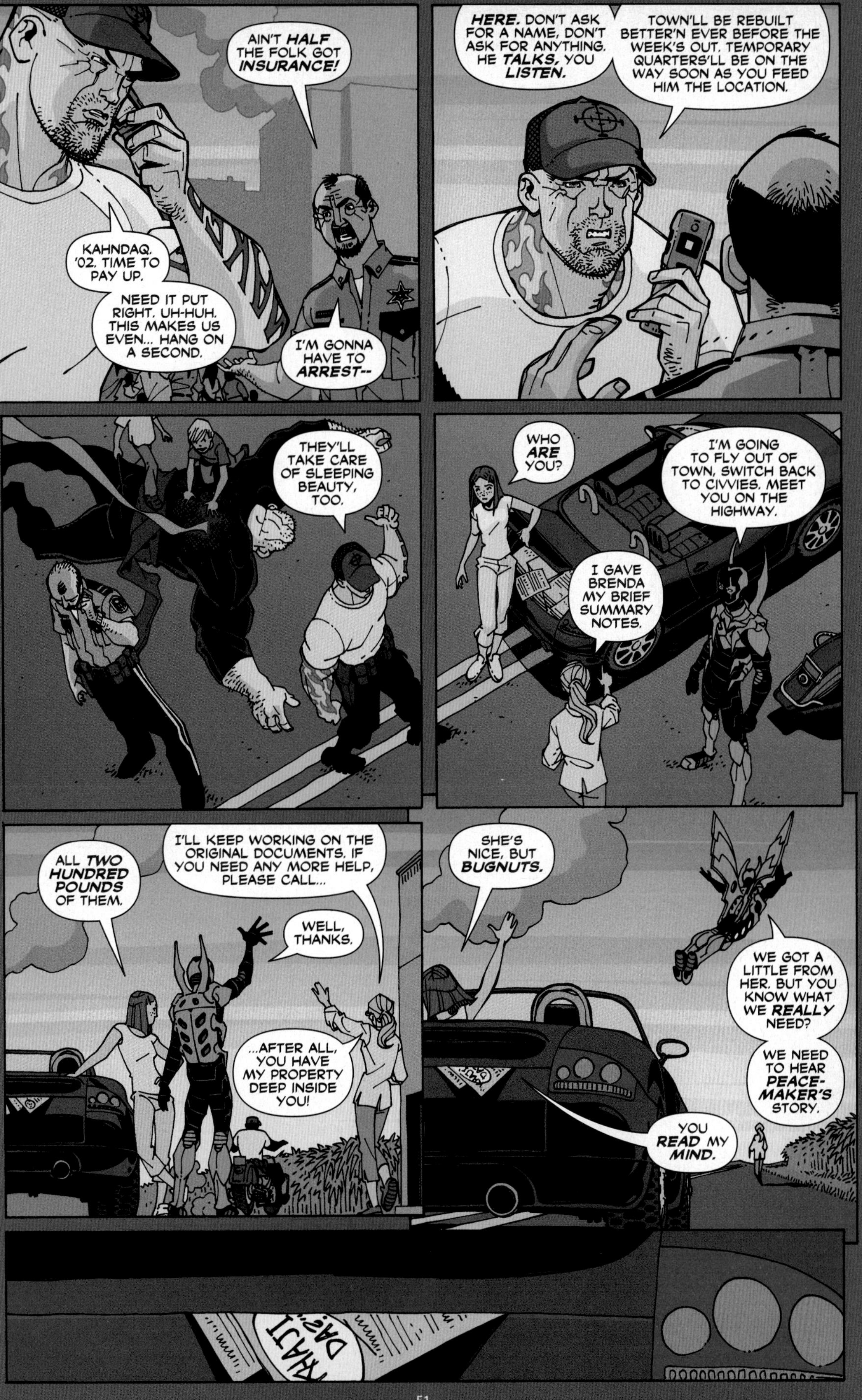
AIN'T HALF THE FOLK GOT INSURANCE!
KAHNDAQ. '02. TIME TO PAY UP.
NEED IT PUT RIGHT. UH-HUH. THIS MAKES US EVEN... HANG ON A SECOND.
I'M GONNA HAVE TO ARREST--
HERE. DON'T ASK FOR A NAME, DON'T ASK FOR ANYTHING. HE TALKS, YOU LISTEN.
TOWN'LL BE REBUILT BETTER'N EVER BEFORE THE WEEK'S OUT. TEMPORARY QUARTERS'LL BE ON THE WAY SOON AS YOU FEED HIM THE LOCATION.
THEY'LL TAKE CARE OF SLEEPING BEAUTY, TOO.
WHO ARE YOU?
I'M GOING TO FLY OUT OF TOWN, SWITCH BACK TO CIVVIES. MEET YOU ON THE HIGHWAY.
I GAVE BRENDA MY BRIEF SUMMARY NOTES.
ALL TWO HUNDRED POUNDS OF THEM.
I'LL KEEP WORKING ON THE ORIGINAL DOCUMENTS. IF YOU NEED ANY MORE HELP, PLEASE CALL...
WELL, THANKS.
...AFTER ALL, YOU HAVE MY PROPERTY DEEP INSIDE YOU!
SHE'S NICE, BUT BUGNUTS.
WE GOT A LITTLE FROM HER. BUT YOU KNOW WHAT WE REALLY NEED?
WE NEED TO HEAR PEACE-MAKER'S STORY.
YOU READ MY MIND.

BLUE BEETLE #9 Written by Keith Giffen & John Rogers Cover and interior art by Duncan Rouleau

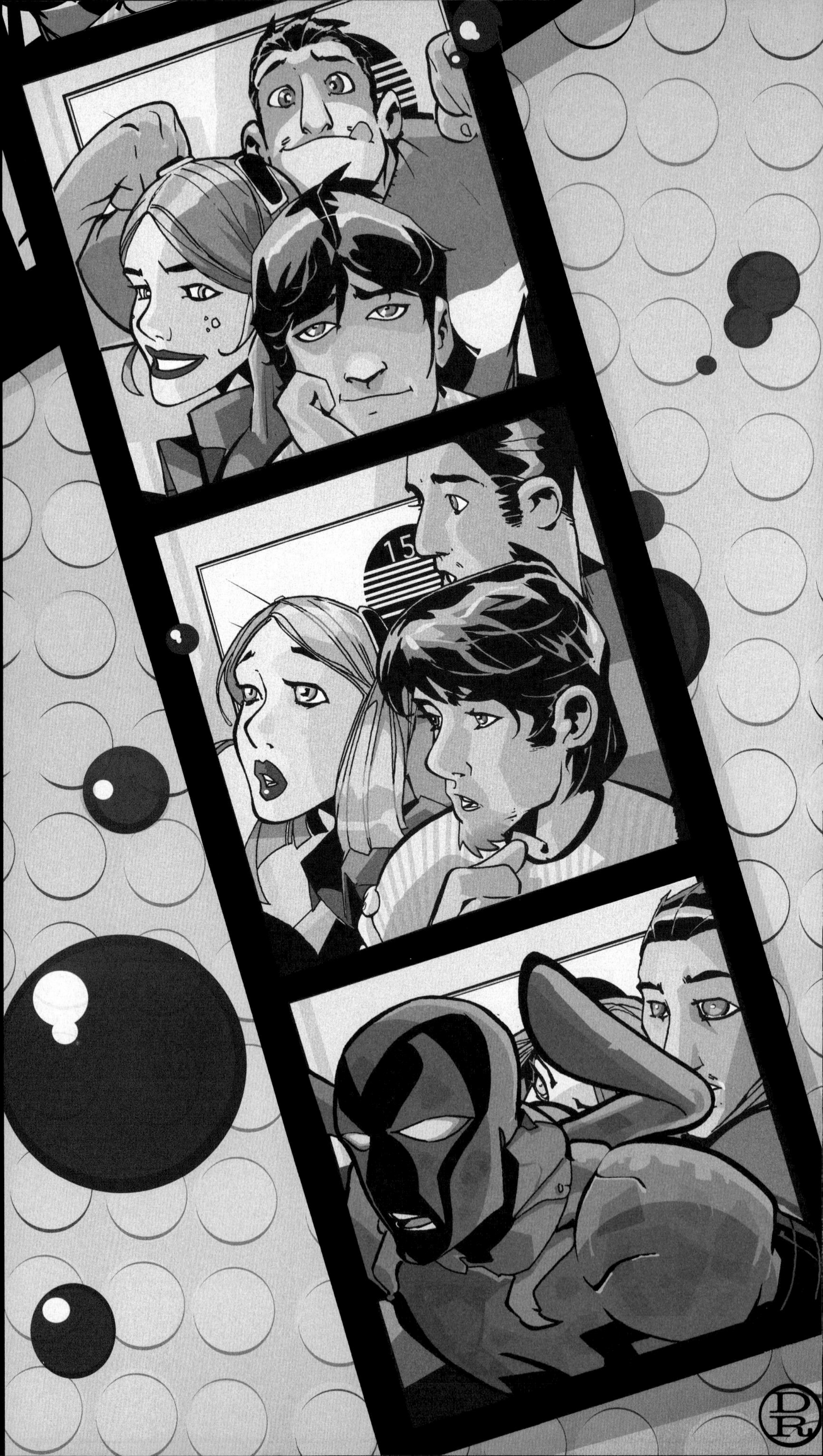
15

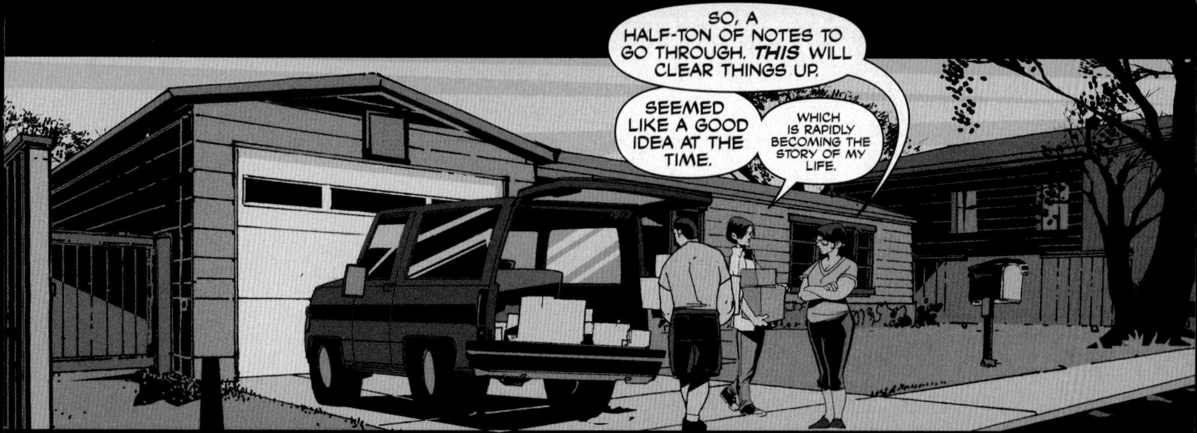
SO, A HALF-TON OF NOTES TO GO THROUGH. THIS WILL CLEAR THINGS UP.
SEEMED LIKE A GOOD IDEA AT THE TIME.
WHICH IS RAPIDLY BECOMING THE STORY OF MY LIFE.

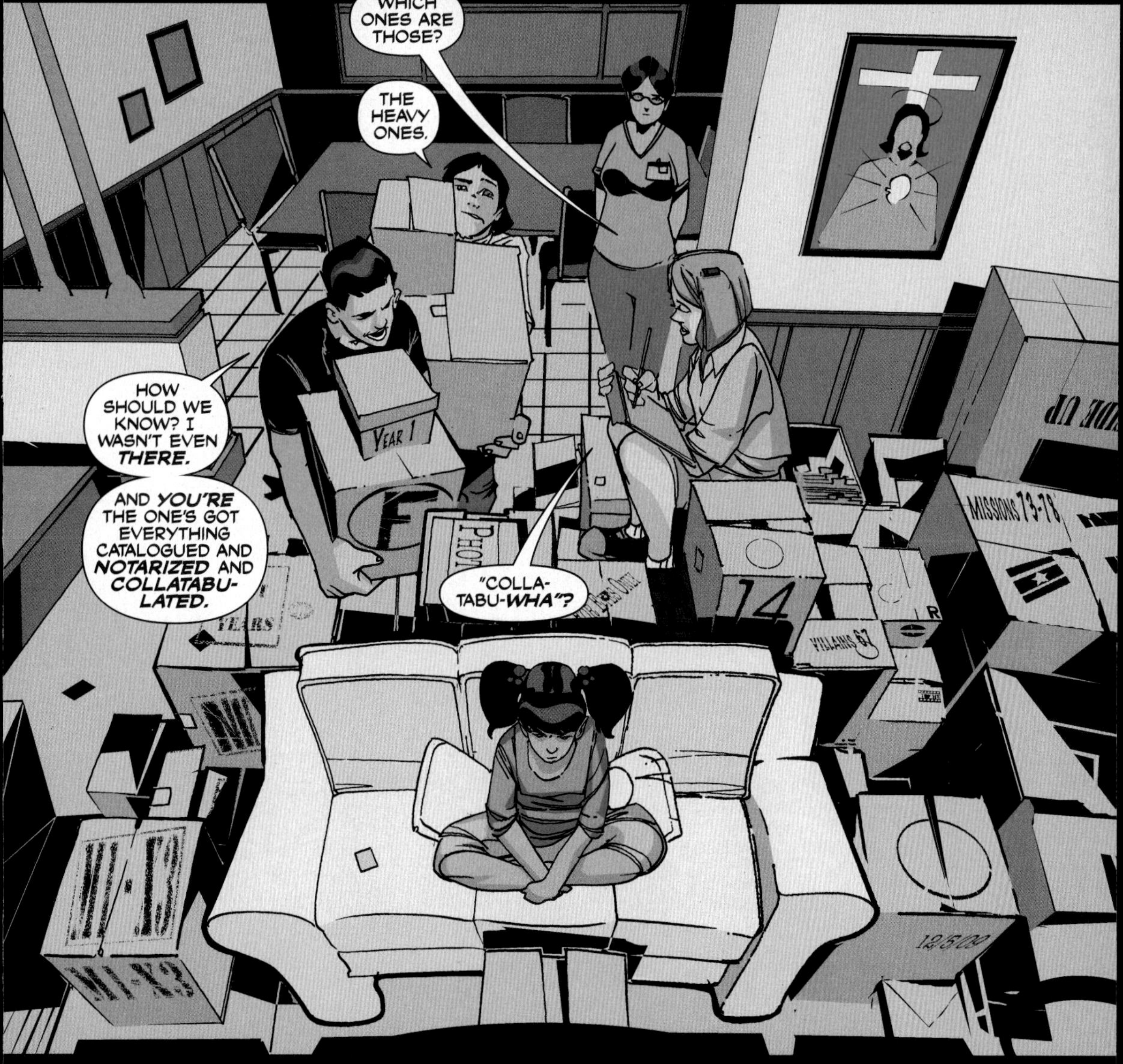
WHICH ONES ARE THOSE?
THE HEAVY ONES.
HOW SHOULD WE KNOW? I WASN'T EVEN THERE.
AND YOU'RE THE ONE'S GOT EVERYTHING CATALOGUED AND NOTARIZED AND COLLATABULATED.
"COLLA-TABU-WHA"?
YEAR 1
MISSIONS 73-78
VILLAINS 67

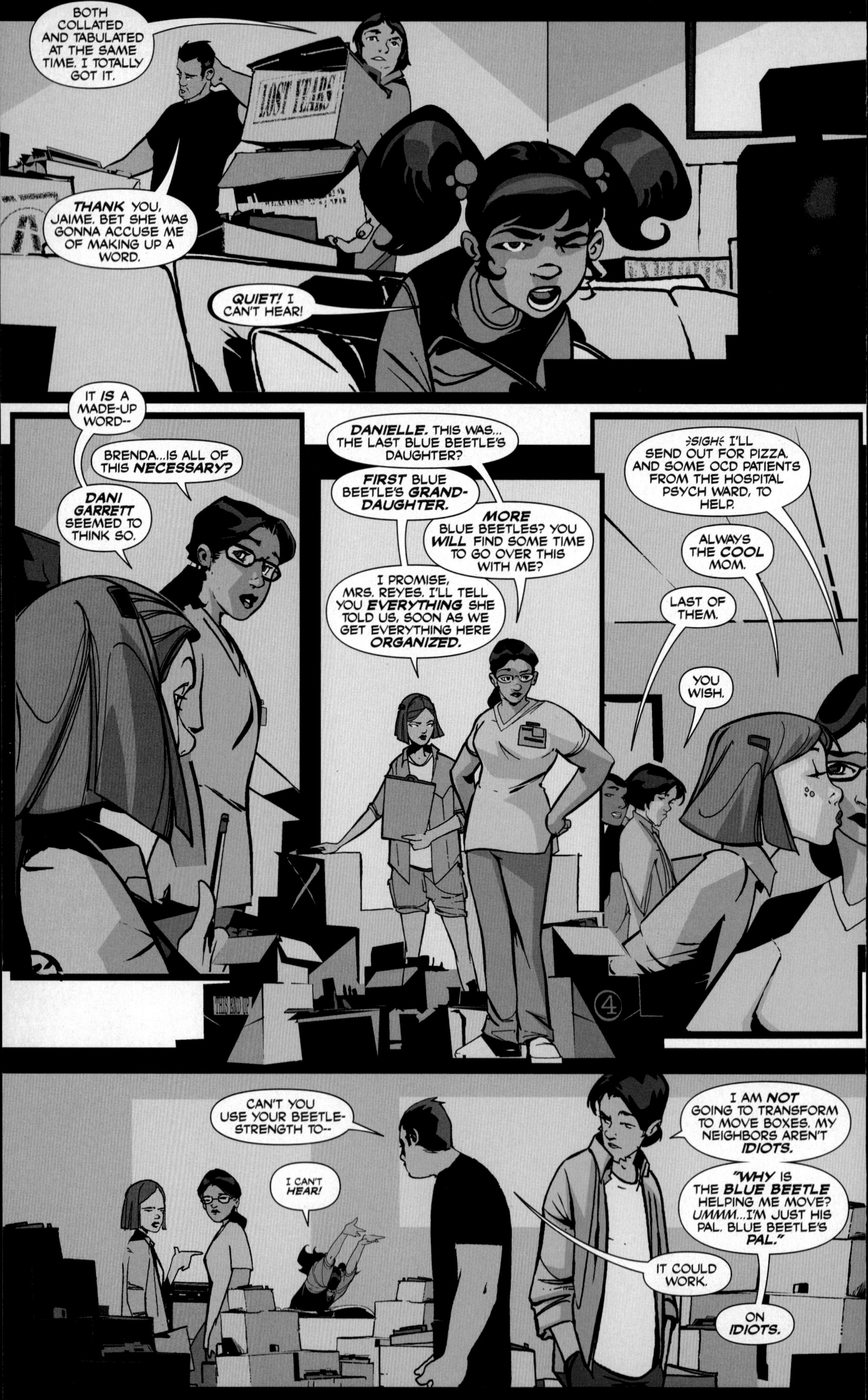
BOTH COLLATED AND TABULATED AT THE SAME TIME. I TOTALLY GOT IT.
LOST YEARS
THANK YOU, JAIME. BET SHE WAS GONNA ACCUSE ME OF MAKING UP A WORD.
QUIET! I CAN'T HEAR!
IT *IS* A MADE-UP WORD--
BRENDA...IS ALL OF THIS *NECESSARY?*
DANI GARRETT SEEMED TO THINK SO.
DANIELLE. THIS WAS... THE LAST BLUE BEETLE'S DAUGHTER?
FIRST BLUE BEETLE'S *GRAND-DAUGHTER.*
MORE BLUE BEETLES? YOU *WILL* FIND SOME TIME TO GO OVER THIS WITH ME?
I PROMISE, MRS. REYES. I'LL TELL YOU *EVERYTHING* SHE TOLD US, SOON AS WE GET EVERYTHING HERE *ORGANIZED.*
THIS END UP
4
SIGH I'LL SEND OUT FOR PIZZA. AND SOME OCD PATIENTS FROM THE HOSPITAL PSYCH WARD, TO HELP.
ALWAYS THE *COOL* MOM.
LAST OF THEM.
YOU WISH.
CAN'T YOU USE YOUR BEETLE-STRENGTH TO--
I CAN'T *HEAR!*
I AM *NOT* GOING TO TRANSFORM TO MOVE BOXES. MY NEIGHBORS AREN'T *IDIOTS.*
"WHY IS THE *BLUE BEETLE* HELPING ME MOVE? *UMMM*...I'M JUST HIS PAL. BLUE BEETLE'S *PAL."*
IT COULD WORK.
ON *IDIOTS.*

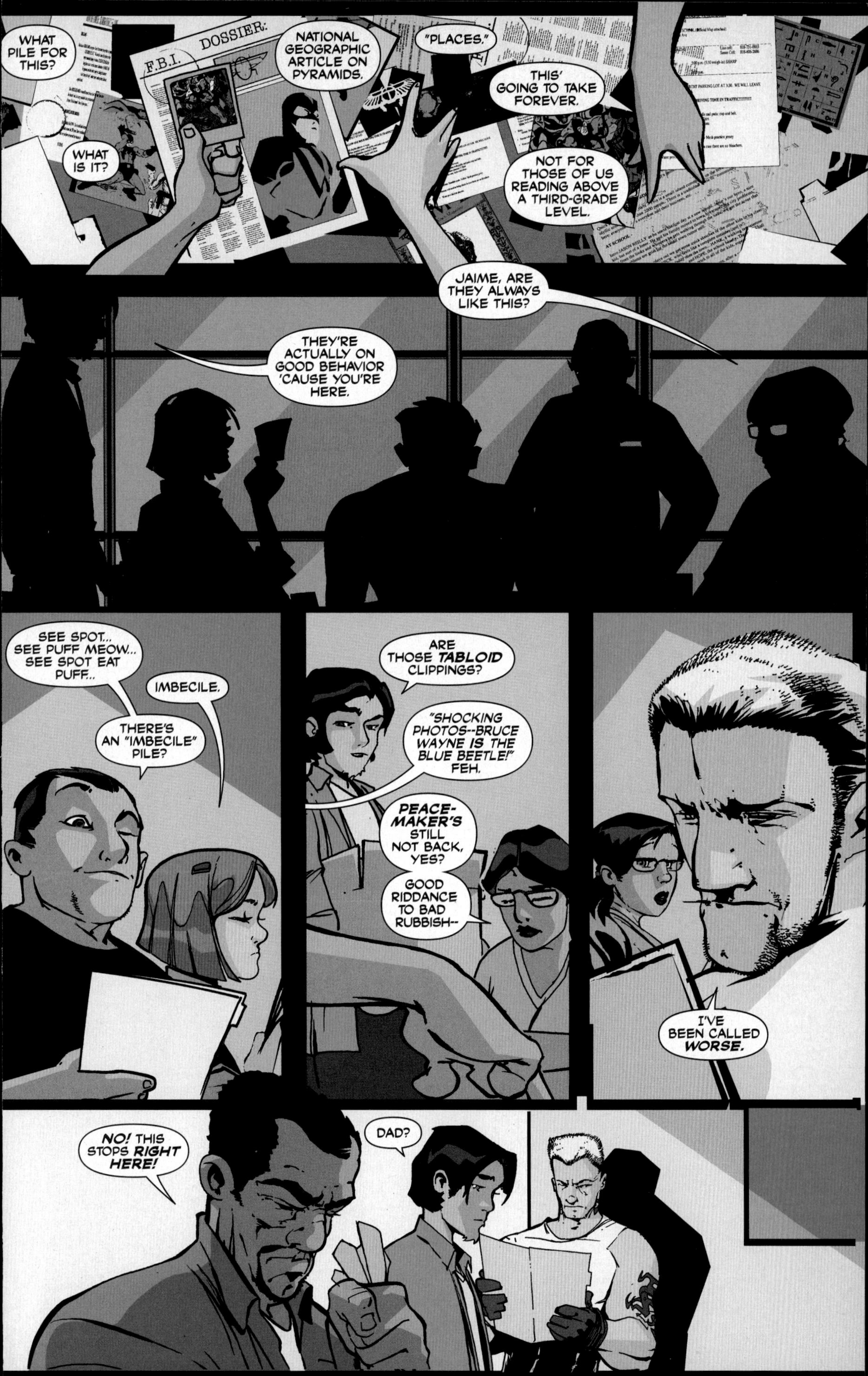
WHAT PILE FOR THIS?
WHAT IS IT?
DOSSIER:
F.B.I.
NATIONAL GEOGRAPHIC ARTICLE ON PYRAMIDS.
"PLACES."
THIS' GOING TO TAKE FOREVER.
NOT FOR THOSE OF US READING ABOVE A THIRD-GRADE LEVEL.
JAIME, ARE THEY ALWAYS LIKE THIS?
THEY'RE ACTUALLY ON GOOD BEHAVIOR 'CAUSE YOU'RE HERE.
SEE SPOT... SEE PUFF MEOW... SEE SPOT EAT PUFF...
IMBECILE.
THERE'S AN "IMBECILE" PILE?
ARE THOSE *TABLOID* CLIPPINGS?
"SHOCKING PHOTOS--BRUCE WAYNE *IS* THE BLUE BEETLE!" FEH.
PEACE-MAKER'S STILL NOT BACK, YES?
GOOD RIDDANCE TO BAD RUBBISH--
I'VE BEEN CALLED *WORSE.*
NO! THIS STOPS *RIGHT HERE!*
DAD?

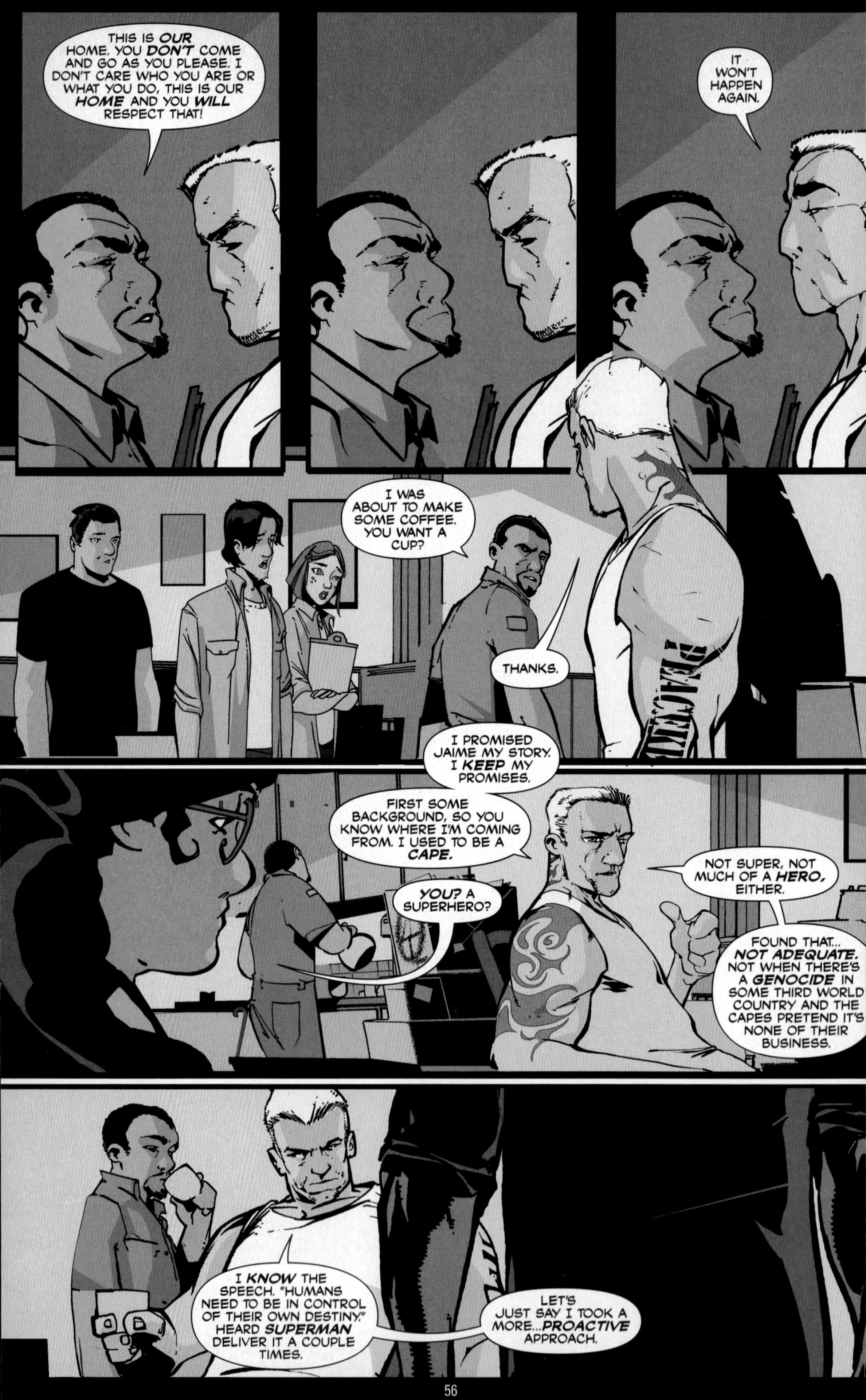
THIS IS OUR HOME. YOU DON'T COME AND GO AS YOU PLEASE. I DON'T CARE WHO YOU ARE OR WHAT YOU DO, THIS IS OUR HOME AND YOU WILL RESPECT THAT!
IT WON'T HAPPEN AGAIN.
I WAS ABOUT TO MAKE SOME COFFEE. YOU WANT A CUP?
THANKS.
I PROMISED JAIME MY STORY. I KEEP MY PROMISES.
FIRST SOME BACKGROUND, SO YOU KNOW WHERE I'M COMING FROM. I USED TO BE A CAPE.
YOU? A SUPERHERO?
NOT SUPER, NOT MUCH OF A HERO, EITHER.
FOUND THAT... NOT ADEQUATE. NOT WHEN THERE'S A GENOCIDE IN SOME THIRD WORLD COUNTRY AND THE CAPES PRETEND IT'S NONE OF THEIR BUSINESS.
I KNOW THE SPEECH. "HUMANS NEED TO BE IN CONTROL OF THEIR OWN DESTINY." HEARD SUPERMAN DELIVER IT A COUPLE TIMES.
LET'S JUST SAY I TOOK A MORE...PROACTIVE APPROACH.

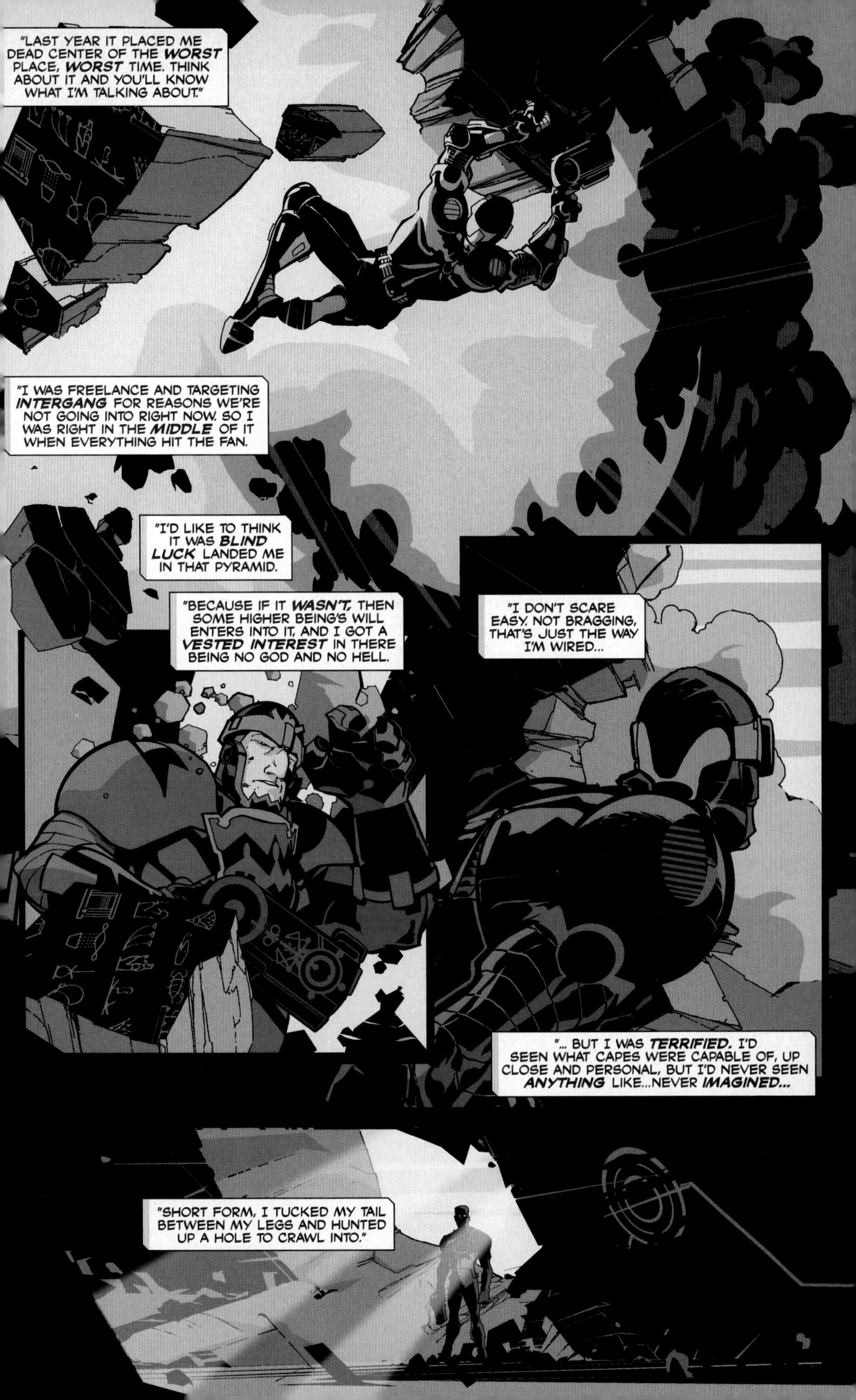
"LAST YEAR IT PLACED ME DEAD CENTER OF THE WORST PLACE, WORST TIME. THINK ABOUT IT AND YOU'LL KNOW WHAT I'M TALKING ABOUT."
"I WAS FREELANCE AND TARGETING INTERGANG FOR REASONS WE'RE NOT GOING INTO RIGHT NOW. SO I WAS RIGHT IN THE MIDDLE OF IT WHEN EVERYTHING HIT THE FAN.
"I'D LIKE TO THINK IT WAS BLIND LUCK LANDED ME IN THAT PYRAMID.
"BECAUSE IF IT WASN'T, THEN SOME HIGHER BEING'S WILL ENTERS INTO IT, AND I GOT A VESTED INTEREST IN THERE BEING NO GOD AND NO HELL.
"I DON'T SCARE EASY. NOT BRAGGING, THAT'S JUST THE WAY I'M WIRED...
"... BUT I WAS TERRIFIED. I'D SEEN WHAT CAPES WERE CAPABLE OF, UP CLOSE AND PERSONAL, BUT I'D NEVER SEEN ANYTHING LIKE...NEVER IMAGINED...
"SHORT FORM, I TUCKED MY TAIL BETWEEN MY LEGS AND HUNTED UP A HOLE TO CRAWL INTO."

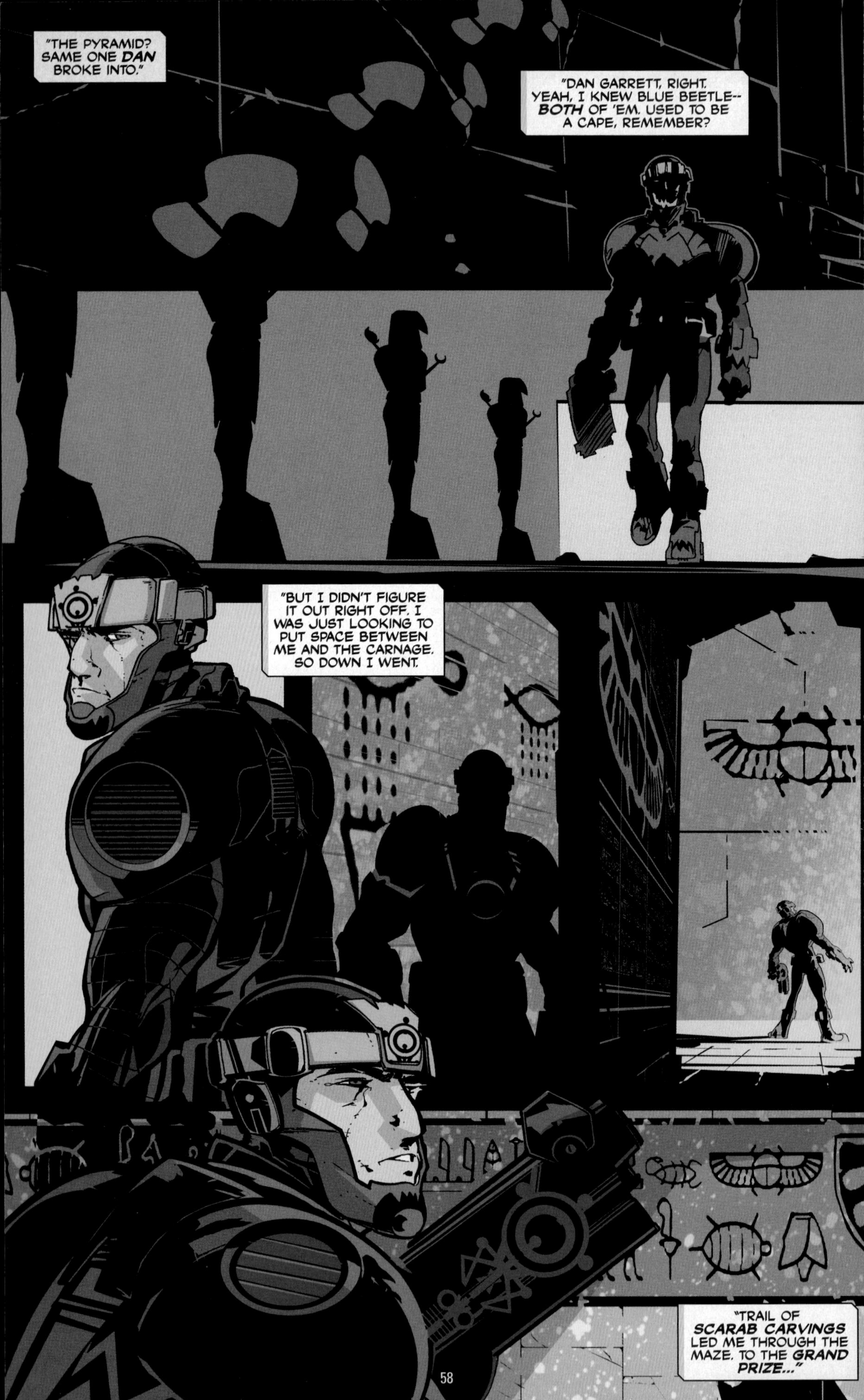

"THE PYRAMID? SAME ONE DAN BROKE INTO."
"DAN GARRETT, RIGHT. YEAH, I KNEW BLUE BEETLE-- BOTH OF 'EM. USED TO BE A CAPE, REMEMBER?
"BUT I DIDN'T FIGURE IT OUT RIGHT OFF. I WAS JUST LOOKING TO PUT SPACE BETWEEN ME AND THE CARNAGE. SO DOWN I WENT.
"TRAIL OF SCARAB CARVINGS LED ME THROUGH THE MAZE. TO THE GRAND PRIZE..."

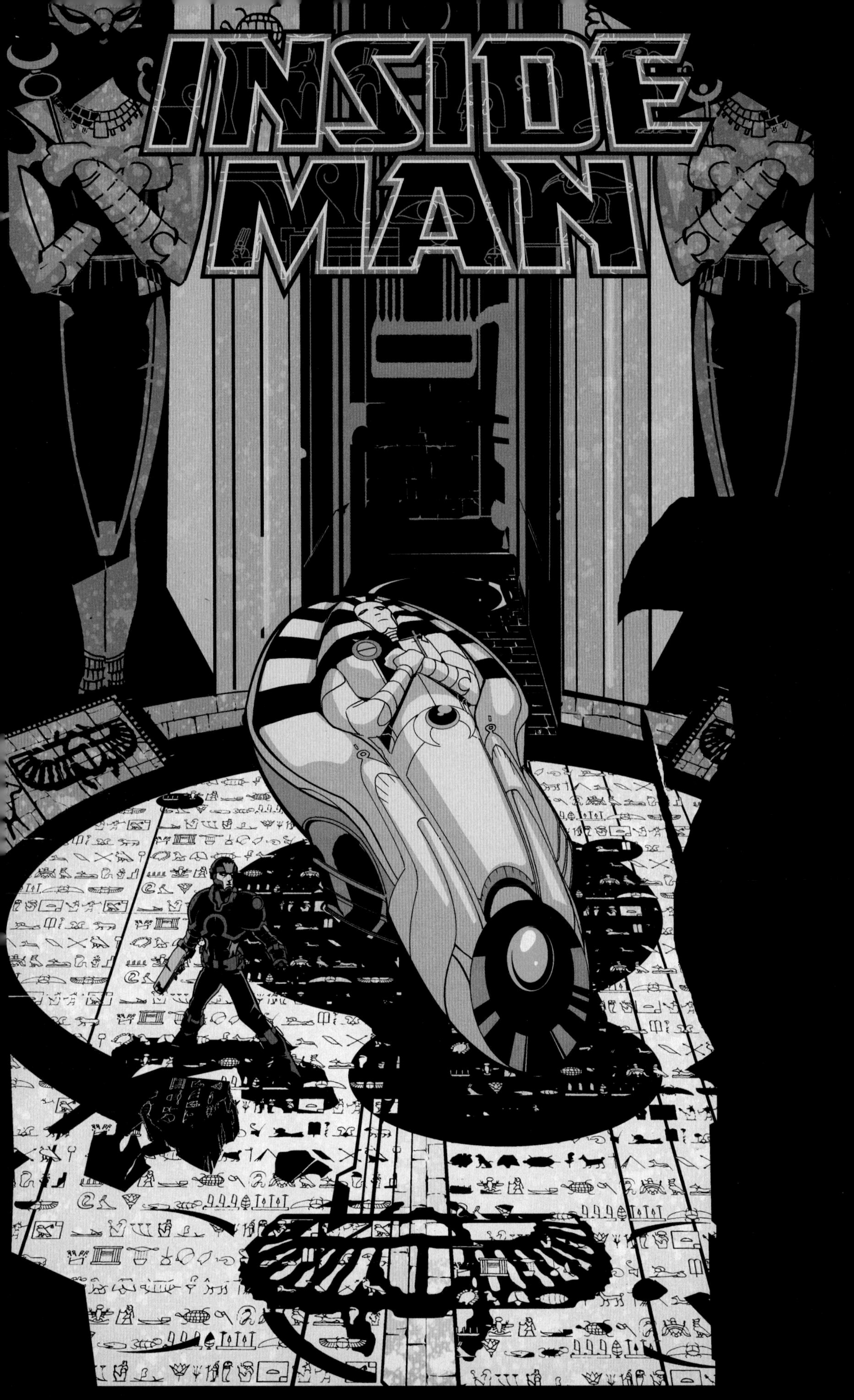
INSIDE MAN

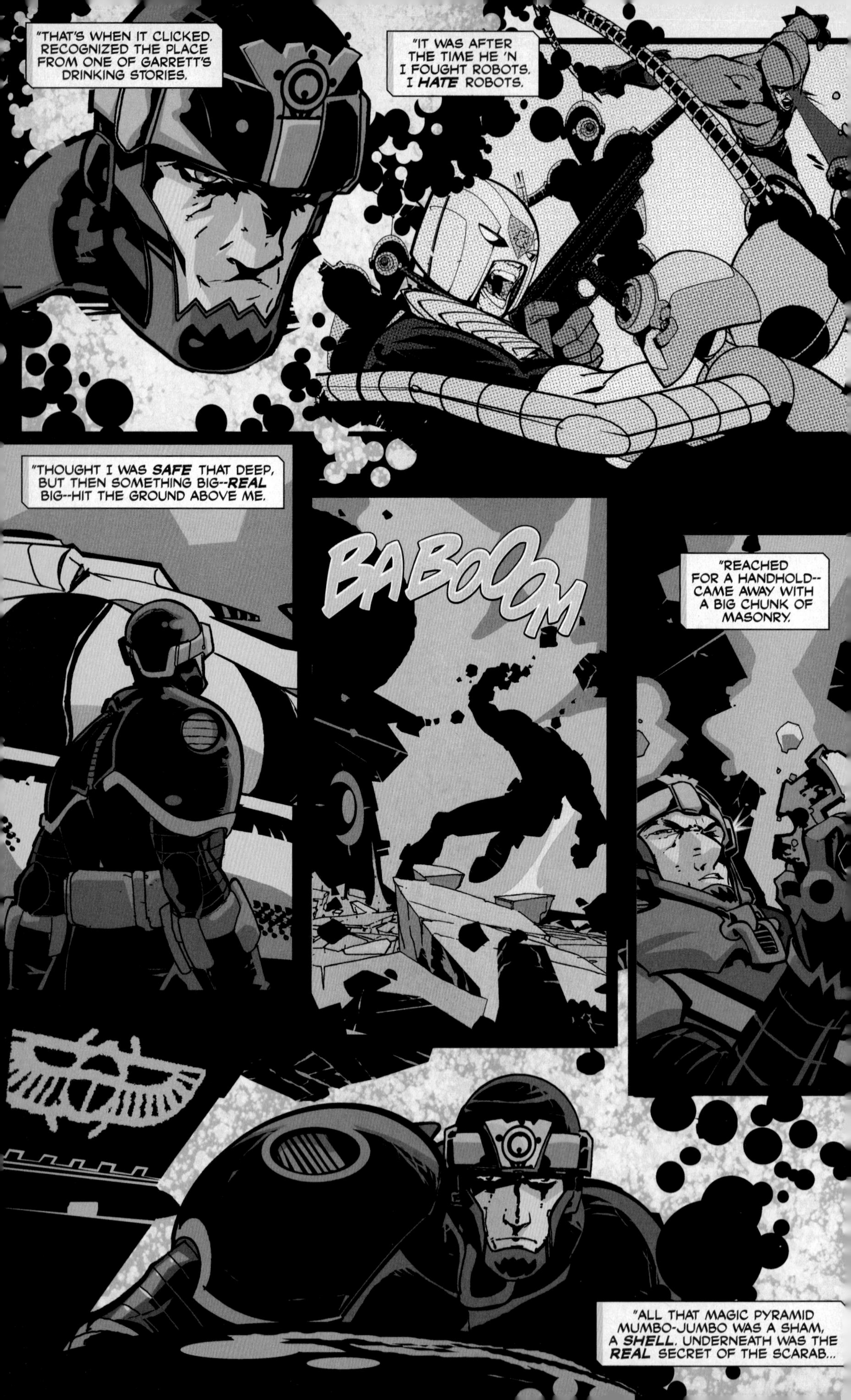
"THAT'S WHEN IT CLICKED. RECOGNIZED THE PLACE FROM ONE OF GARRETT'S DRINKING STORIES.
"IT WAS AFTER THE TIME HE 'N I FOUGHT ROBOTS. I **HATE** ROBOTS.
"THOUGHT I WAS **SAFE** THAT DEEP, BUT THEN SOMETHING BIG--**REAL** BIG--HIT THE GROUND ABOVE ME.
BABOOOM
"REACHED FOR A HANDHOLD--CAME AWAY WITH A BIG CHUNK OF MASONRY.
"ALL THAT MAGIC PYRAMID MUMBO-JUMBO WAS A SHAM, A **SHELL**. UNDERNEATH WAS THE **REAL** SECRET OF THE SCARAB...

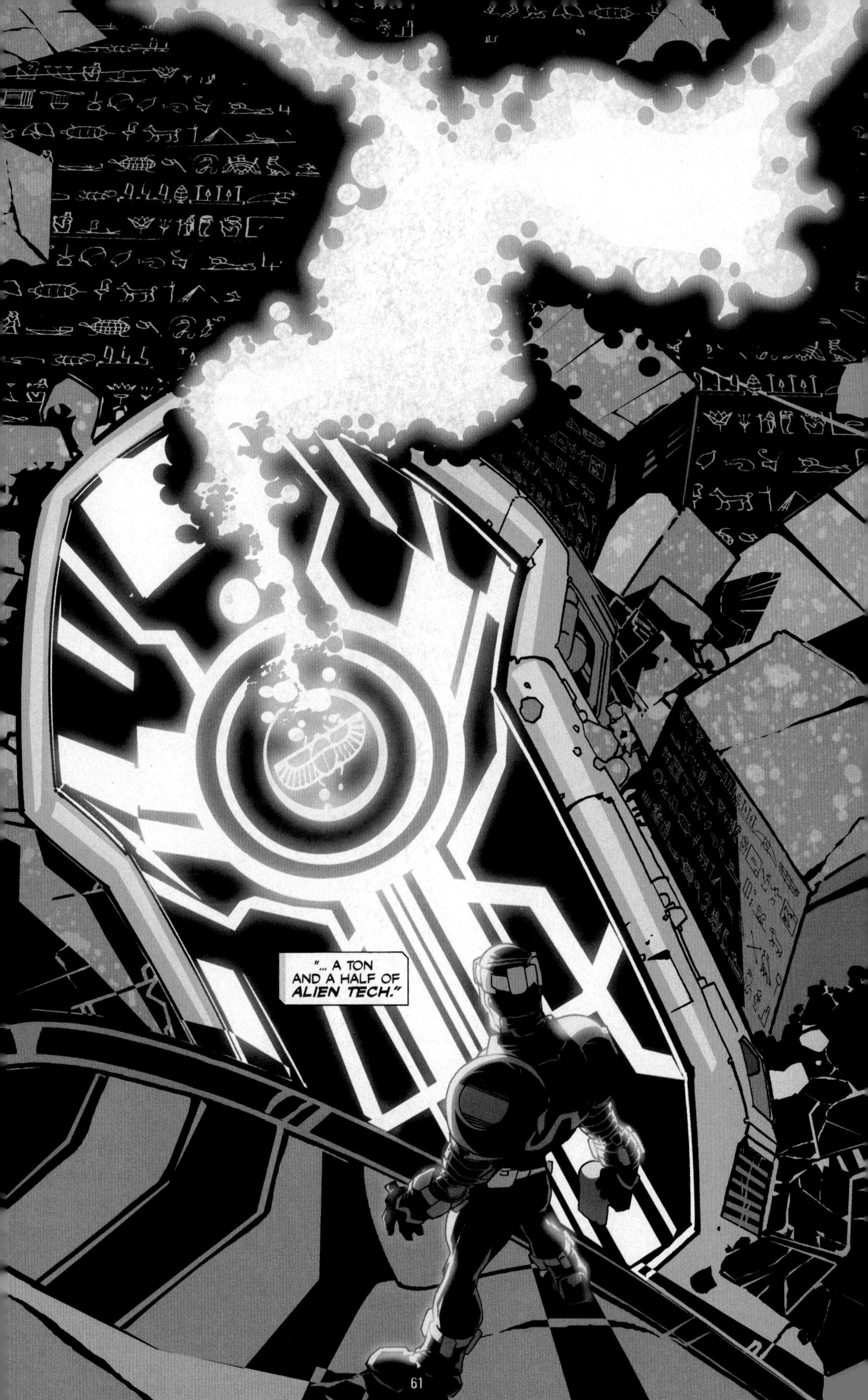
"... A TON AND A HALF OF ALIEN TECH."

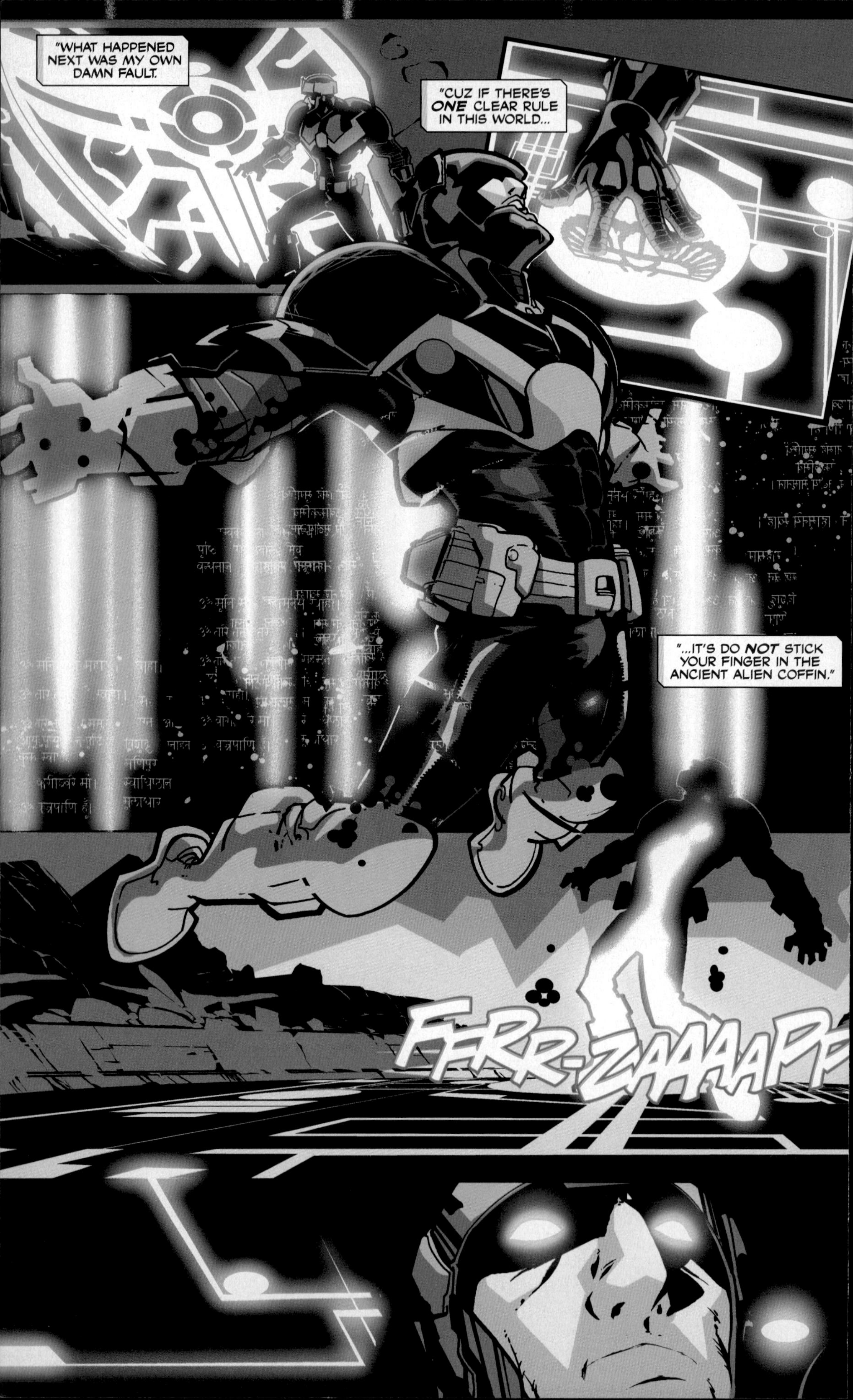
"WHAT HAPPENED NEXT WAS MY OWN DAMN FAULT.
"CUZ IF THERE'S ONE CLEAR RULE IN THIS WORLD...
"...IT'S DO NOT STICK YOUR FINGER IN THE ANCIENT ALIEN COFFIN."
FFRR-ZAAAAPP

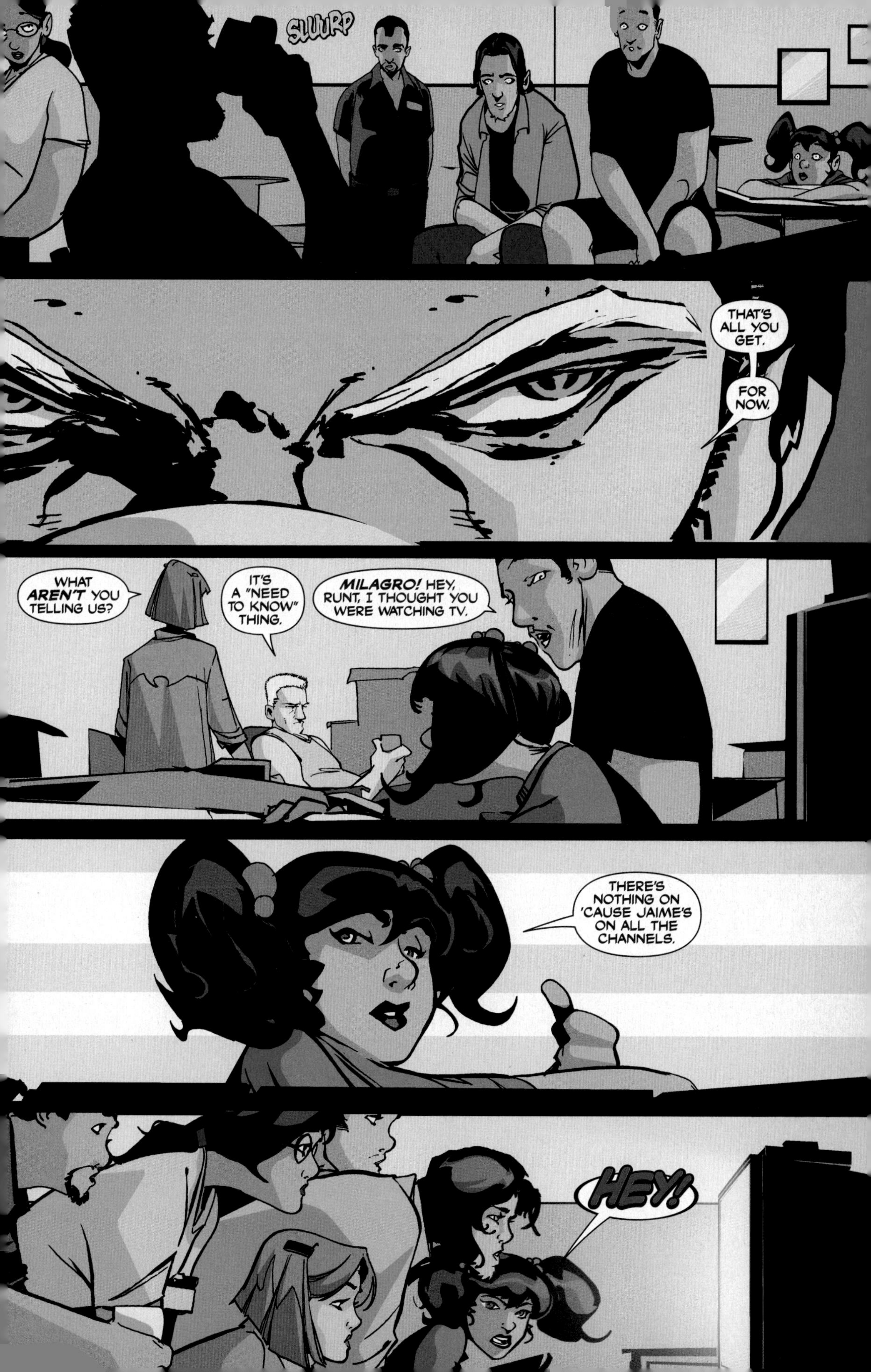
SLUURP
THAT'S ALL YOU GET.
FOR NOW.
WHAT AREN'T YOU TELLING US?
IT'S A "NEED TO KNOW" THING.
MILAGRO! HEY, RUNT, I THOUGHT YOU WERE WATCHING TV.
THERE'S NOTHING ON 'CAUSE JAIME'S ON ALL THE CHANNELS.
HEY!

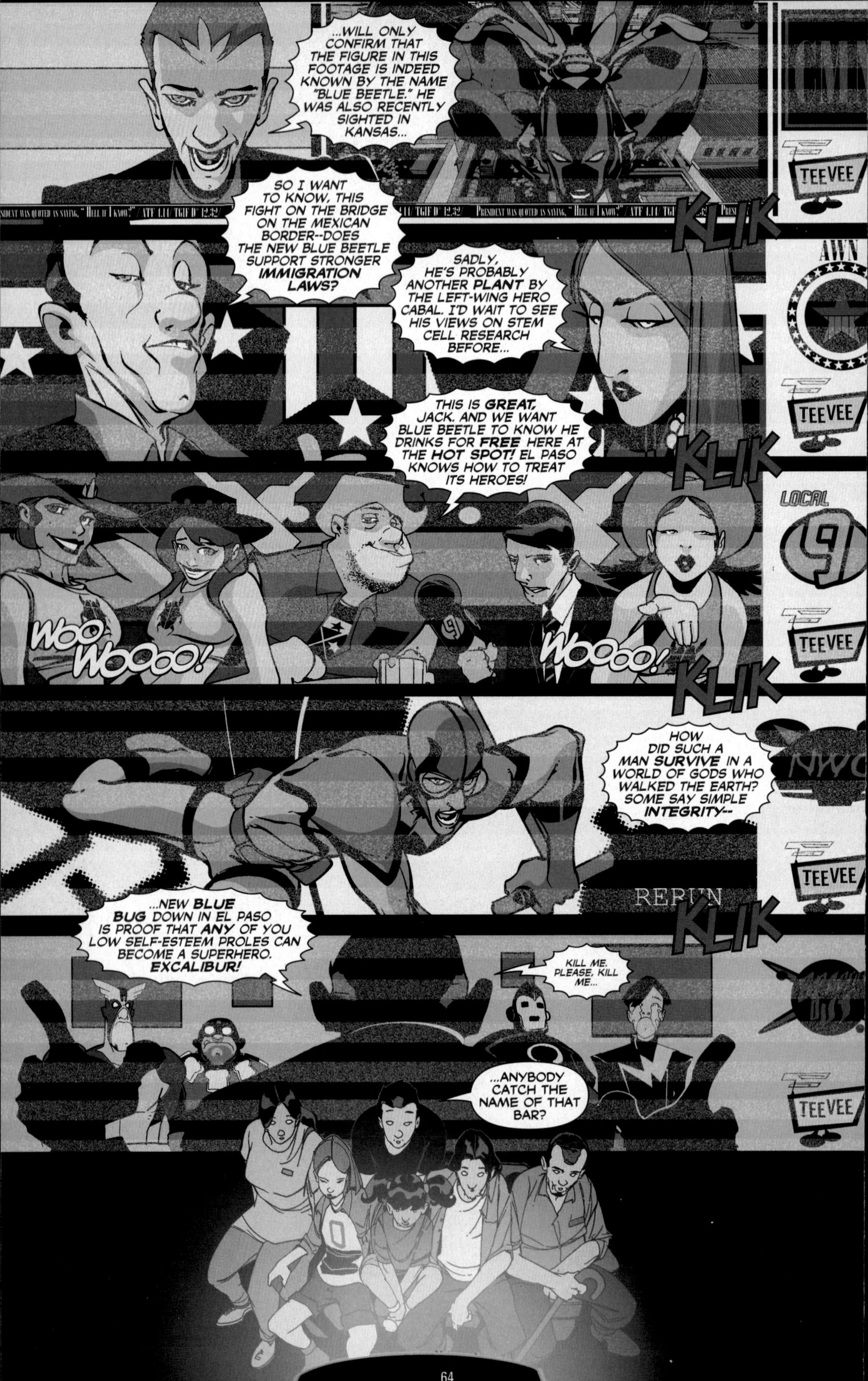
...WILL ONLY CONFIRM THAT THE FIGURE IN THIS FOOTAGE IS INDEED KNOWN BY THE NAME "BLUE BEETLE." HE WAS ALSO RECENTLY SIGHTED IN KANSAS...
TEEVEE
PRESIDENT WAS QUOTED AS SAYING, "HELL IF I KNOW?" / ATF 1.14/ TGIF D 12.32/
SO I WANT TO KNOW, THIS FIGHT ON THE BRIDGE ON THE MEXICAN BORDER--DOES THE NEW BLUE BEETLE SUPPORT STRONGER IMMIGRATION LAWS?
KLIK
AWN
SADLY, HE'S PROBABLY ANOTHER PLANT BY THE LEFT-WING HERO CABAL. I'D WAIT TO SEE HIS VIEWS ON STEM CELL RESEARCH BEFORE...
TEEVEE
KLIK
THIS IS GREAT, JACK. AND WE WANT BLUE BEETLE TO KNOW HE DRINKS FOR FREE HERE AT THE HOT SPOT! EL PASO KNOWS HOW TO TREAT ITS HEROES!
LOCAL 9
WOO WOOOOO!
WOOOO!
TEEVEE
KLIK
HOW DID SUCH A MAN SURVIVE IN A WORLD OF GODS WHO WALKED THE EARTH? SOME SAY SIMPLE INTEGRITY--
TEEVEE
KLIK
...NEW BLUE BUG DOWN IN EL PASO IS PROOF THAT ANY OF YOU LOW SELF-ESTEEM PROLES CAN BECOME A SUPERHERO. EXCALIBUR!
KILL ME. PLEASE, KILL ME...
...ANYBODY CATCH THE NAME OF THAT BAR?
TEEVEE

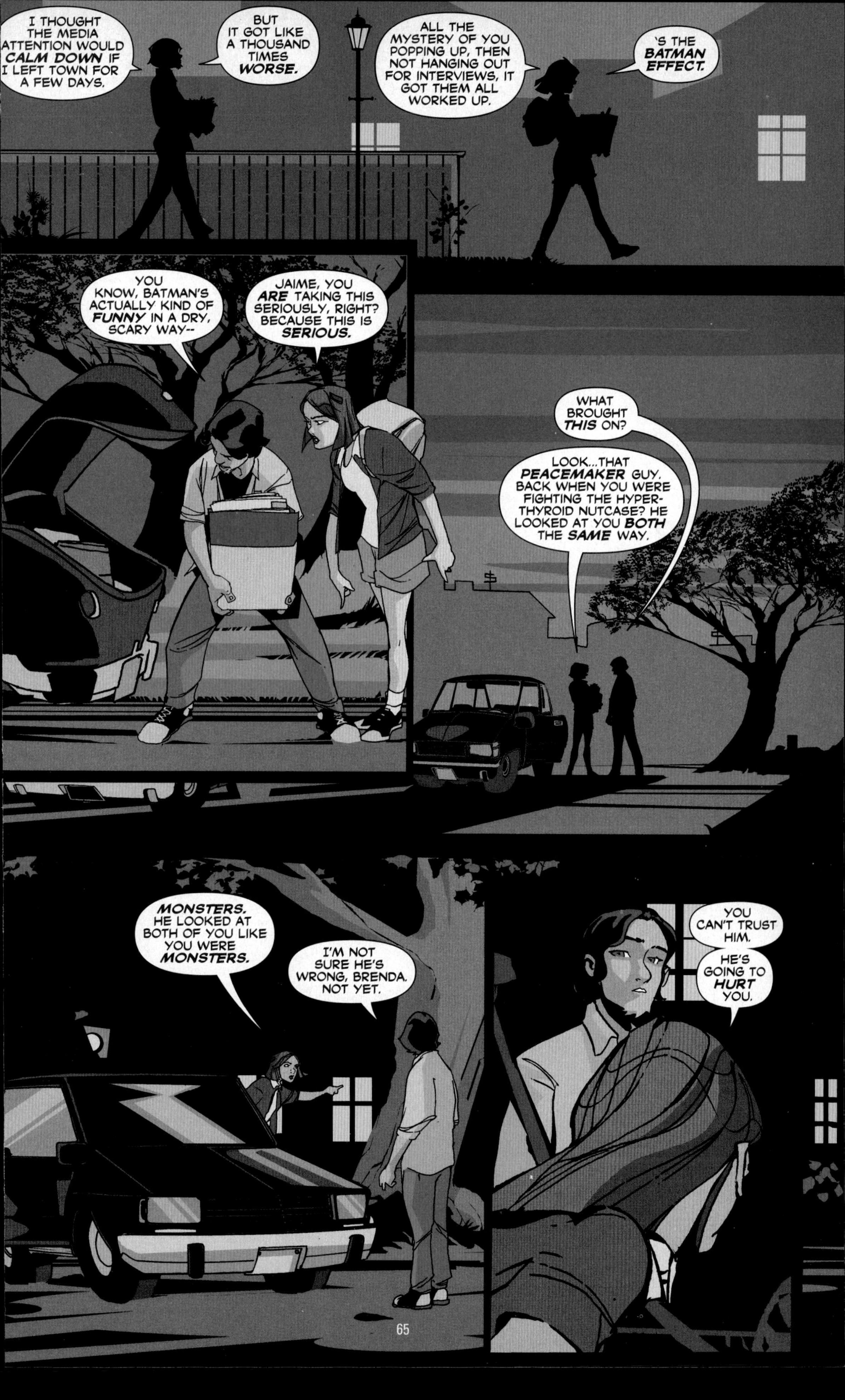
I THOUGHT THE MEDIA ATTENTION WOULD CALM DOWN IF I LEFT TOWN FOR A FEW DAYS.
BUT IT GOT LIKE A THOUSAND TIMES WORSE.
ALL THE MYSTERY OF YOU POPPING UP, THEN NOT HANGING OUT FOR INTERVIEWS, IT GOT THEM ALL WORKED UP.
'S THE BATMAN EFFECT.
YOU KNOW, BATMAN'S ACTUALLY KIND OF FUNNY IN A DRY, SCARY WAY--
JAIME, YOU ARE TAKING THIS SERIOUSLY, RIGHT? BECAUSE THIS IS SERIOUS.
WHAT BROUGHT THIS ON?
LOOK...THAT PEACEMAKER GUY. BACK WHEN YOU WERE FIGHTING THE HYPER-THYROID NUTCASE? HE LOOKED AT YOU BOTH THE SAME WAY.
MONSTERS. HE LOOKED AT BOTH OF YOU LIKE YOU WERE MONSTERS.
I'M NOT SURE HE'S WRONG, BRENDA. NOT YET.
YOU CAN'T TRUST HIM.
HE'S GOING TO HURT YOU.

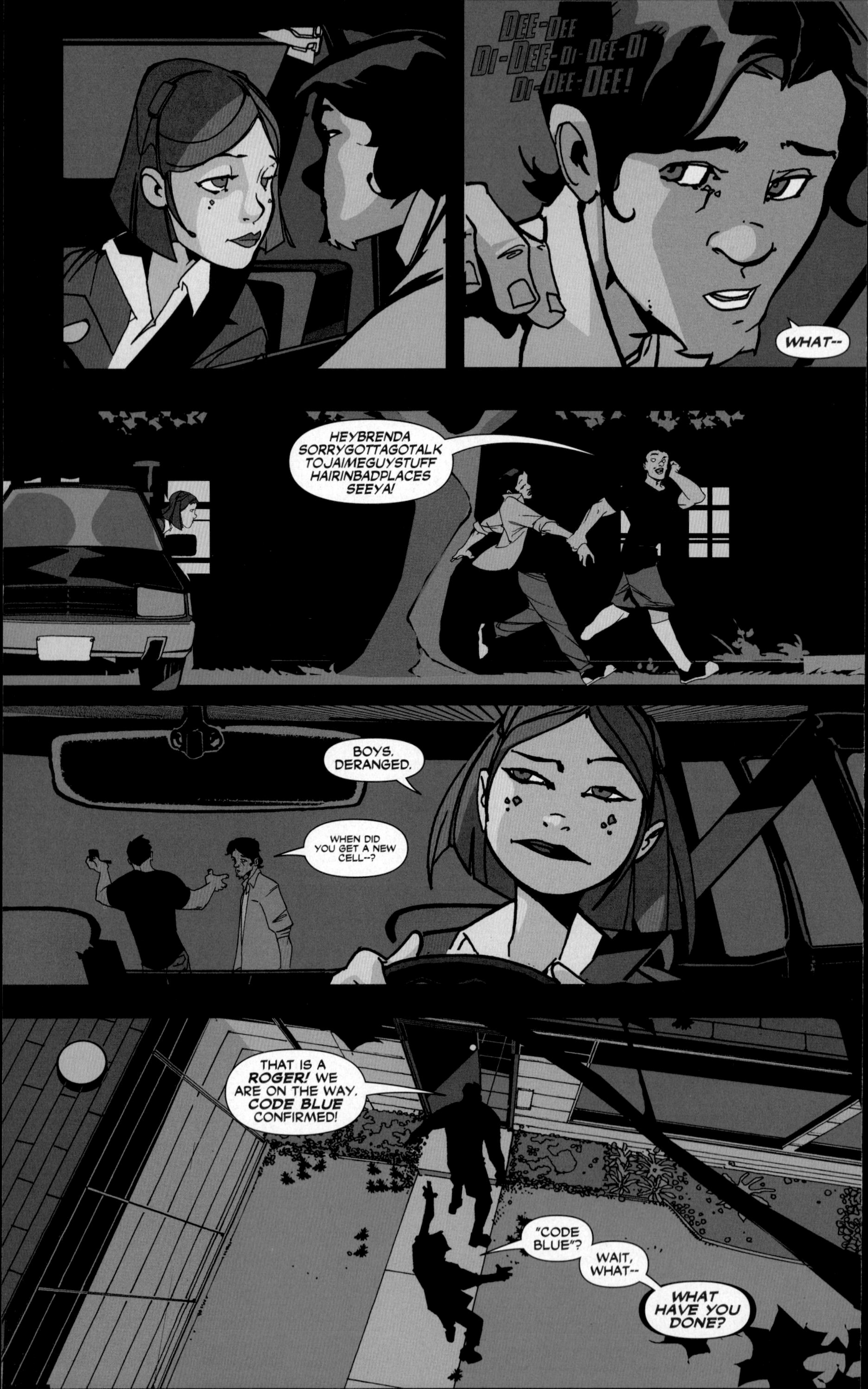
DEE-DEE DI-DEE-DI-DEE-DI DI-DEE-DEE!
WHAT--
HEYBRENDA SORRYGOTTAGOTALK TOJAIMEGUYSTUFF HAIRINBADPLACES SEEYA!
BOYS. DERANGED.
WHEN DID YOU GET A NEW CELL--?
THAT IS A ROGER! WE ARE ON THE WAY. CODE BLUE CONFIRMED!
"CODE BLUE"?
WAIT, WHAT--
WHAT HAVE YOU DONE?

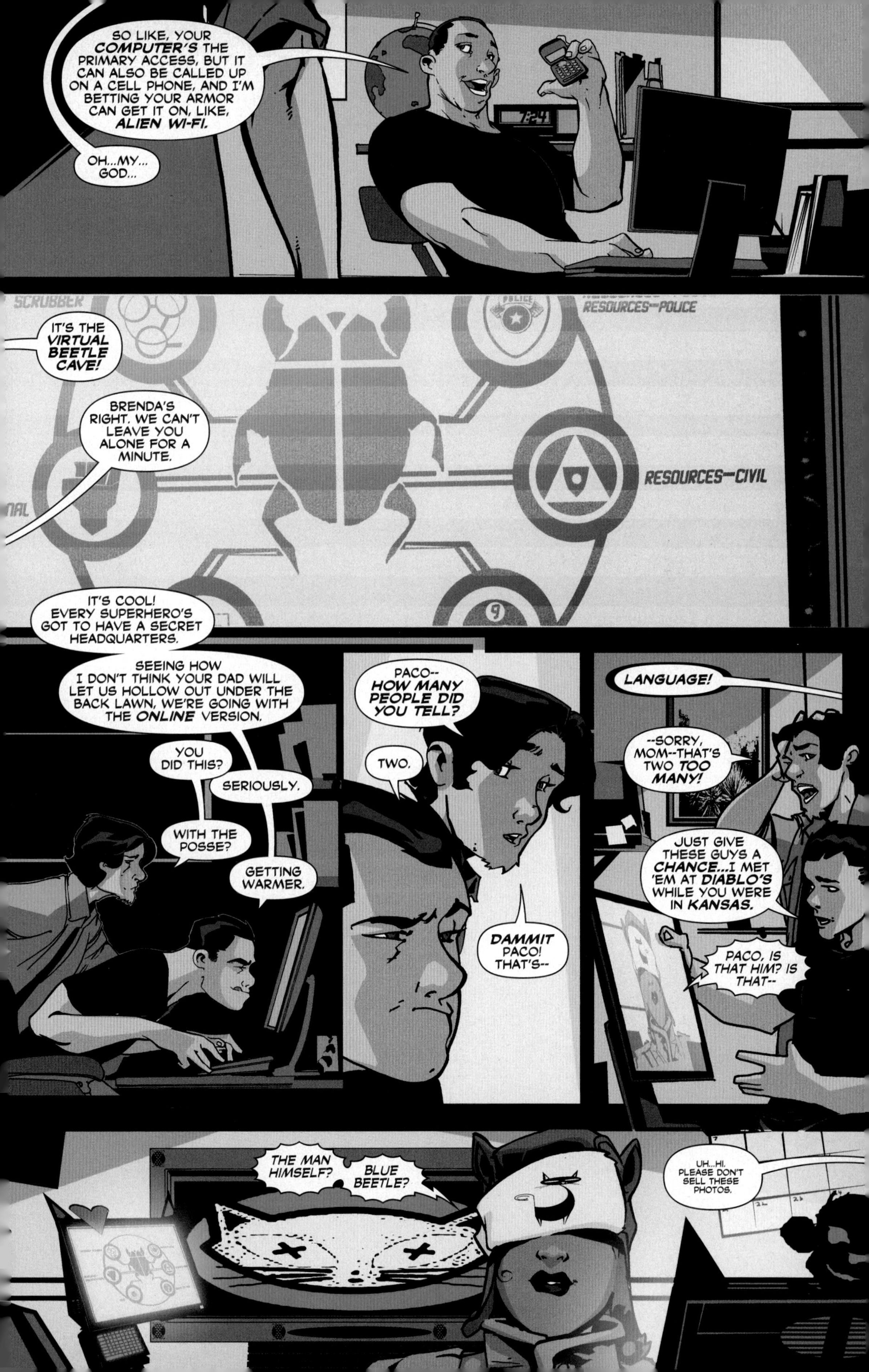
SO LIKE, YOUR COMPUTER'S THE PRIMARY ACCESS, BUT IT CAN ALSO BE CALLED UP ON A CELL PHONE, AND I'M BETTING YOUR ARMOR CAN GET IT ON, LIKE, ALIEN WI-FI.
OH...MY... GOD...
7:24
SCRUBBER
RESOURCES—POLICE
POLICE
IT'S THE VIRTUAL BEETLE CAVE!
BRENDA'S RIGHT. WE CAN'T LEAVE YOU ALONE FOR A MINUTE.
RESOURCES—CIVIL
IT'S COOL! EVERY SUPERHERO'S GOT TO HAVE A SECRET HEADQUARTERS.
SEEING HOW I DON'T THINK YOUR DAD WILL LET US HOLLOW OUT UNDER THE BACK LAWN, WE'RE GOING WITH THE ONLINE VERSION.
YOU DID THIS?
SERIOUSLY.
WITH THE POSSE?
GETTING WARMER.
PACO-- HOW MANY PEOPLE DID YOU TELL?
TWO.
DAMMIT PACO! THAT'S--
LANGUAGE!
--SORRY, MOM--THAT'S TWO TOO MANY!
JUST GIVE THESE GUYS A CHANCE...I MET 'EM AT DIABLO'S WHILE YOU WERE IN KANSAS.
PACO, IS THAT HIM? IS THAT--
THE MAN HIMSELF?
BLUE BEETLE?
UH...HI. PLEASE DON'T SELL THESE PHOTOS.

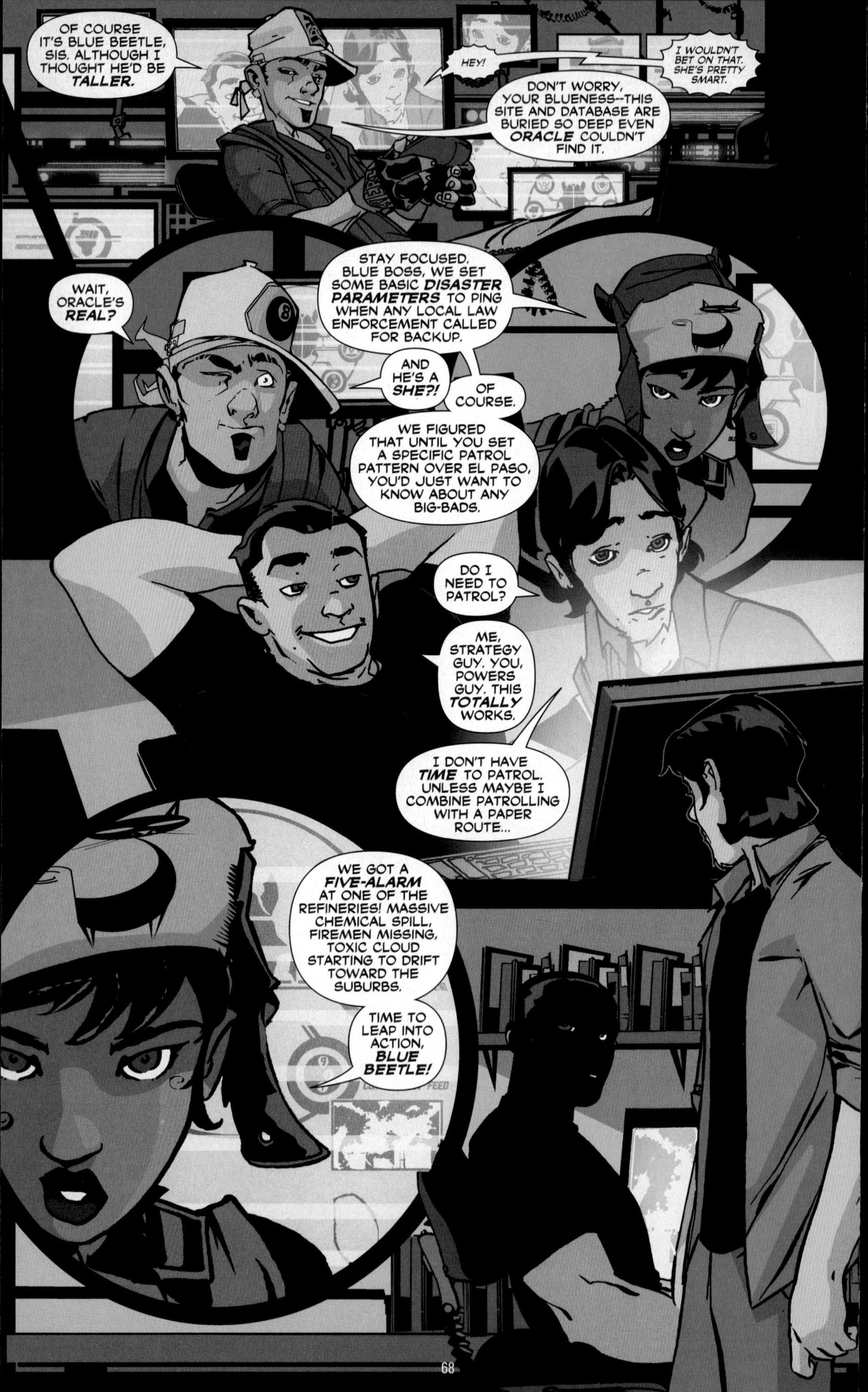
OF COURSE IT'S BLUE BEETLE, SIS. ALTHOUGH I THOUGHT HE'D BE *TALLER.*
HEY!
I WOULDN'T BET ON THAT. SHE'S PRETTY SMART.
DON'T WORRY, YOUR BLUENESS--THIS SITE AND DATABASE ARE BURIED SO DEEP EVEN *ORACLE* COULDN'T FIND IT.
WAIT, ORACLE'S *REAL?*
STAY FOCUSED, BLUE BOSS. WE SET SOME BASIC *DISASTER PARAMETERS* TO PING WHEN ANY LOCAL LAW ENFORCEMENT CALLED FOR BACKUP.
AND HE'S A *SHE?!*
OF COURSE.
WE FIGURED THAT UNTIL YOU SET A SPECIFIC PATROL PATTERN OVER EL PASO, YOU'D JUST WANT TO KNOW ABOUT ANY BIG-BADS.
DO I NEED TO PATROL?
ME, STRATEGY GUY. YOU, POWERS GUY. THIS *TOTALLY* WORKS.
I DON'T HAVE *TIME* TO PATROL. UNLESS MAYBE I COMBINE PATROLLING WITH A PAPER ROUTE...
WE GOT A *FIVE-ALARM* AT ONE OF THE REFINERIES! MASSIVE CHEMICAL SPILL, FIREMEN MISSING, TOXIC CLOUD STARTING TO DRIFT TOWARD THE SUBURBS.
TIME TO LEAP INTO ACTION, *BLUE BEETLE!*

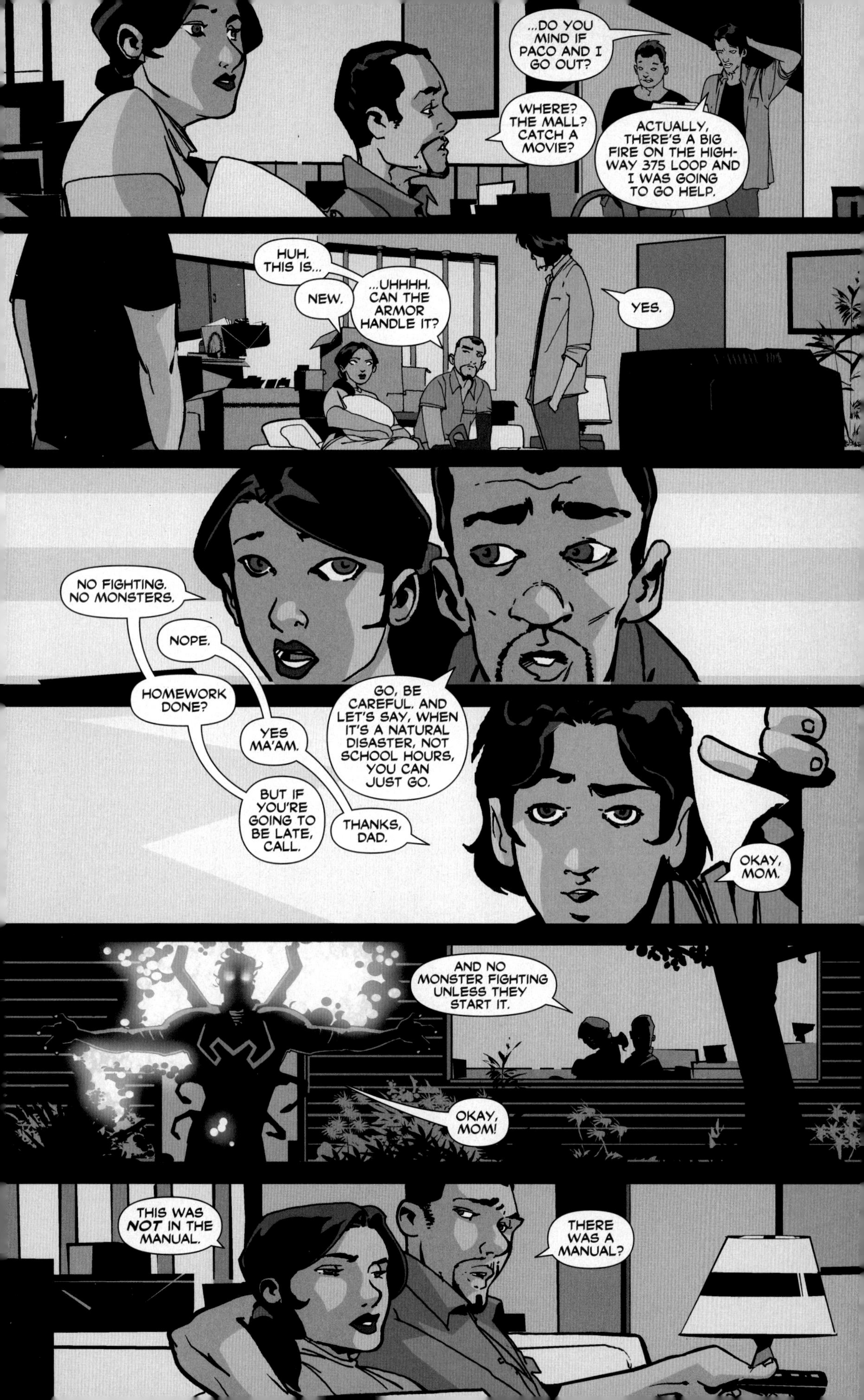
...DO YOU MIND IF PACO AND I GO OUT?
WHERE? THE MALL? CATCH A MOVIE?
ACTUALLY, THERE'S A BIG FIRE ON THE HIGH-WAY 375 LOOP AND I WAS GOING TO GO HELP.
HUH. THIS IS...
NEW.
...UHHHH. CAN THE ARMOR HANDLE IT?
YES.
NO FIGHTING. NO MONSTERS.
NOPE.
HOMEWORK DONE?
YES MA'AM.
BUT IF YOU'RE GOING TO BE LATE, CALL.
GO, BE CAREFUL. AND LET'S SAY, WHEN IT'S A NATURAL DISASTER, NOT SCHOOL HOURS, YOU CAN JUST GO.
THANKS, DAD.
OKAY, MOM.
AND NO MONSTER FIGHTING UNLESS THEY START IT.
OKAY, MOM!
THIS WAS NOT IN THE MANUAL.
THERE WAS A MANUAL?

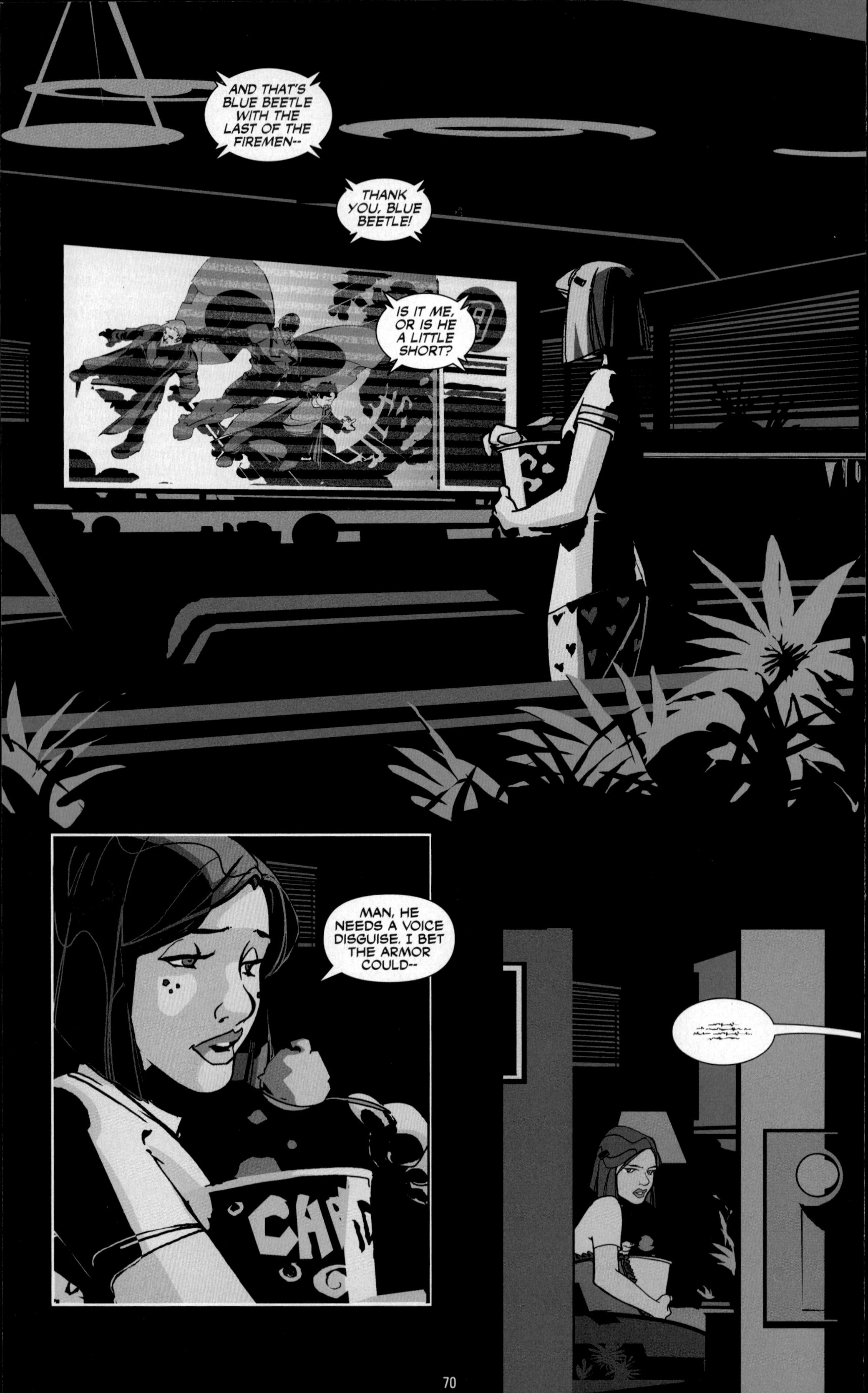
AND THAT'S BLUE BEETLE WITH THE LAST OF THE FIREMEN--
THANK YOU, BLUE BEETLE!
IS IT ME, OR IS HE A LITTLE SHORT?
MAN, HE NEEDS A VOICE DISGUISE. I BET THE ARMOR COULD--
CHA

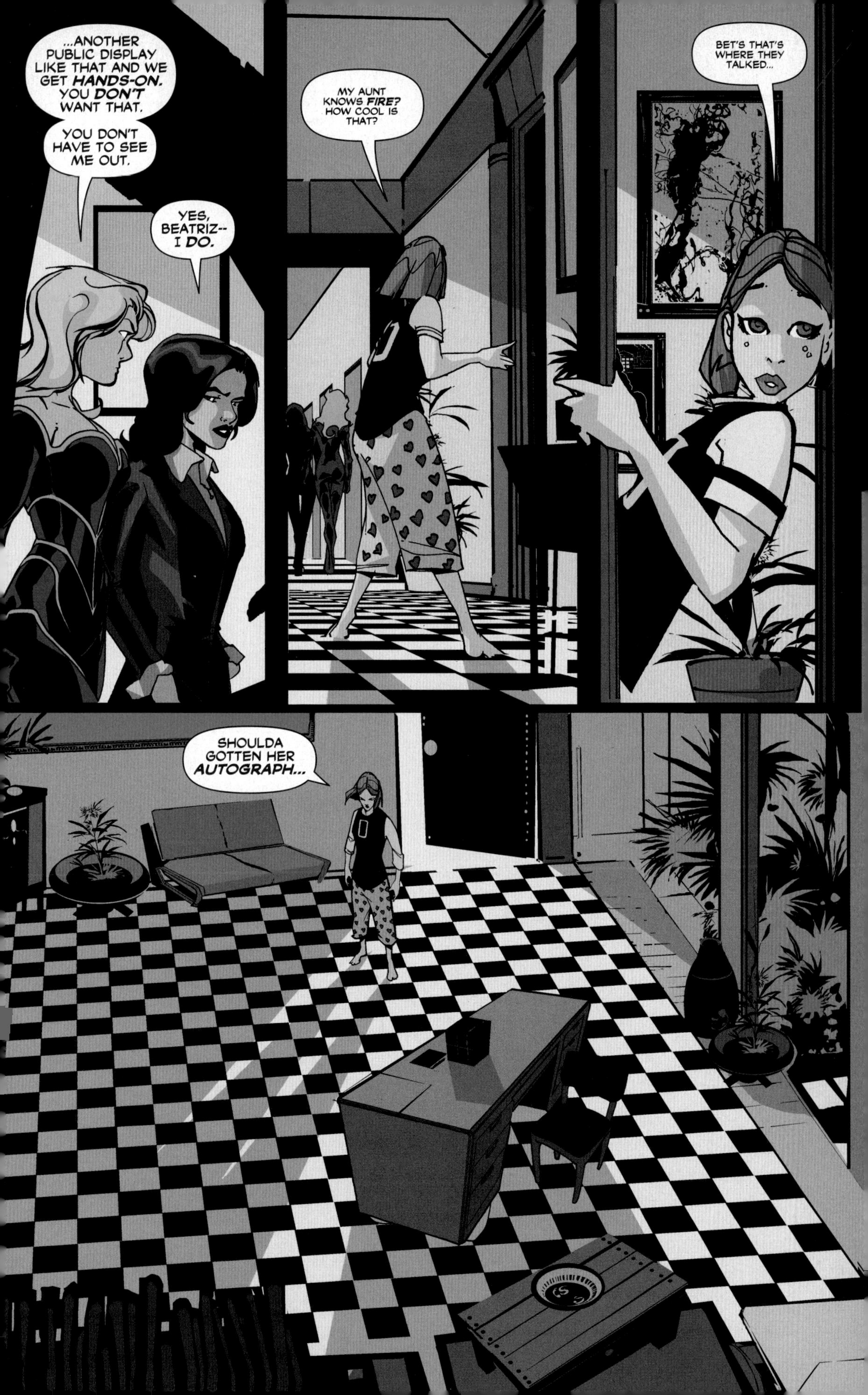
...ANOTHER PUBLIC DISPLAY LIKE THAT AND WE GET HANDS-ON. YOU DON'T WANT THAT.
YOU DON'T HAVE TO SEE ME OUT.
YES, BEATRIZ-- I DO.
MY AUNT KNOWS FIRE? HOW COOL IS THAT?
BET'S THAT'S WHERE THEY TALKED...
SHOULDA GOTTEN HER AUTOGRAPH...

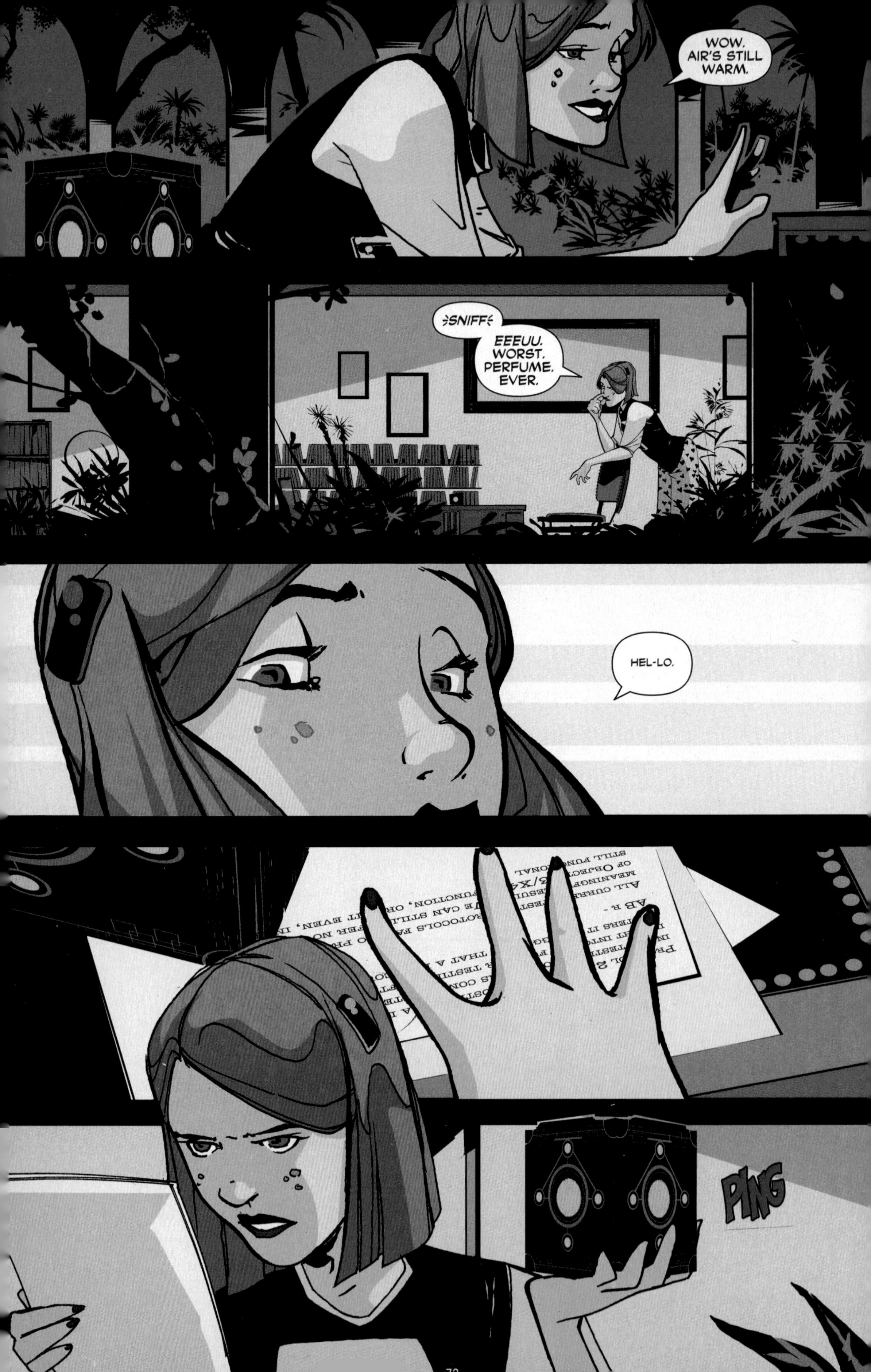
WOW. AIR'S STILL WARM.
SNIFF
EEEUU. WORST. PERFUME. EVER.
HEL-LO.
PING

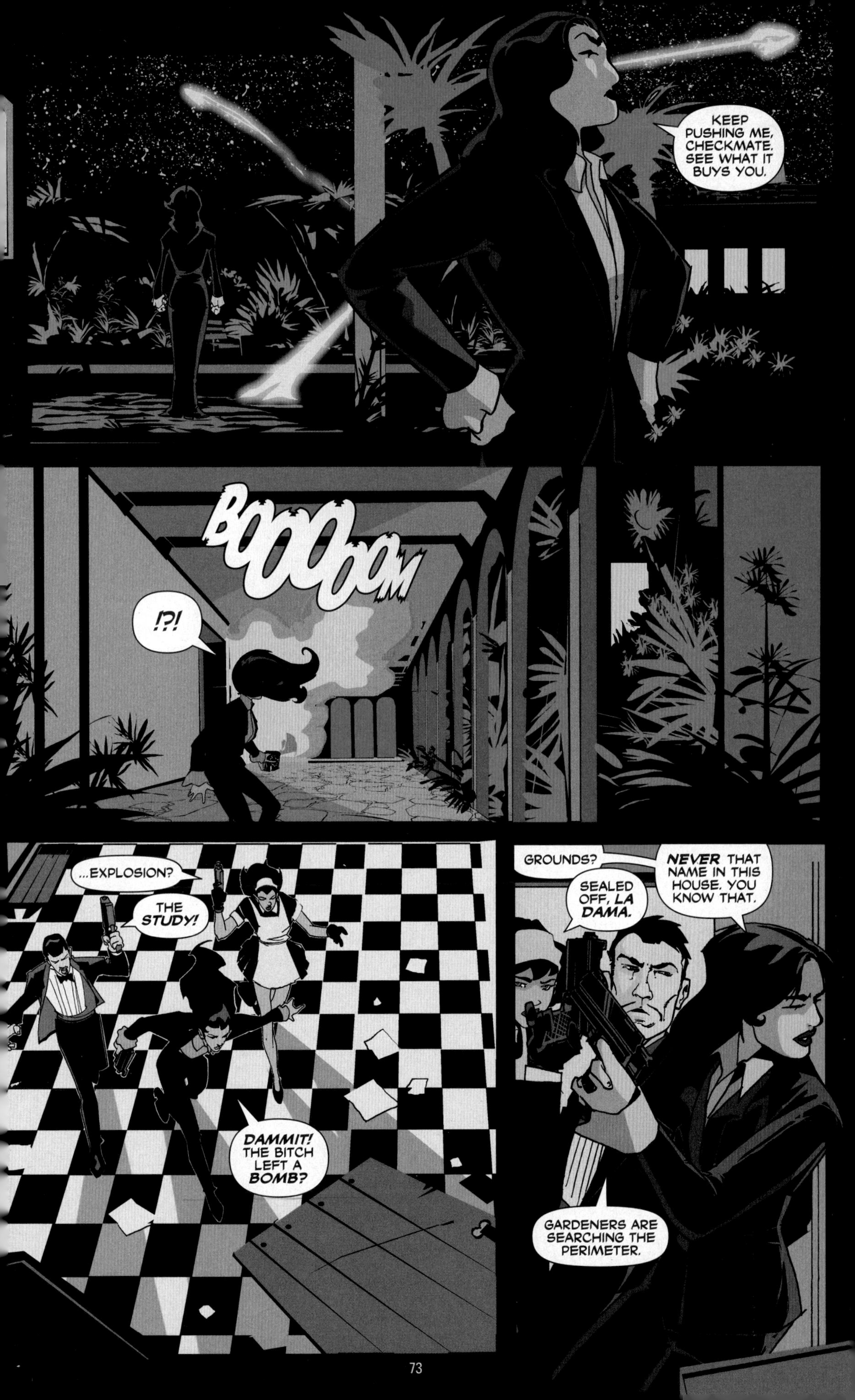
KEEP PUSHING ME, CHECKMATE. SEE WHAT IT BUYS YOU.
BOOOOOOM
!?!
...EXPLOSION?
THE STUDY!
DAMMIT! THE BITCH LEFT A BOMB?
GROUNDS?
SEALED OFF, LA DAMA.
NEVER THAT NAME IN THIS HOUSE. YOU KNOW THAT.
GARDENERS ARE SEARCHING THE PERIMETER.

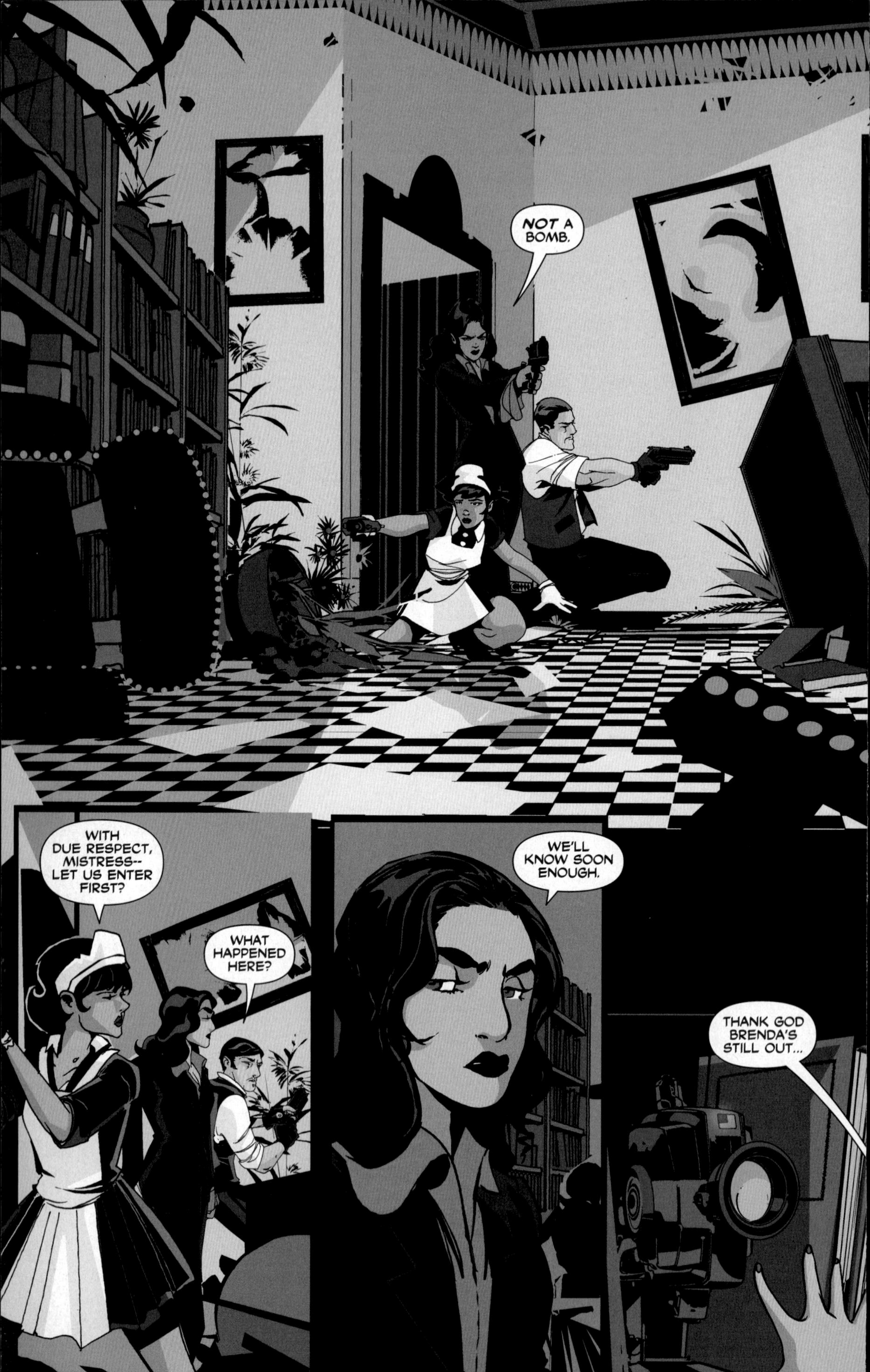
NOT A BOMB.
WITH DUE RESPECT, MISTRESS-- LET US ENTER FIRST?
WHAT HAPPENED HERE?
WE'LL KNOW SOON ENOUGH.
THANK GOD BRENDA'S STILL OUT...

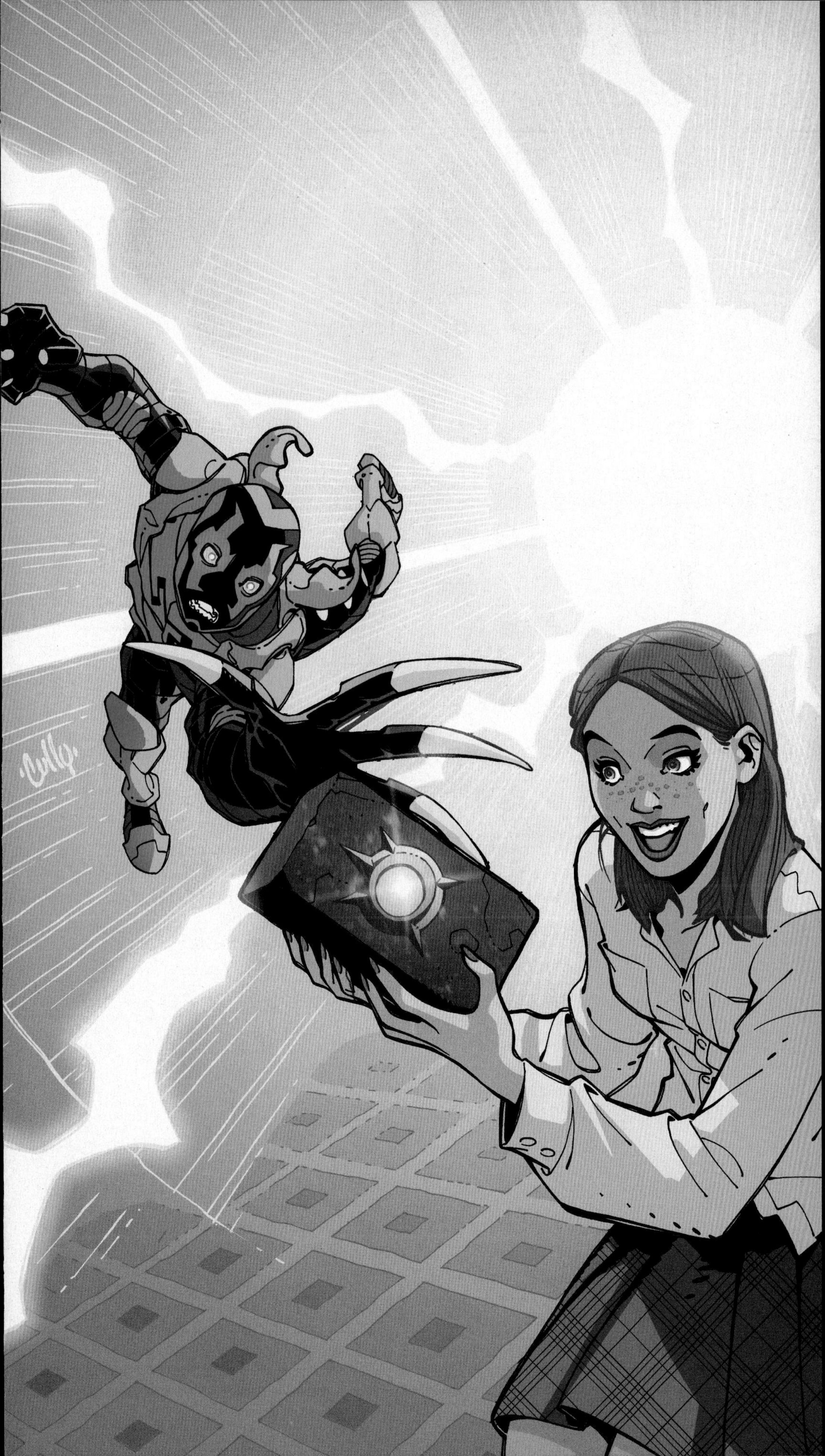

BLUE BEETLE #10 Written by Keith Giffen & John Rogers Cover by Cully Hamner Interior art by Cully Hamner with Rafael Albuquerque

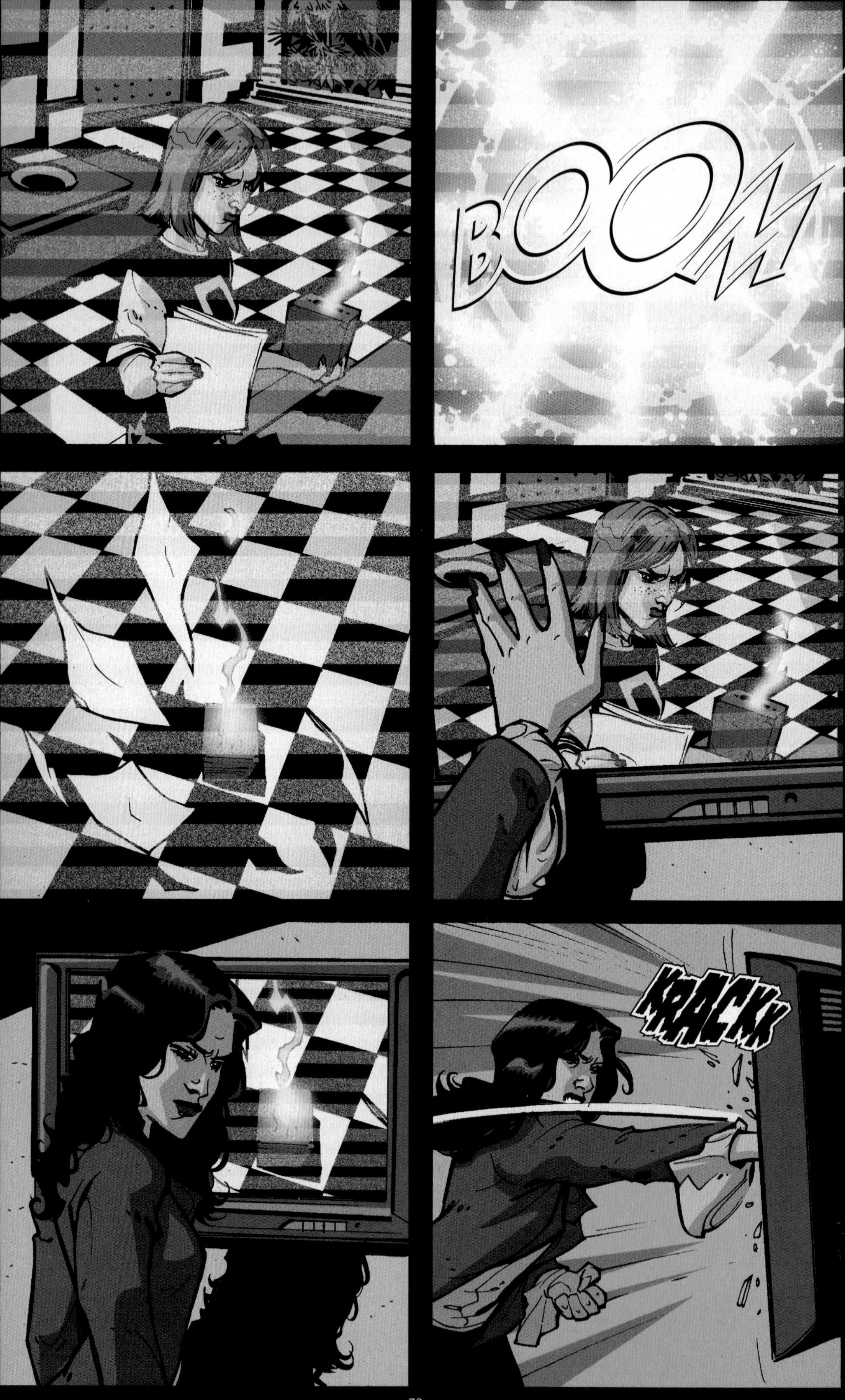
BOOM
KRACKK

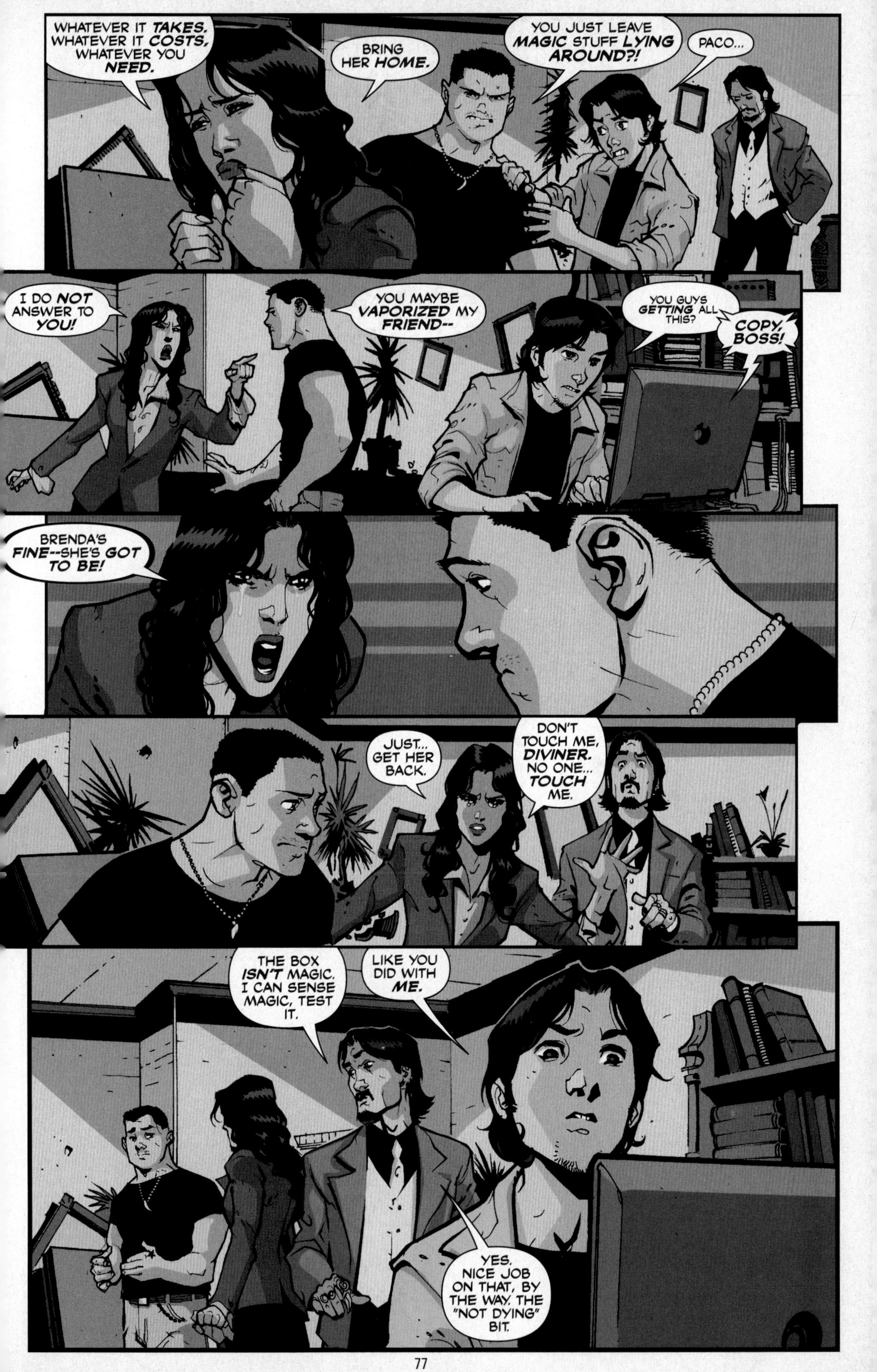

WHATEVER IT TAKES. WHATEVER IT COSTS, WHATEVER YOU NEED.
BRING HER HOME.
YOU JUST LEAVE MAGIC STUFF LYING AROUND?!
PACO...
I DO NOT ANSWER TO YOU!
YOU MAYBE VAPORIZED MY FRIEND--
YOU GUYS GETTING ALL THIS?
COPY, BOSS!
BRENDA'S FINE--SHE'S GOT TO BE!
JUST... GET HER BACK.
DON'T TOUCH ME, DIVINER. NO ONE... TOUCH ME.
THE BOX ISN'T MAGIC. I CAN SENSE MAGIC, TEST IT.
LIKE YOU DID WITH ME.
YES, NICE JOB ON THAT, BY THE WAY. THE "NOT DYING" BIT.

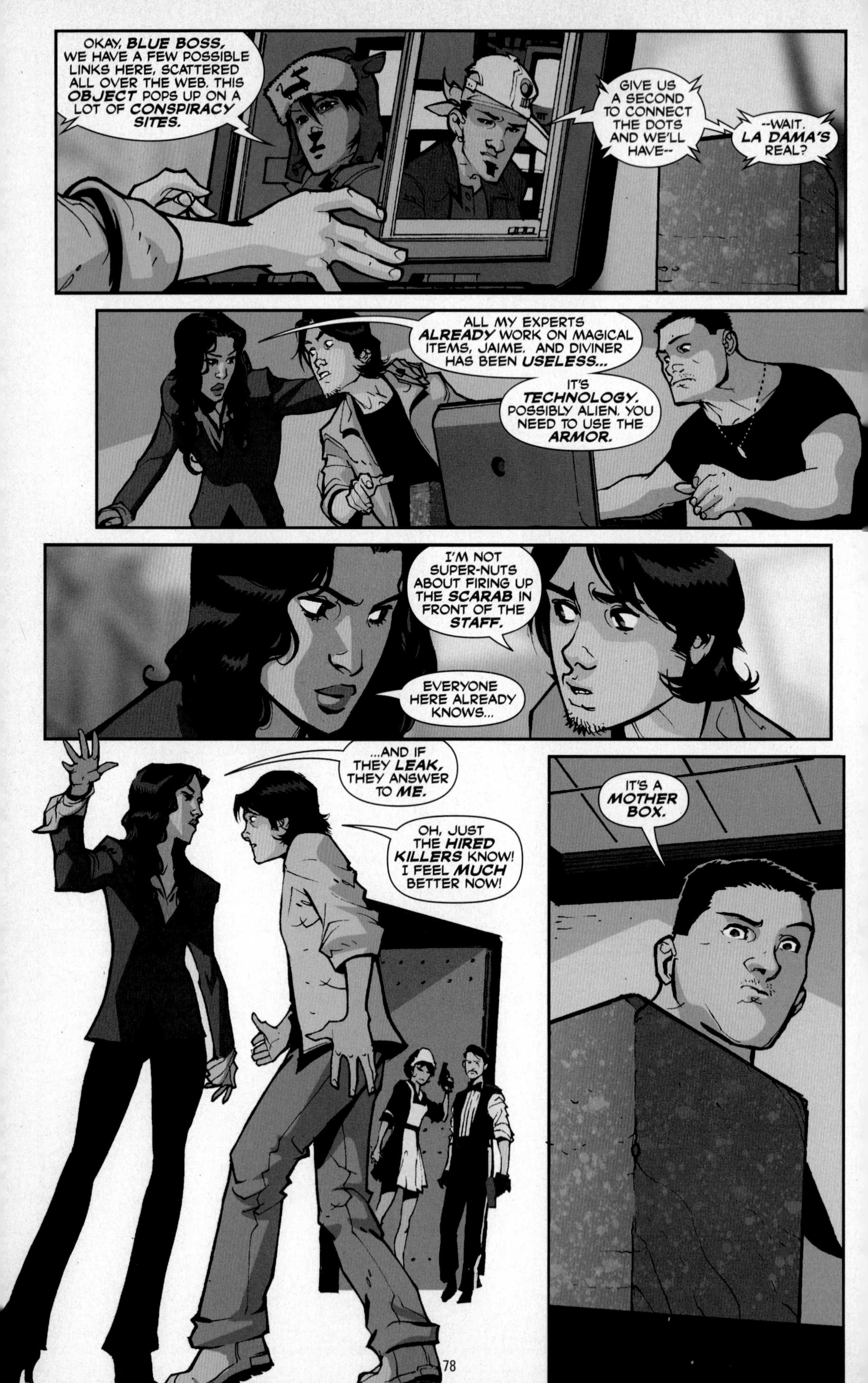
OKAY, BLUE BOSS, WE HAVE A FEW POSSIBLE LINKS HERE, SCATTERED ALL OVER THE WEB. THIS OBJECT POPS UP ON A LOT OF CONSPIRACY SITES.
GIVE US A SECOND TO CONNECT THE DOTS AND WE'LL HAVE--
--WAIT. LA DAMA'S REAL?
ALL MY EXPERTS ALREADY WORK ON MAGICAL ITEMS, JAIME. AND DIVINER HAS BEEN USELESS...
IT'S TECHNOLOGY. POSSIBLY ALIEN. YOU NEED TO USE THE ARMOR.
I'M NOT SUPER-NUTS ABOUT FIRING UP THE SCARAB IN FRONT OF THE STAFF.
EVERYONE HERE ALREADY KNOWS...
...AND IF THEY LEAK, THEY ANSWER TO ME.
OH, JUST THE HIRED KILLERS KNOW! I FEEL MUCH BETTER NOW!
IT'S A MOTHER BOX.

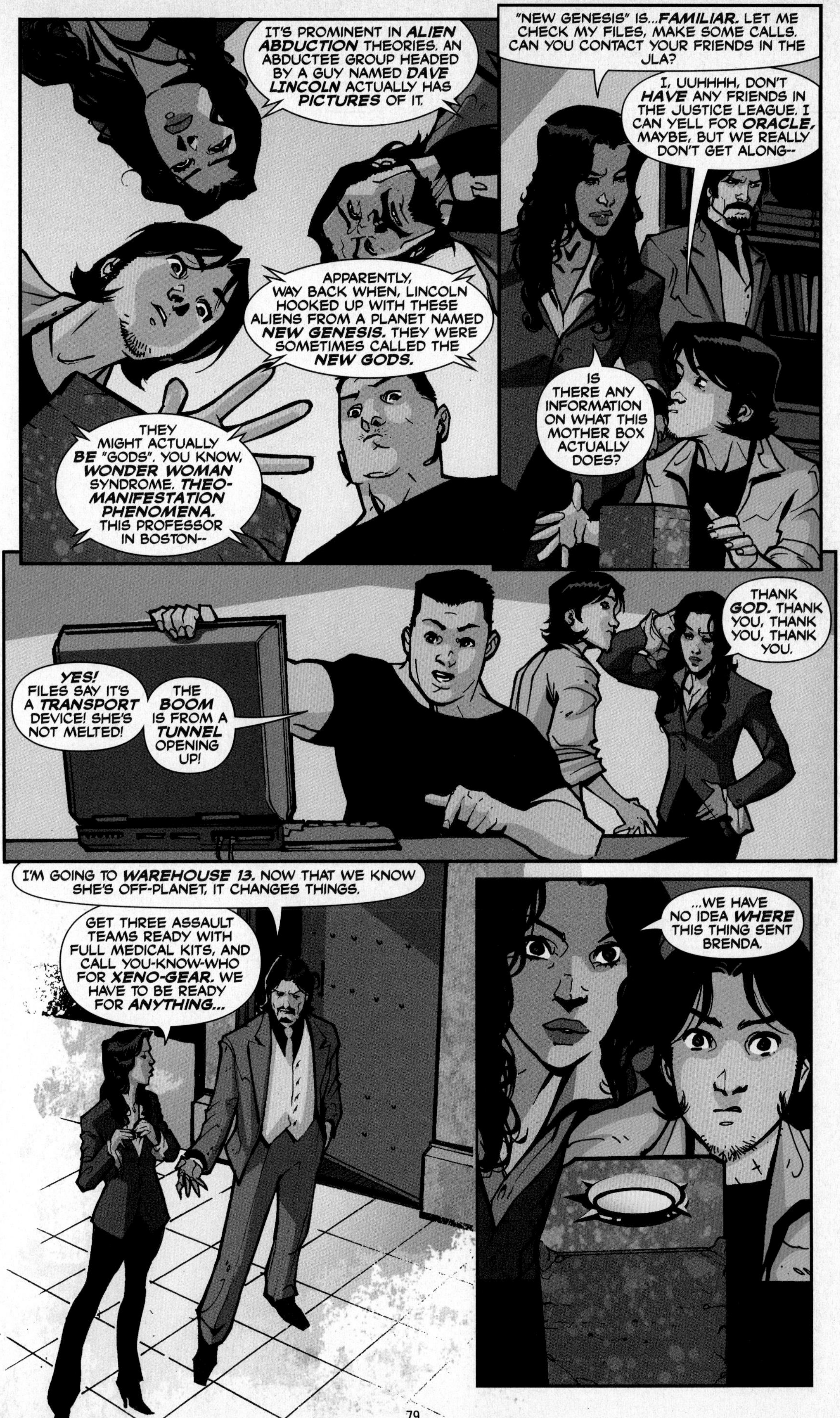
IT'S PROMINENT IN ALIEN ABDUCTION THEORIES. AN ABDUCTEE GROUP HEADED BY A GUY NAMED DAVE LINCOLN ACTUALLY HAS PICTURES OF IT.
APPARENTLY, WAY BACK WHEN, LINCOLN HOOKED UP WITH THESE ALIENS FROM A PLANET NAMED NEW GENESIS. THEY WERE SOMETIMES CALLED THE NEW GODS.
THEY MIGHT ACTUALLY BE "GODS", YOU KNOW. WONDER WOMAN SYNDROME. THEO-MANIFESTATION PHENOMENA. THIS PROFESSOR IN BOSTON--
"NEW GENESIS" IS...FAMILIAR. LET ME CHECK MY FILES, MAKE SOME CALLS. CAN YOU CONTACT YOUR FRIENDS IN THE JLA?
I, UUHHHH, DON'T HAVE ANY FRIENDS IN THE JUSTICE LEAGUE. I CAN YELL FOR ORACLE, MAYBE, BUT WE REALLY DON'T GET ALONG--
IS THERE ANY INFORMATION ON WHAT THIS MOTHER BOX ACTUALLY DOES?
YES! FILES SAY IT'S A TRANSPORT DEVICE! SHE'S NOT MELTED!
THE BOOM IS FROM A TUNNEL OPENING UP!
THANK GOD. THANK YOU, THANK YOU, THANK YOU.
I'M GOING TO WAREHOUSE 13. NOW THAT WE KNOW SHE'S OFF-PLANET, IT CHANGES THINGS.
GET THREE ASSAULT TEAMS READY WITH FULL MEDICAL KITS, AND CALL YOU-KNOW-WHO FOR XENO-GEAR. WE HAVE TO BE READY FOR ANYTHING...
...WE HAVE NO IDEA WHERE THIS THING SENT BRENDA.

SHOULD'VE TAKEN THAT LEFT TURN

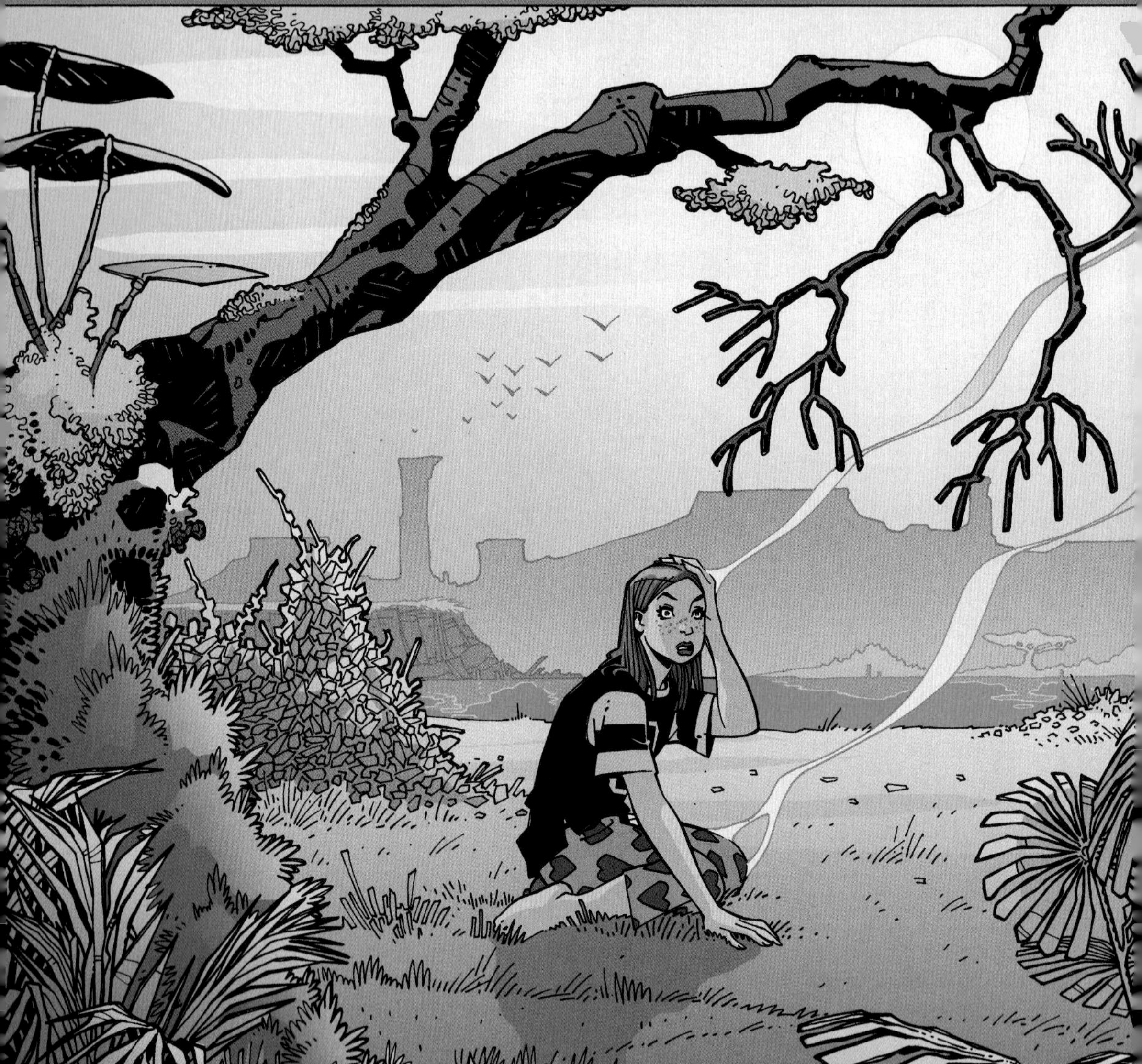

AT ALBUQUERQUE...

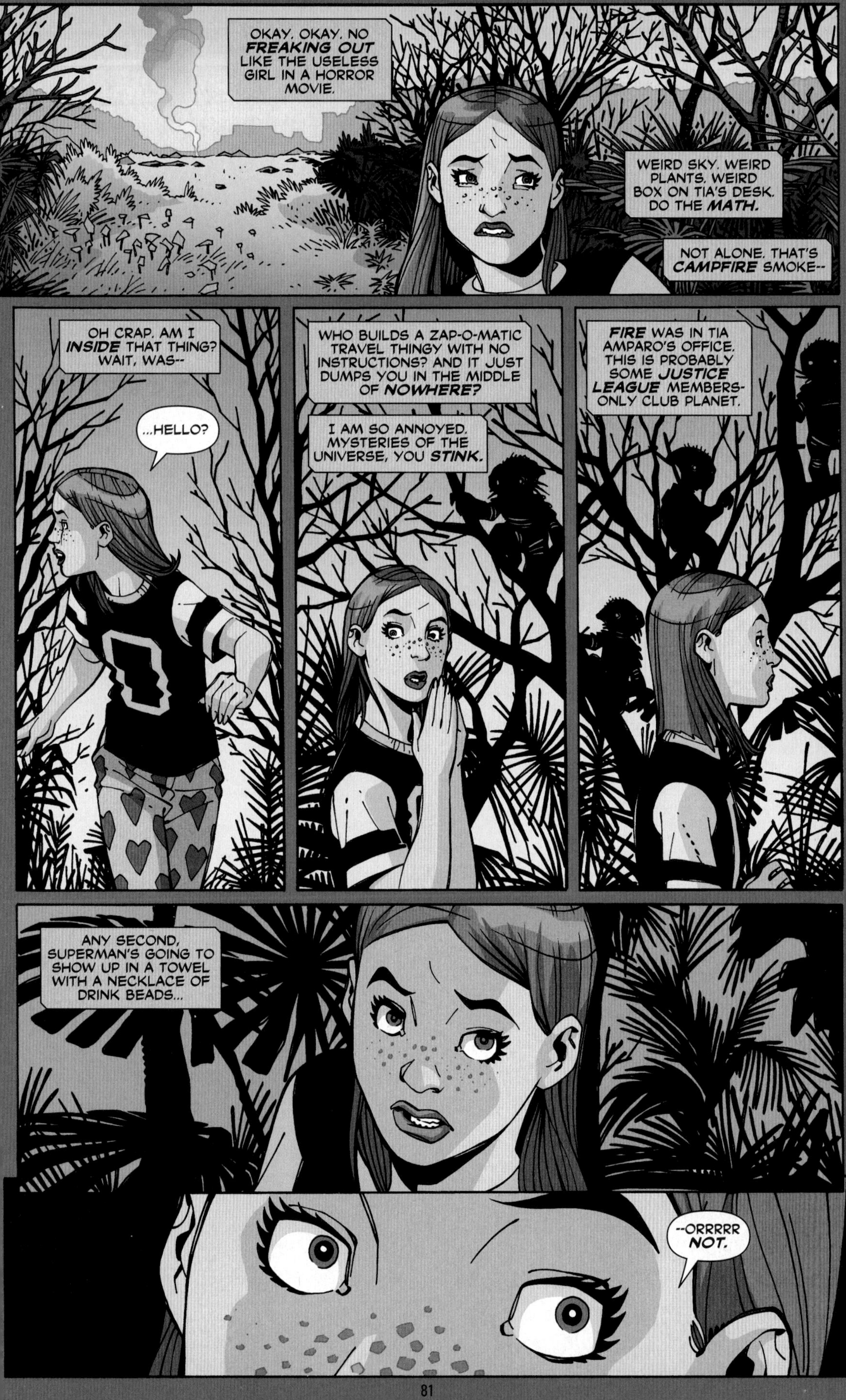
OKAY, OKAY. NO FREAKING OUT LIKE THE USELESS GIRL IN A HORROR MOVIE.
WEIRD SKY. WEIRD PLANTS. WEIRD BOX ON TIA'S DESK. DO THE MATH.
NOT ALONE. THAT'S CAMPFIRE SMOKE--
OH CRAP. AM I INSIDE THAT THING? WAIT, WAS--
...HELLO?
WHO BUILDS A ZAP-O-MATIC TRAVEL THINGY WITH NO INSTRUCTIONS? AND IT JUST DUMPS YOU IN THE MIDDLE OF NOWHERE?
I AM SO ANNOYED. MYSTERIES OF THE UNIVERSE, YOU STINK.
FIRE WAS IN TIA AMPARO'S OFFICE. THIS IS PROBABLY SOME JUSTICE LEAGUE MEMBERS-ONLY CLUB PLANET.
ANY SECOND, SUPERMAN'S GOING TO SHOW UP IN A TOWEL WITH A NECKLACE OF DRINK BEADS...
--ORRRRR NOT.

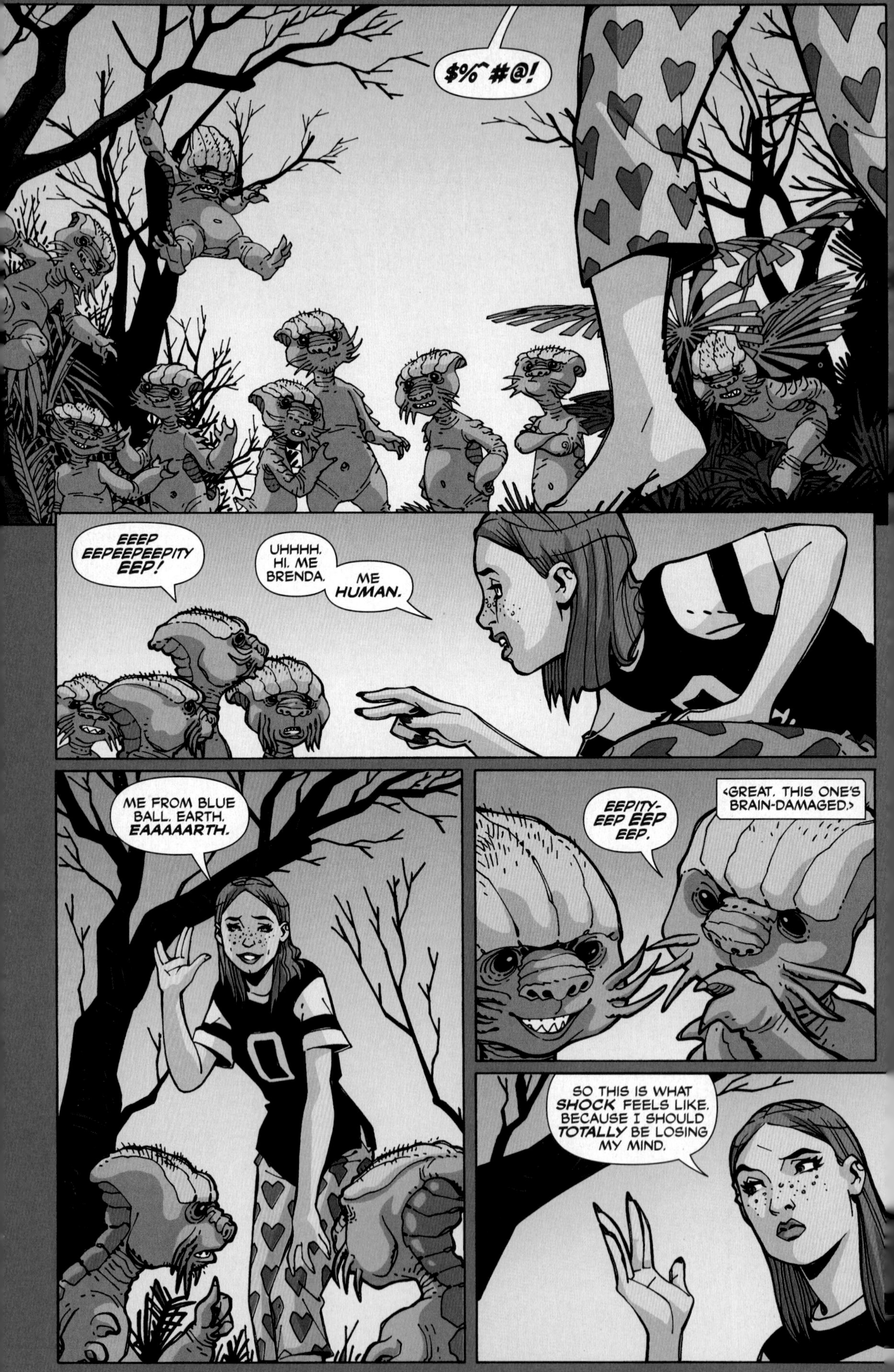
$%^#@!
EEEP EEPEEPEEPITY EEP!
UHHHH. HI. ME BRENDA.
ME HUMAN.
ME FROM BLUE BALL. EARTH. EAAAAARTH.
EEPITY-EEP EEP EEP.
<GREAT. THIS ONE'S BRAIN-DAMAGED.>
SO THIS IS WHAT SHOCK FEELS LIKE. BECAUSE I SHOULD TOTALLY BE LOSING MY MIND.

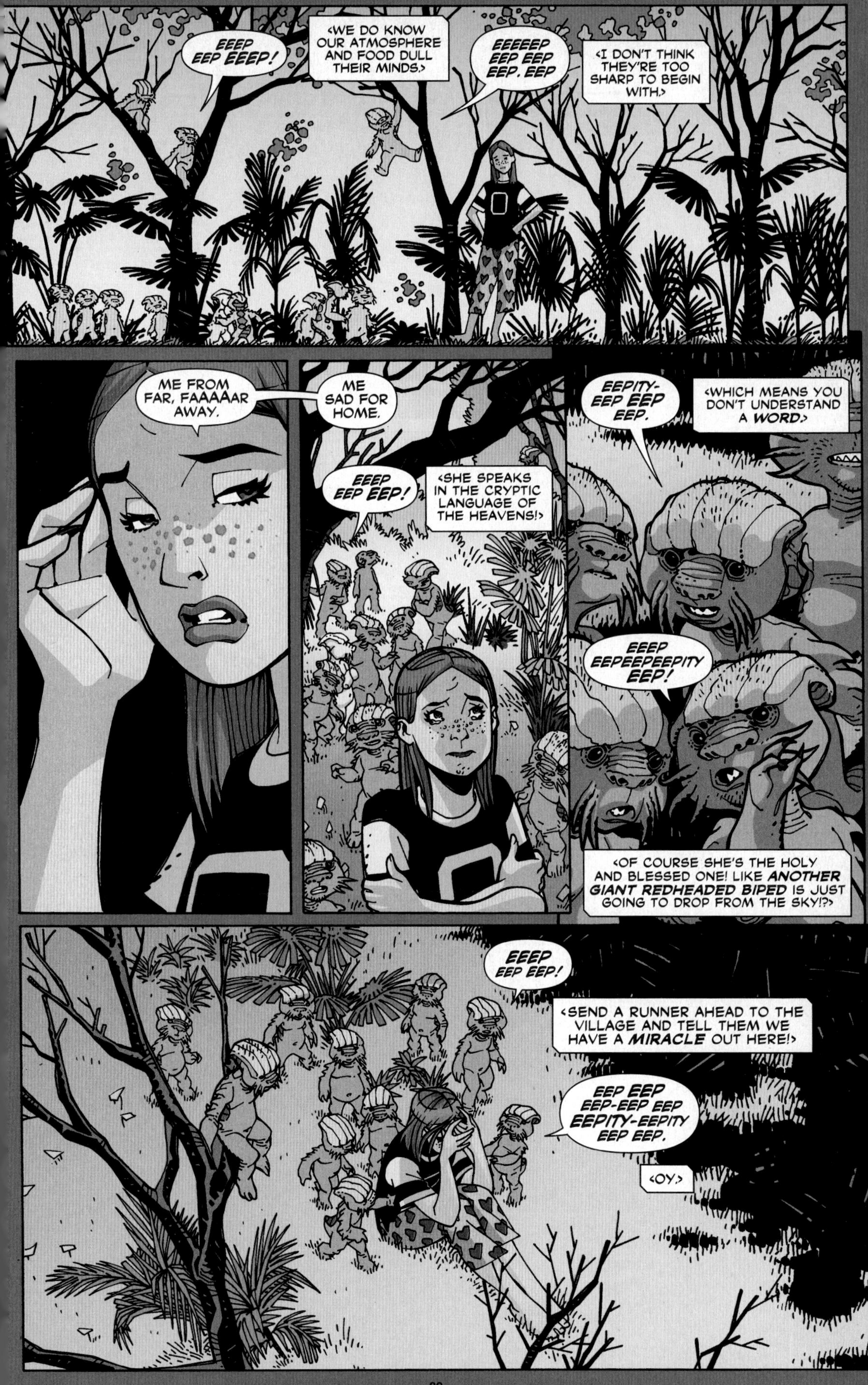
EEEP EEP EEEP!
‹WE DO KNOW OUR ATMOSPHERE AND FOOD DULL THEIR MINDS.›
EEEEEP EEP EEP EEP. EEP
‹I DON'T THINK THEY'RE TOO SHARP TO BEGIN WITH.›
ME FROM FAR, FAAAAAR AWAY.
ME SAD FOR HOME.
EEEP EEP EEP!
‹SHE SPEAKS IN THE CRYPTIC LANGUAGE OF THE HEAVENS!›
EEPITY-EEP EEP EEP.
‹WHICH MEANS YOU DON'T UNDERSTAND A WORD.›
EEEP EEPEEPEEPITY EEP!
‹OF COURSE SHE'S THE HOLY AND BLESSED ONE! LIKE ANOTHER GIANT REDHEADED BIPED IS JUST GOING TO DROP FROM THE SKY!?›
EEEP EEP EEP!
‹SEND A RUNNER AHEAD TO THE VILLAGE AND TELL THEM WE HAVE A MIRACLE OUT HERE!›
EEP EEP EEP-EEP EEP EEPITY-EEPITY EEP EEP.
‹OY.›

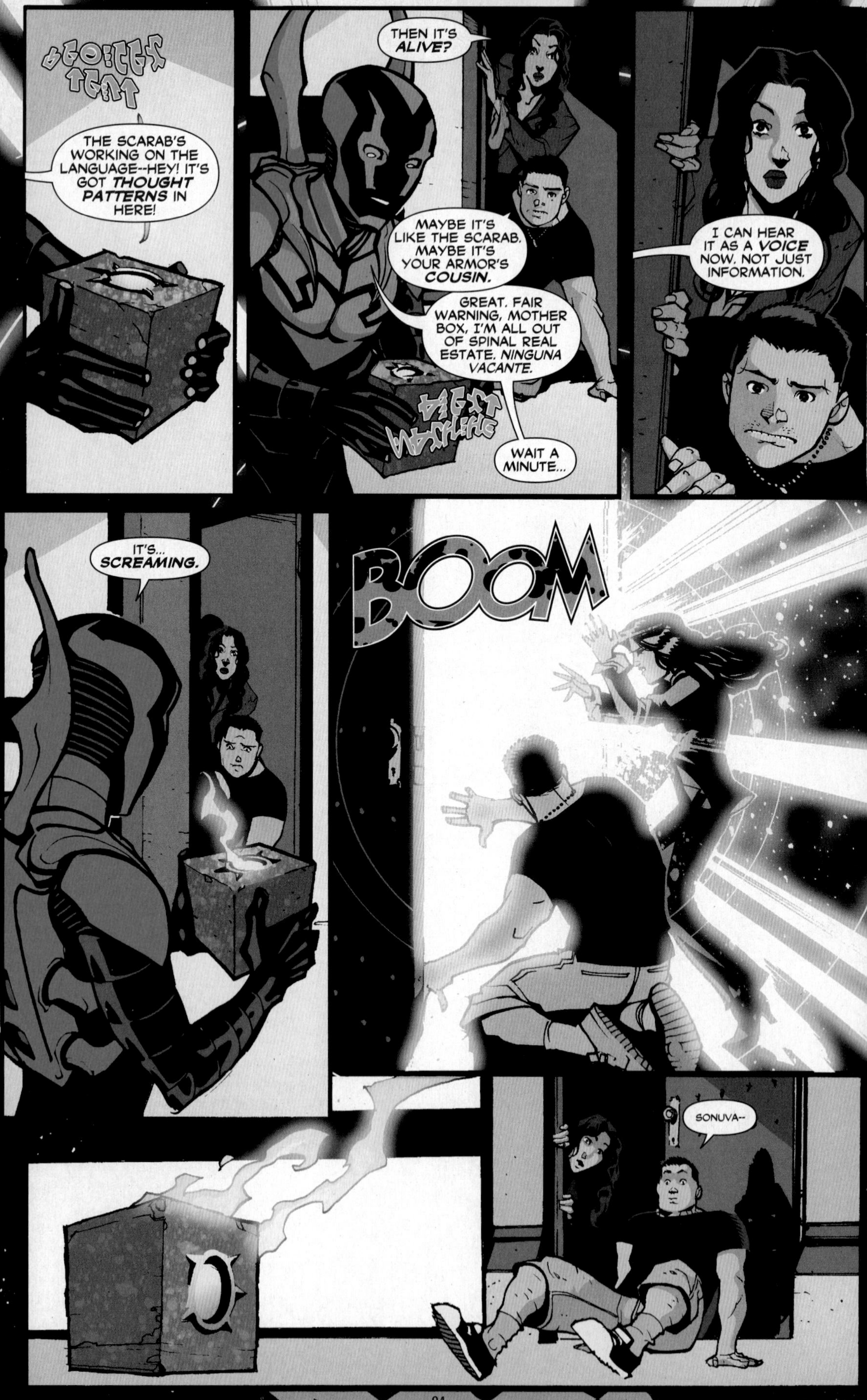

THE SCARAB'S WORKING ON THE LANGUAGE--HEY! IT'S GOT *THOUGHT PATTERNS* IN HERE!
THEN IT'S *ALIVE?*
MAYBE IT'S LIKE THE SCARAB. MAYBE IT'S YOUR ARMOR'S *COUSIN.*
GREAT. FAIR WARNING, MOTHER BOX, I'M ALL OUT OF SPINAL REAL ESTATE. *NINGUNA VACANTE.*
WAIT A MINUTE...
I CAN HEAR IT AS A *VOICE* NOW. NOT JUST INFORMATION.
IT'S... *SCREAMING.*
BOOM
SONUVA--

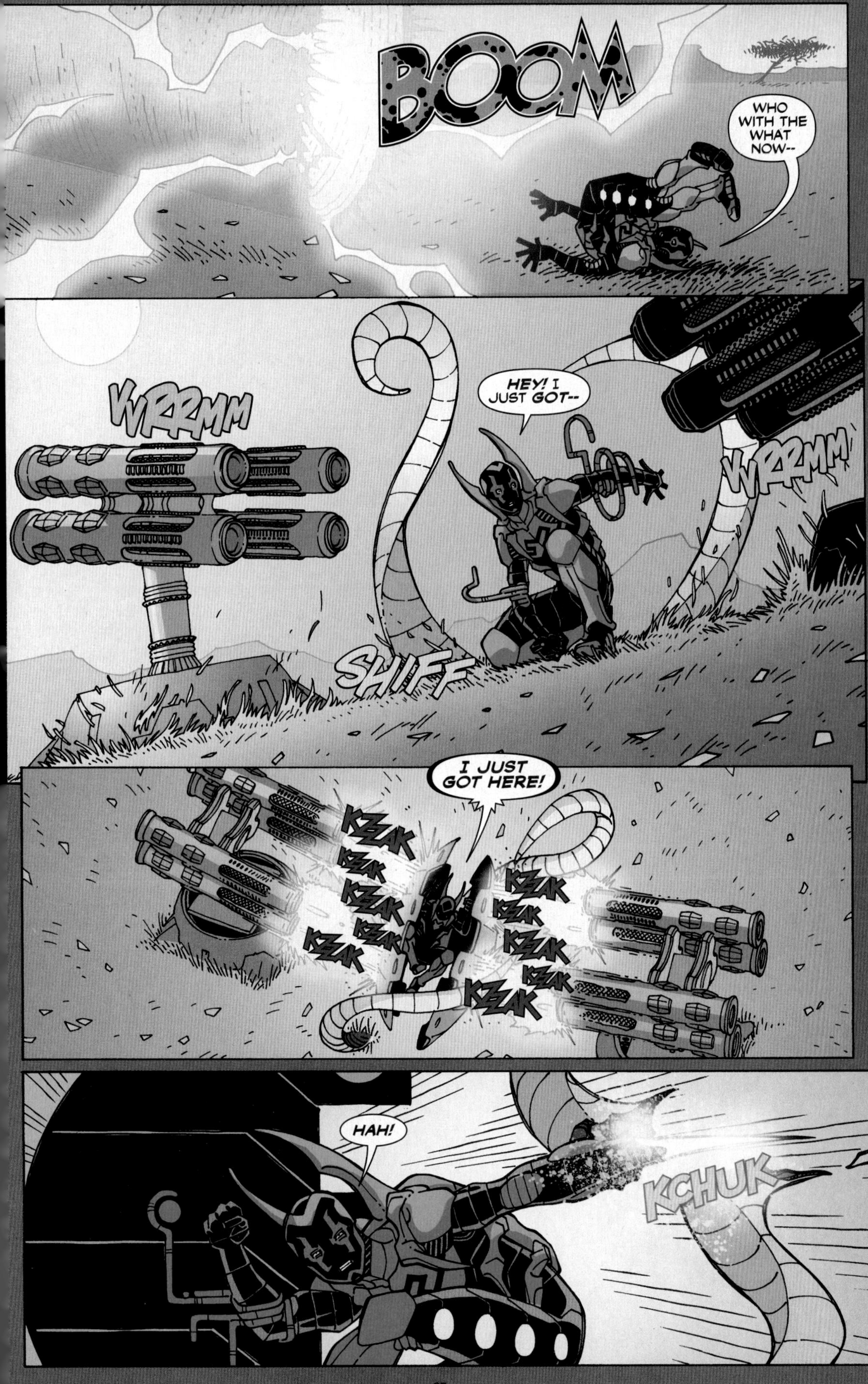
BOOM
WHO WITH THE WHAT NOW--
VVRRMM
HEY! I JUST GOT--
VVRRMM
SHIFF
I JUST GOT HERE!
KZZAK
KZZAK
KZZAK
KZZAK
KZZAK
KZZAK
KZZAK
KZZAK
KZZAK
KZZAK
HAH!
KCHUK

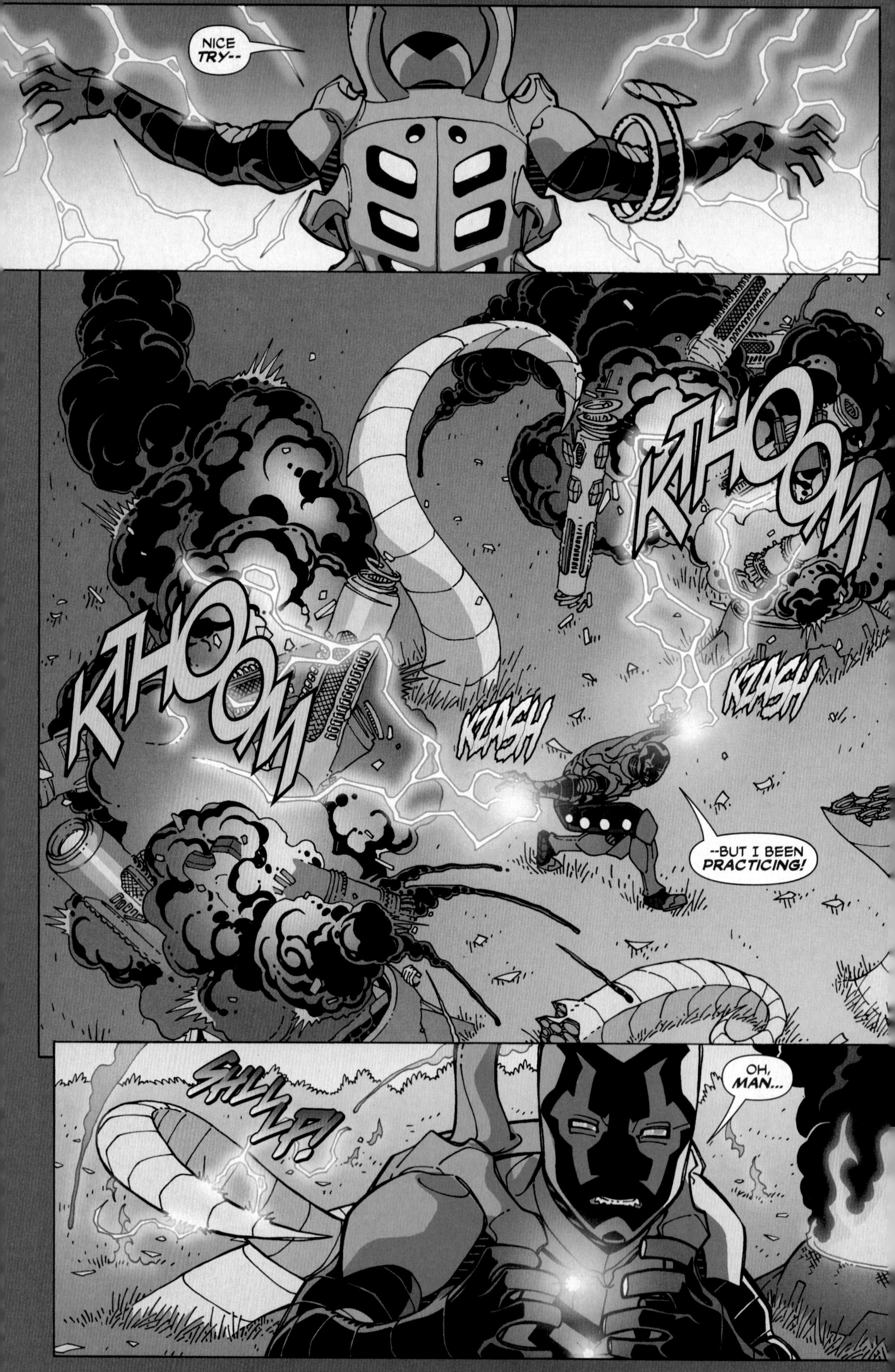
NICE *TRY--*
KTHOOM
KTHOOM
KZASH
KZASH
--BUT I BEEN *PRACTICING!*
SHWAP!
OH, *MAN...*

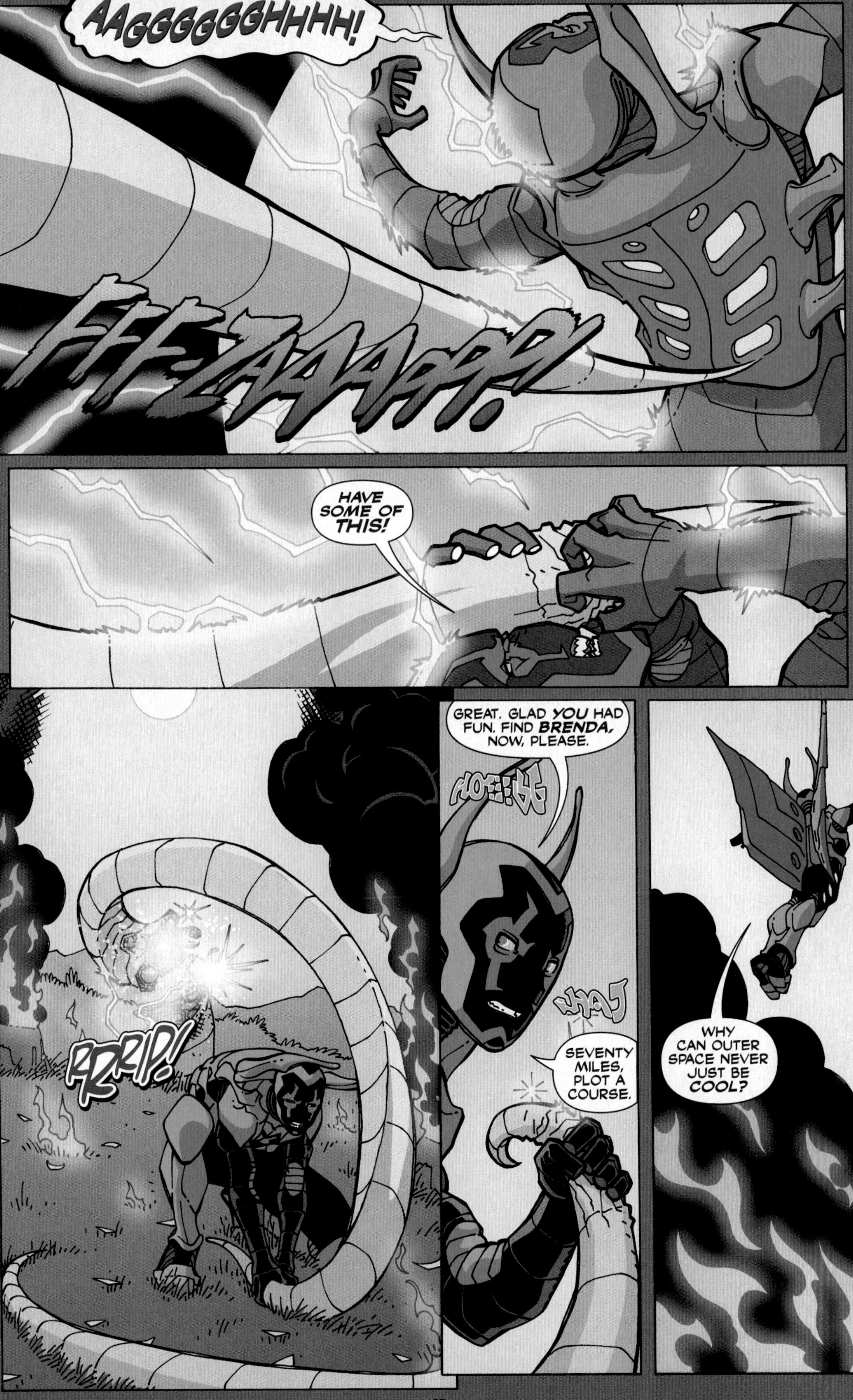
AAGGGGGGHHHH!
FFFZAAAPP!
HAVE SOME OF THIS!
RRRIP!
GREAT. GLAD YOU HAD FUN. FIND BRENDA, NOW, PLEASE.
SEVENTY MILES, PLOT A COURSE.
WHY CAN OUTER SPACE NEVER JUST BE COOL?

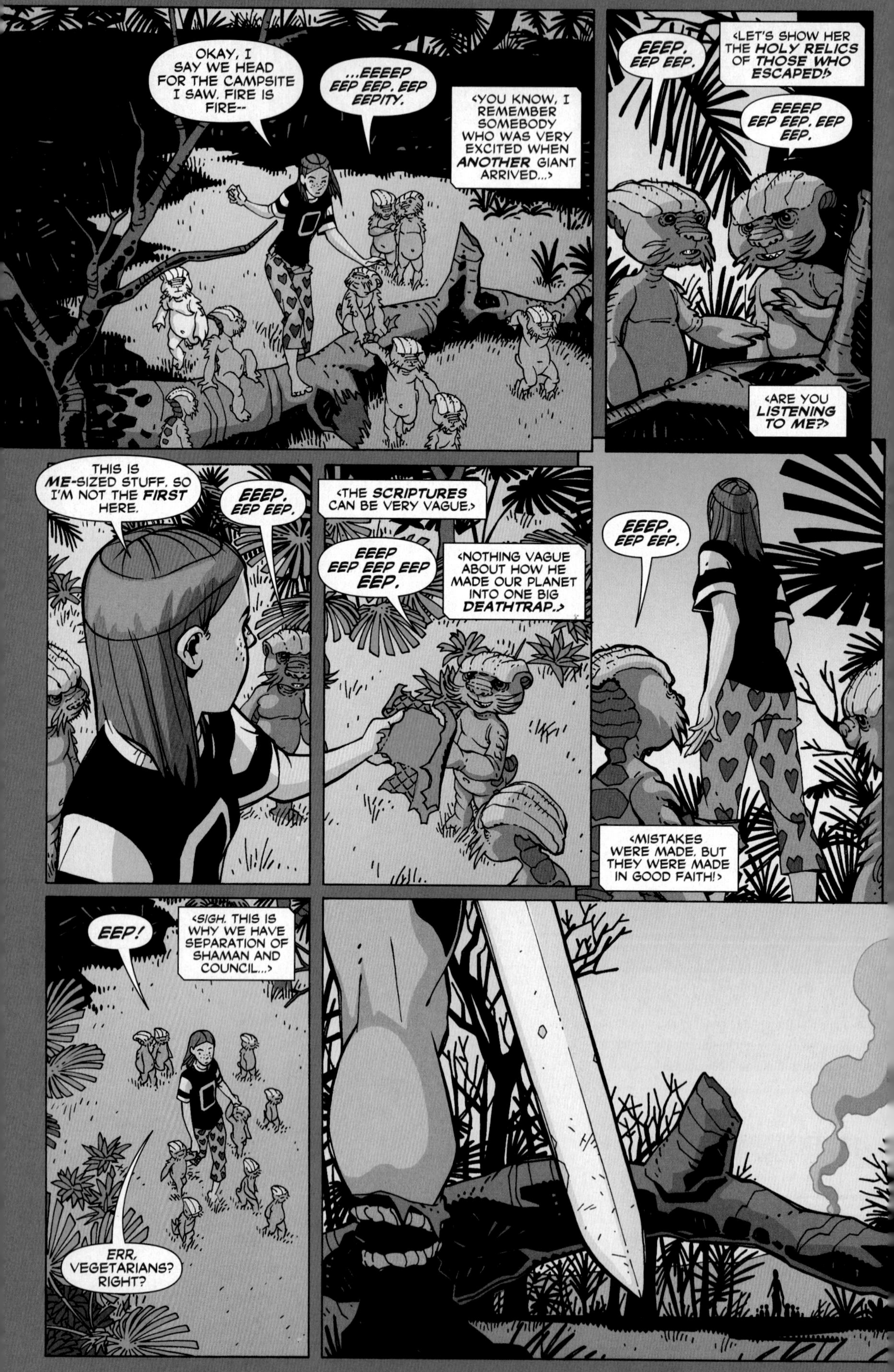
OKAY, I SAY WE HEAD FOR THE CAMPSITE I SAW. FIRE IS FIRE--
...EEEEP EEP EEP. EEP EEPITY.
‹YOU KNOW, I REMEMBER SOMEBODY WHO WAS VERY EXCITED WHEN ANOTHER GIANT ARRIVED...›
EEEP. EEP EEP.
‹LET'S SHOW HER THE HOLY RELICS OF THOSE WHO ESCAPED!›
EEEEP EEP EEP. EEP EEP.
‹ARE YOU LISTENING TO ME?›
THIS IS ME-SIZED STUFF. SO I'M NOT THE FIRST HERE.
EEEP. EEP EEP.
‹THE SCRIPTURES CAN BE VERY VAGUE.›
EEEP EEP EEP EEP EEP.
‹NOTHING VAGUE ABOUT HOW HE MADE OUR PLANET INTO ONE BIG DEATHTRAP.›
EEEP. EEP EEP.
‹MISTAKES WERE MADE. BUT THEY WERE MADE IN GOOD FAITH!›
EEP!
‹SIGH. THIS IS WHY WE HAVE SEPARATION OF SHAMAN AND COUNCIL...›
ERR, VEGETARIANS? RIGHT?

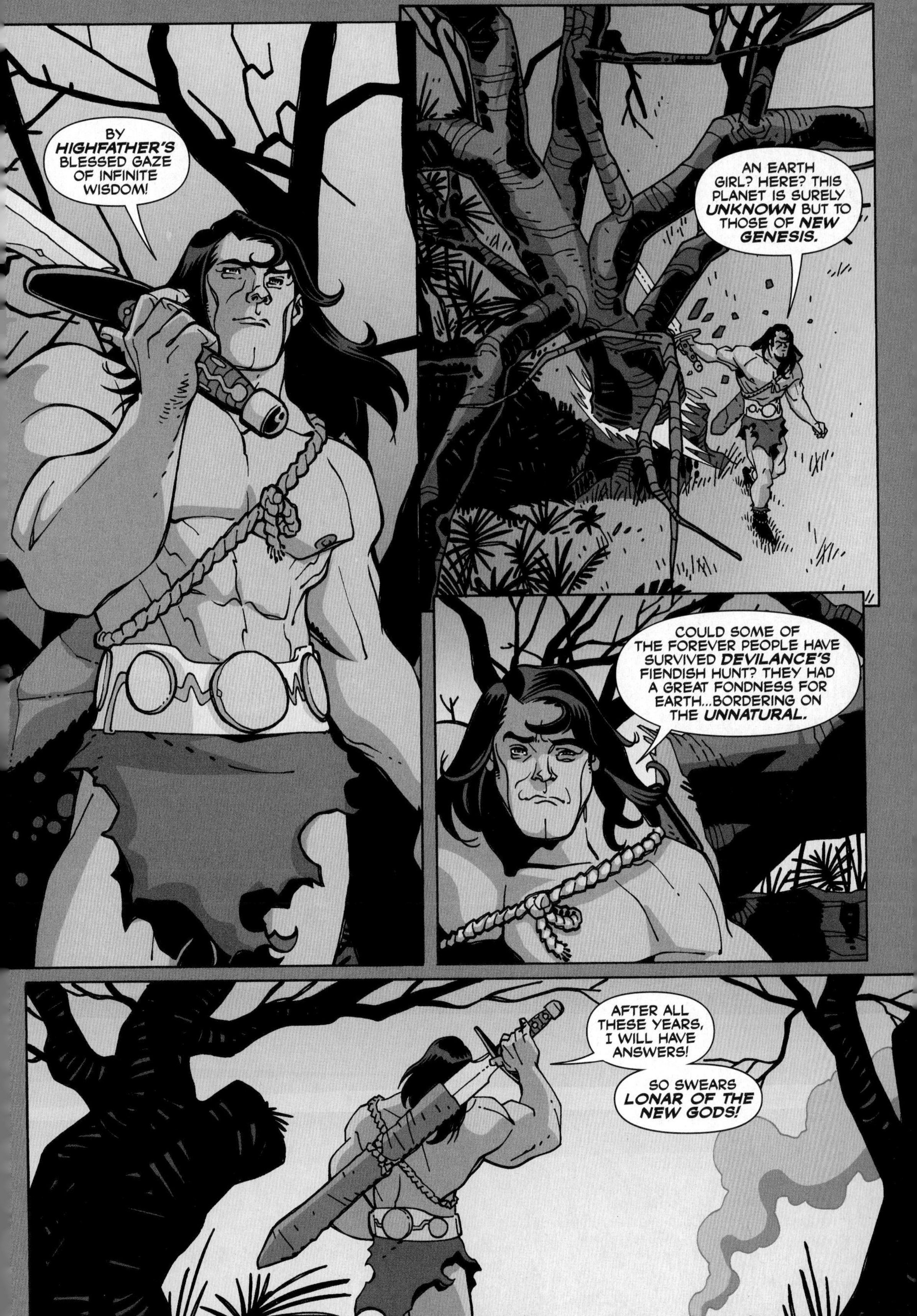
BY HIGHFATHER'S BLESSED GAZE OF INFINITE WISDOM!
AN EARTH GIRL? HERE? THIS PLANET IS SURELY UNKNOWN BUT TO THOSE OF NEW GENESIS.
COULD SOME OF THE FOREVER PEOPLE HAVE SURVIVED DEVILANCE'S FIENDISH HUNT? THEY HAD A GREAT FONDNESS FOR EARTH...BORDERING ON THE UNNATURAL.
AFTER ALL THESE YEARS, I WILL HAVE ANSWERS!
SO SWEARS LONAR OF THE NEW GODS!

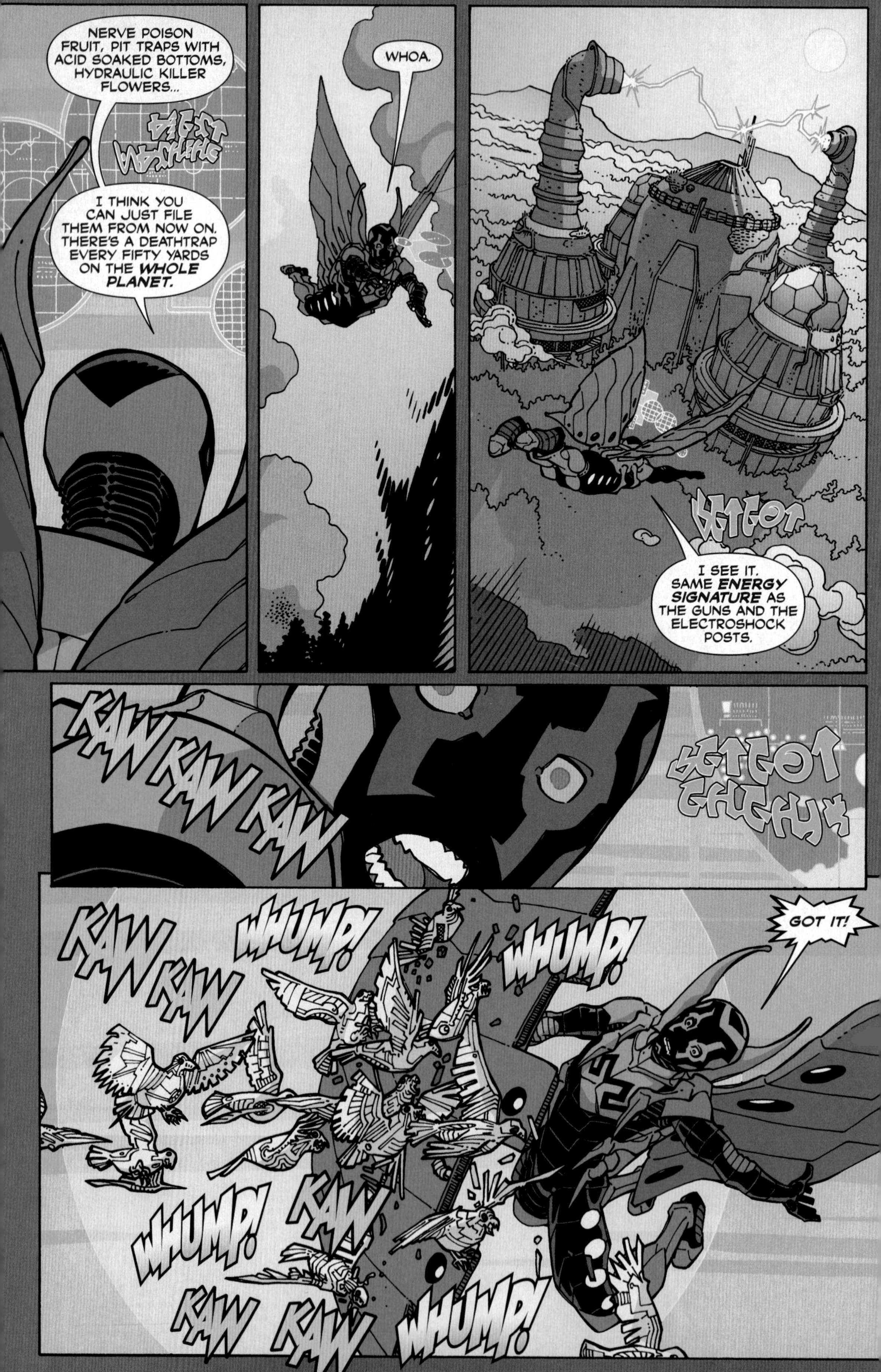
NERVE POISON FRUIT, PIT TRAPS WITH ACID SOAKED BOTTOMS, HYDRAULIC KILLER FLOWERS...
I THINK YOU CAN JUST FILE THEM FROM NOW ON. THERE'S A DEATHTRAP EVERY FIFTY YARDS ON THE WHOLE PLANET.
WHOA.
I SEE IT. SAME ENERGY SIGNATURE AS THE GUNS AND THE ELECTROSHOCK POSTS.
KAW KAW KAW
KAW KAW
WHUMP!
WHUMP!
GOT IT!
WHUMP!
KAW
KAW
KAW
WHUMP!

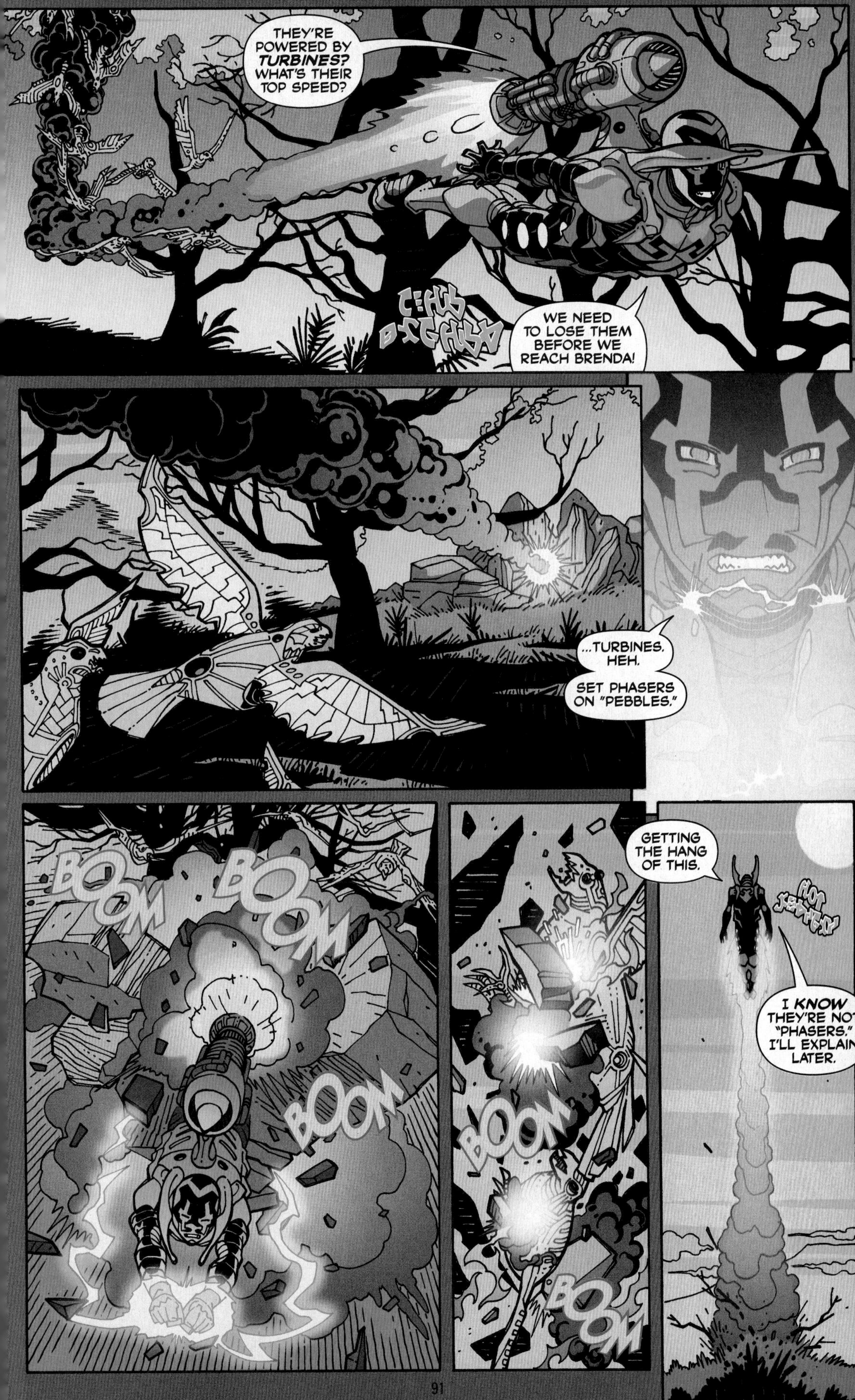
THEY'RE POWERED BY *TURBINES?* WHAT'S THEIR TOP SPEED?
WE NEED TO LOSE THEM BEFORE WE REACH BRENDA!
...TURBINES. HEH.
SET PHASERS ON "PEBBLES."
BOOM
BOOM
BOOM
GETTING THE HANG OF THIS.
BOOM
BOOM
I *KNOW* THEY'RE NOT "PHASERS." I'LL EXPLAIN LATER.

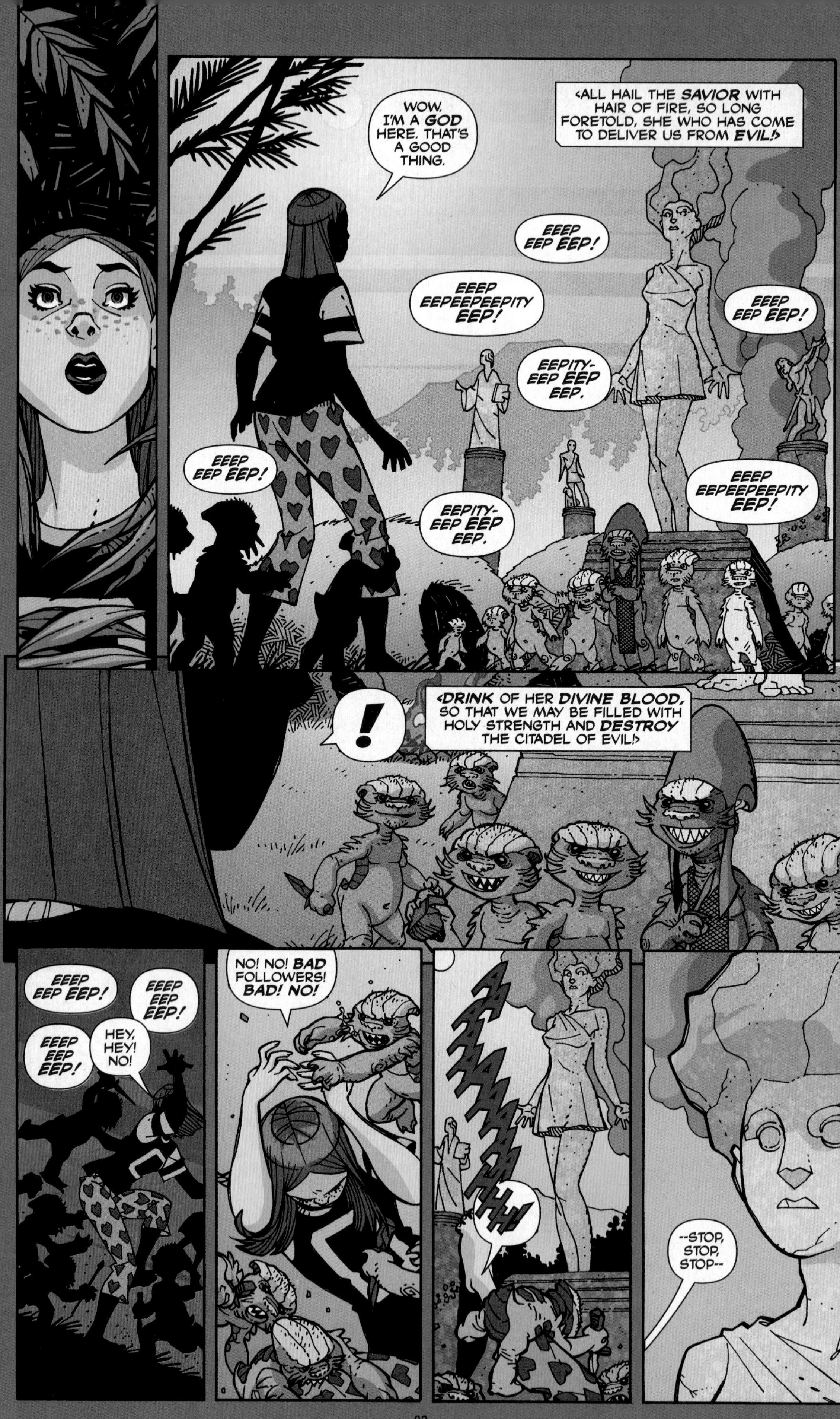
WOW. I'M A GOD HERE. THAT'S A GOOD THING.
<ALL HAIL THE SAVIOR WITH HAIR OF FIRE, SO LONG FORETOLD, SHE WHO HAS COME TO DELIVER US FROM EVIL!>
EEEP EEP EEP!
EEEP EEPEEPEEPITY EEP!
EEEP EEP EEP!
EEPITY-EEP EEP EEP.
EEEP EEP EEP!
EEPITY-EEP EEP EEP.
EEEP EEPEEPEEPITY EEP!
!
<DRINK OF HER DIVINE BLOOD, SO THAT WE MAY BE FILLED WITH HOLY STRENGTH AND DESTROY THE CITADEL OF EVIL!>
EEEP EEP EEP!
EEEP EEP EEP!
EEEP EEP EEP!
HEY, HEY! NO!
NO! NO! BAD FOLLOWERS! BAD! NO!
--STOP, STOP, STOP--

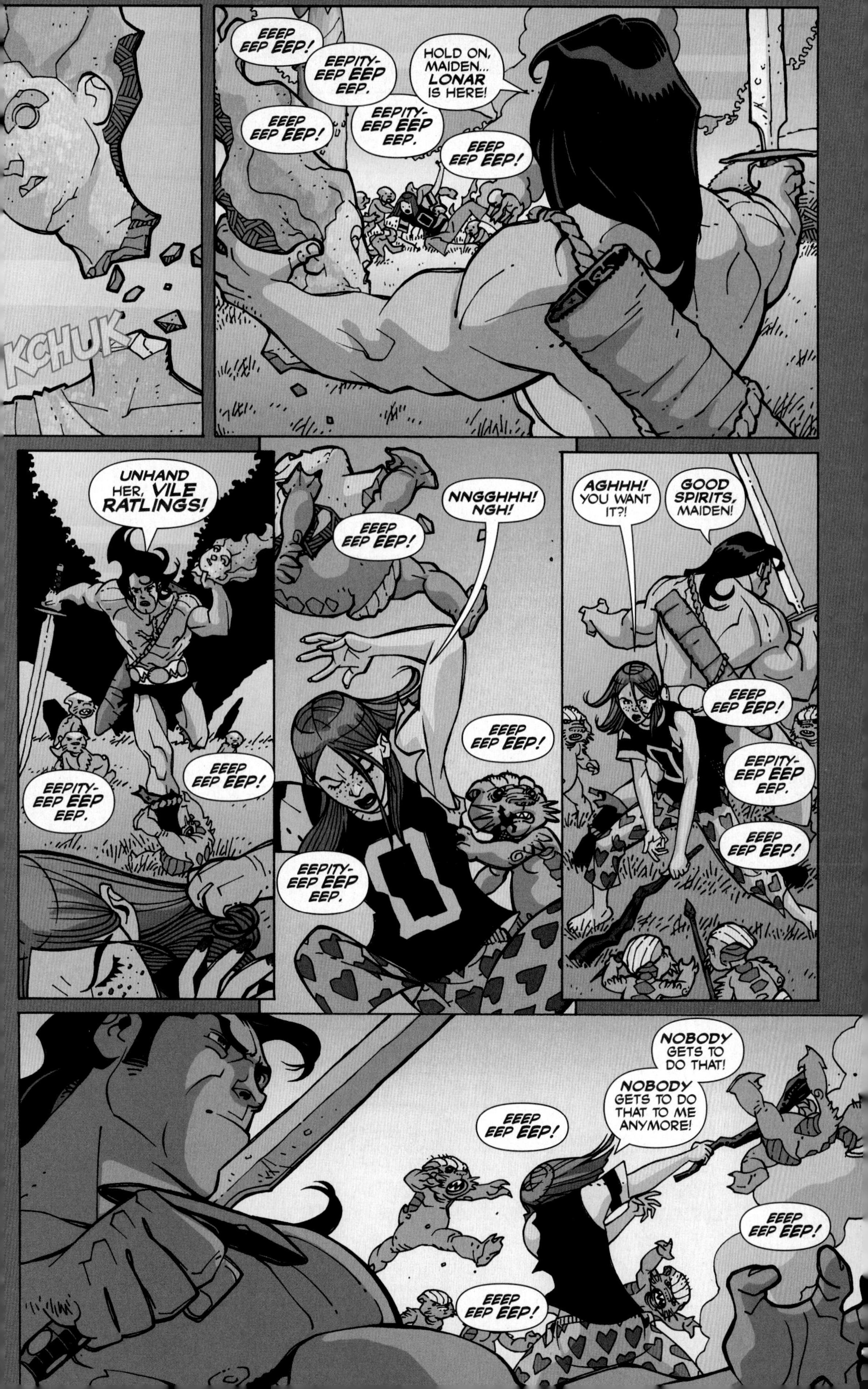
KCHUK
EEEP EEP EEP!
EEPITY-EEP EEP EEP.
HOLD ON, MAIDEN... LONAR IS HERE!
EEEP EEP EEP!
EEPITY-EEP EEP EEP.
EEEP EEP EEP!
UNHAND HER, VILE RATLINGS!
EEEP EEP EEP!
EEPITY-EEP EEP EEP.
NNGGHHH! NGH!
EEEP EEP EEP!
EEEP EEP EEP!
EEPITY-EEP EEP EEP.
AGHHH! YOU WANT IT?!
GOOD SPIRITS, MAIDEN!
EEEP EEP EEP!
EEPITY-EEP EEP EEP.
EEEP EEP EEP!
NOBODY GETS TO DO THAT!
NOBODY GETS TO DO THAT TO ME ANYMORE!
EEEP EEP EEP!
EEEP EEP EEP!
EEEP EEP EEP!

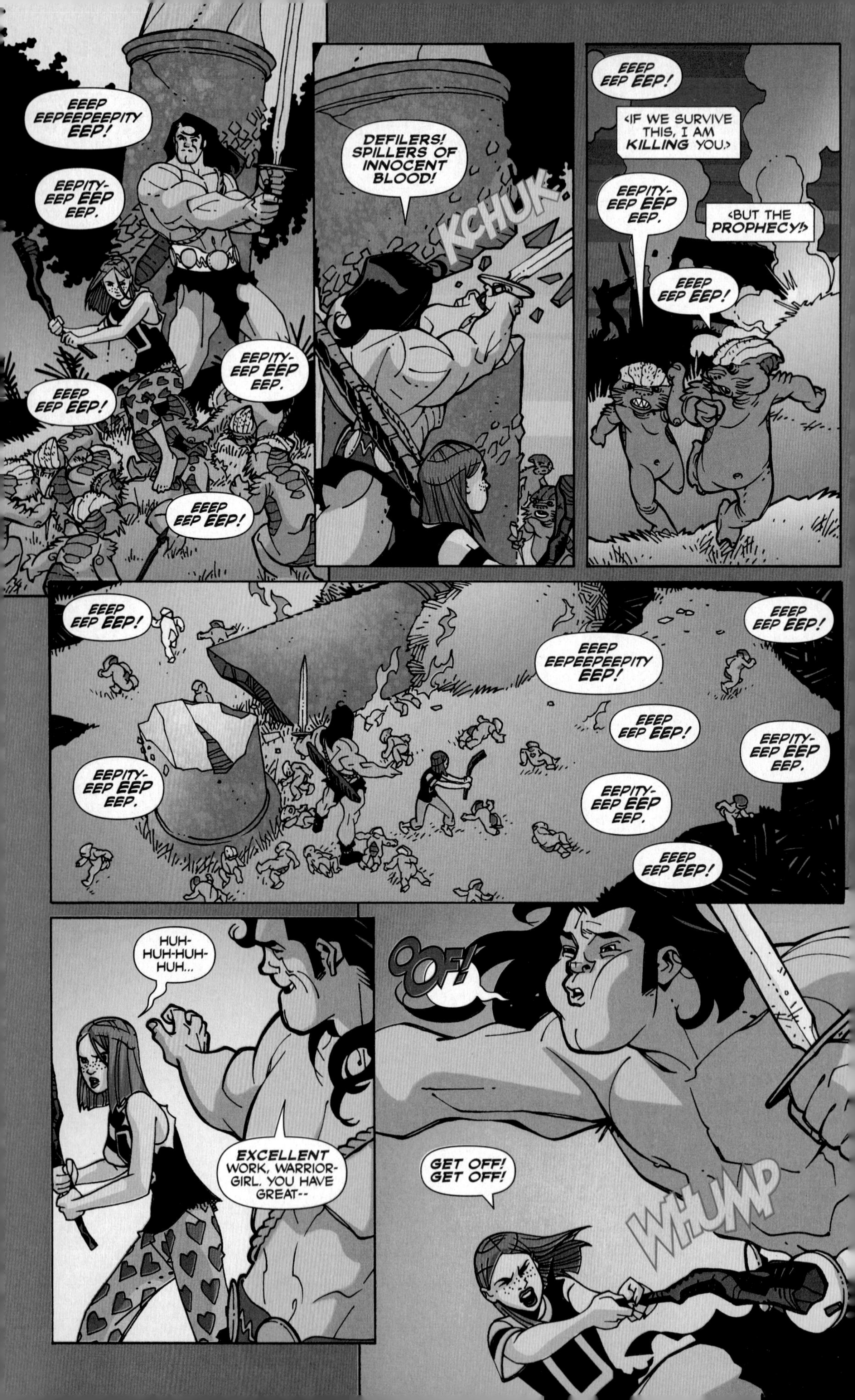
EEEP EEPEEPEEPITY EEP!
EEPITY-EEP EEP EEP.
EEEP EEP EEP!
EEPITY-EEP EEP EEP.
EEEP EEP EEP!
DEFILERS! SPILLERS OF INNOCENT BLOOD!
KCHUK
EEEP EEP EEP!
<IF WE SURVIVE THIS, I AM KILLING YOU.>
EEPITY-EEP EEP EEP.
<BUT THE PROPHECY!>
EEEP EEP EEP!
EEEP EEP EEP!
EEEP EEPEEPEEPITY EEP!
EEEP EEP EEP!
EEEP EEP EEP!
EEPITY-EEP EEP EEP.
EEPITY-EEP EEP EEP.
EEPITY-EEP EEP EEP.
EEEP EEP EEP!
HUH-HUH-HUH-HUH...
EXCELLENT WORK, WARRIOR-GIRL. YOU HAVE GREAT--
OOF!
GET OFF! GET OFF!
WHUMP

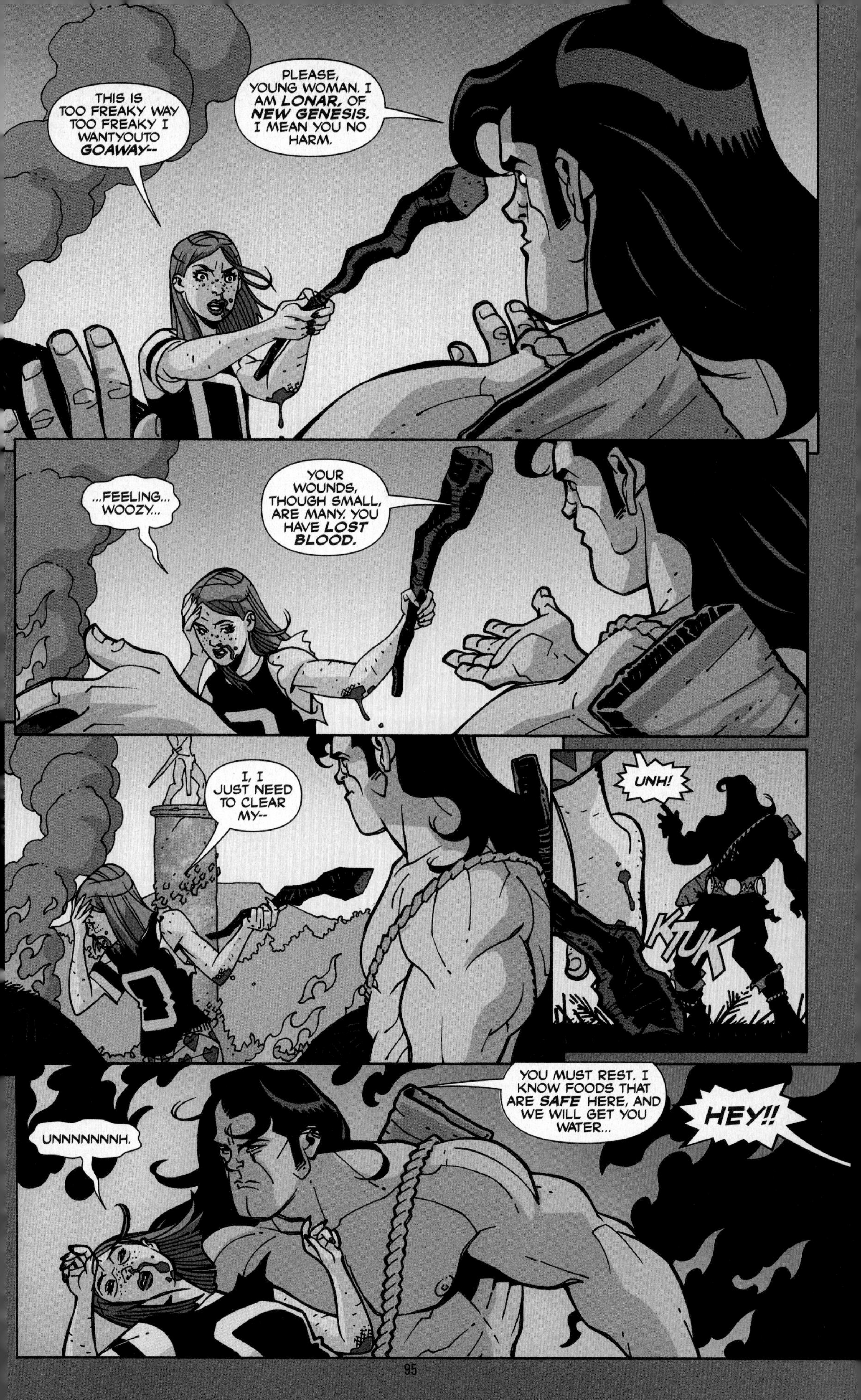
THIS IS TOO FREAKY WAY TOO FREAKY I WANTYOUTO GOAWAY--
PLEASE, YOUNG WOMAN. I AM LONAR, OF NEW GENESIS. I MEAN YOU NO HARM.
...FEELING... WOOZY...
YOUR WOUNDS, THOUGH SMALL, ARE MANY. YOU HAVE LOST BLOOD.
I, I JUST NEED TO CLEAR MY--
UNH!
KTUK
UNNNNNNNH.
YOU MUST REST. I KNOW FOODS THAT ARE SAFE HERE, AND WE WILL GET YOU WATER...
HEY!!

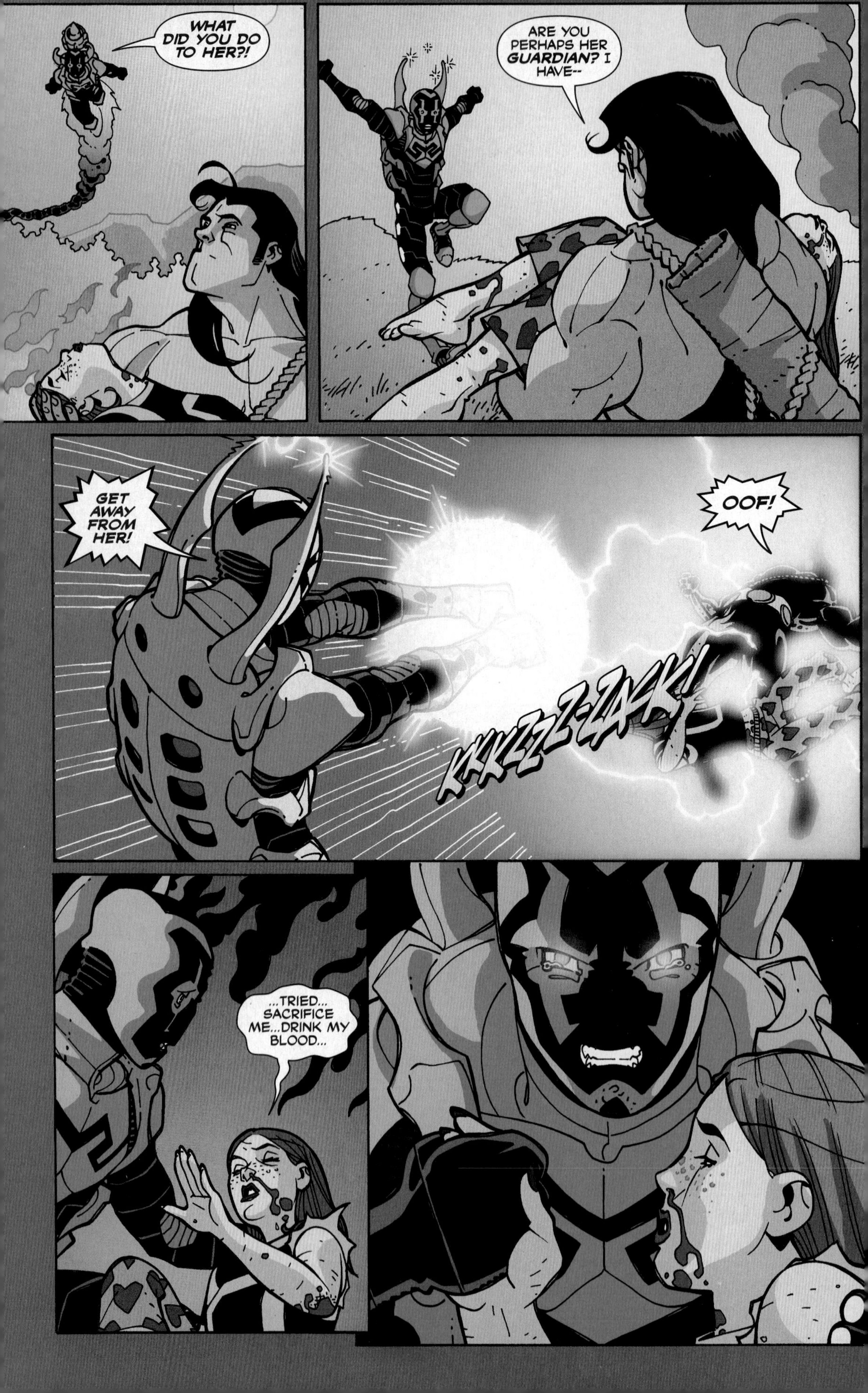
WHAT DID YOU DO TO HER?!
ARE YOU PERHAPS HER GUARDIAN? I HAVE--
GET AWAY FROM HER!
OOF!
KKKZZZZ-ZAK!
...TRIED... SACRIFICE ME...DRINK MY BLOOD...

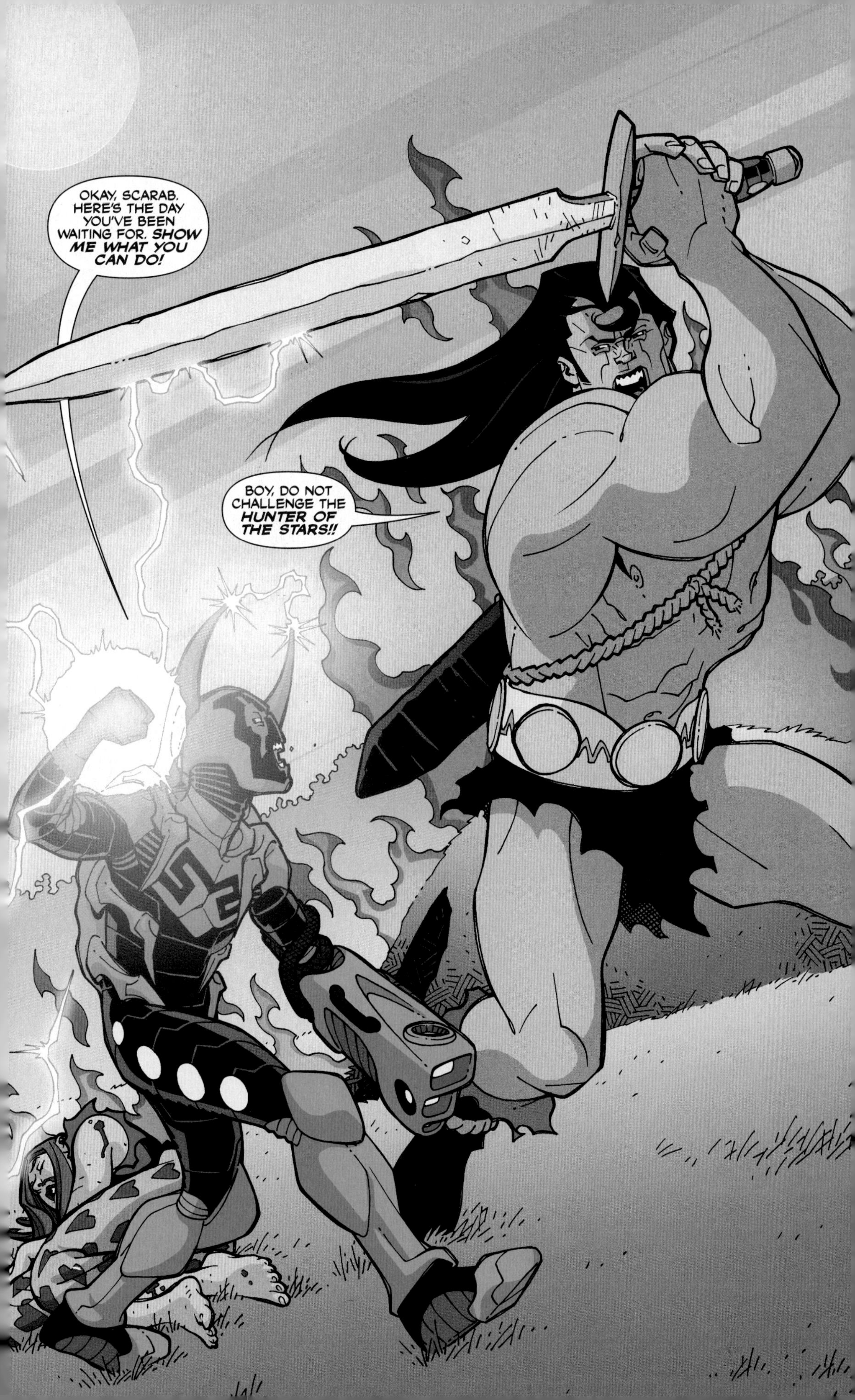
OKAY, SCARAB. HERE'S THE DAY YOU'VE BEEN WAITING FOR. SHOW ME WHAT YOU CAN DO!
BOY, DO NOT CHALLENGE THE HUNTER OF THE STARS!!

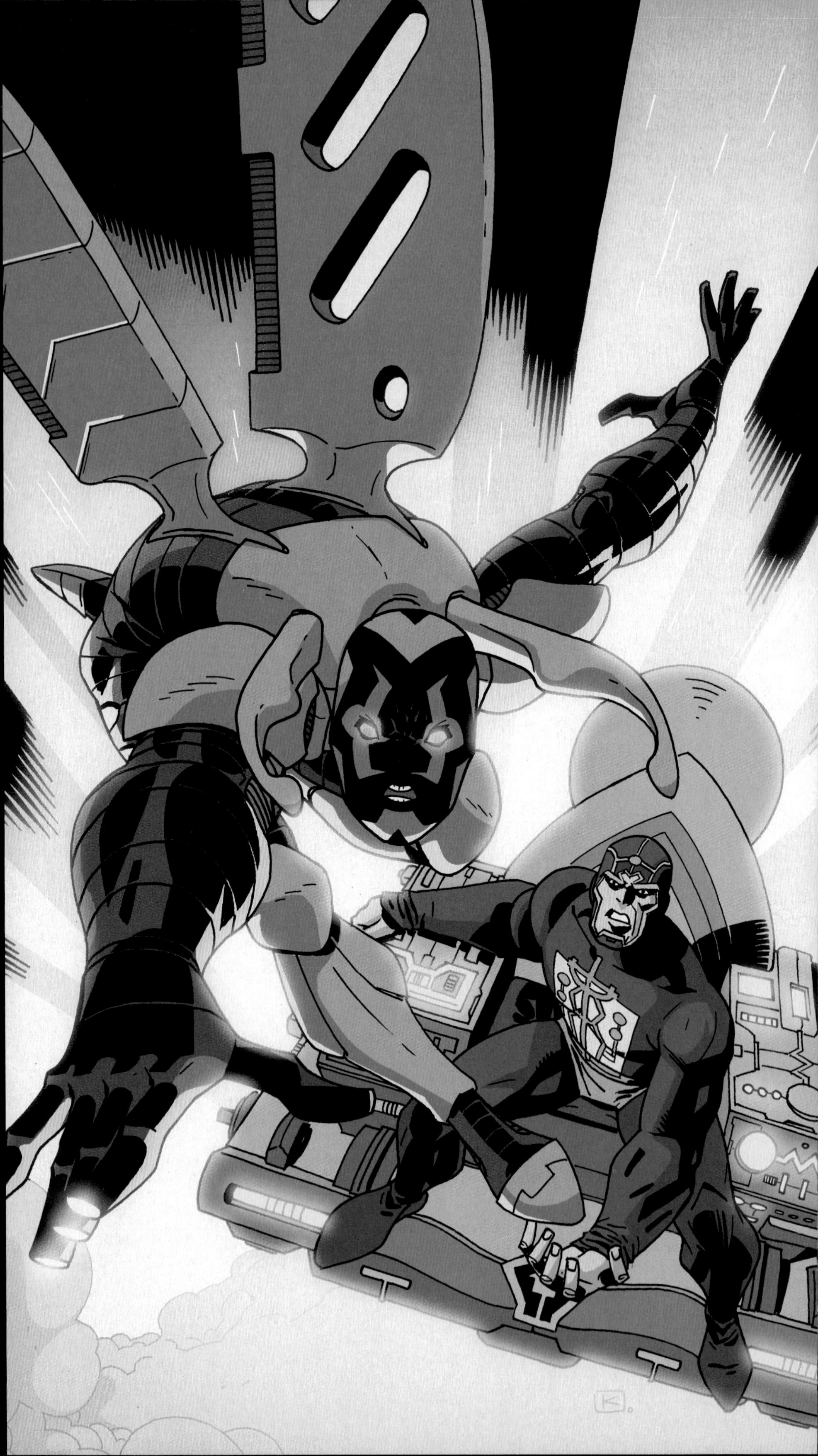

BLUE BEETLE #11 Written by John Rogers Cover by Andy Kuhn Interior art by Rafael Albuquerque

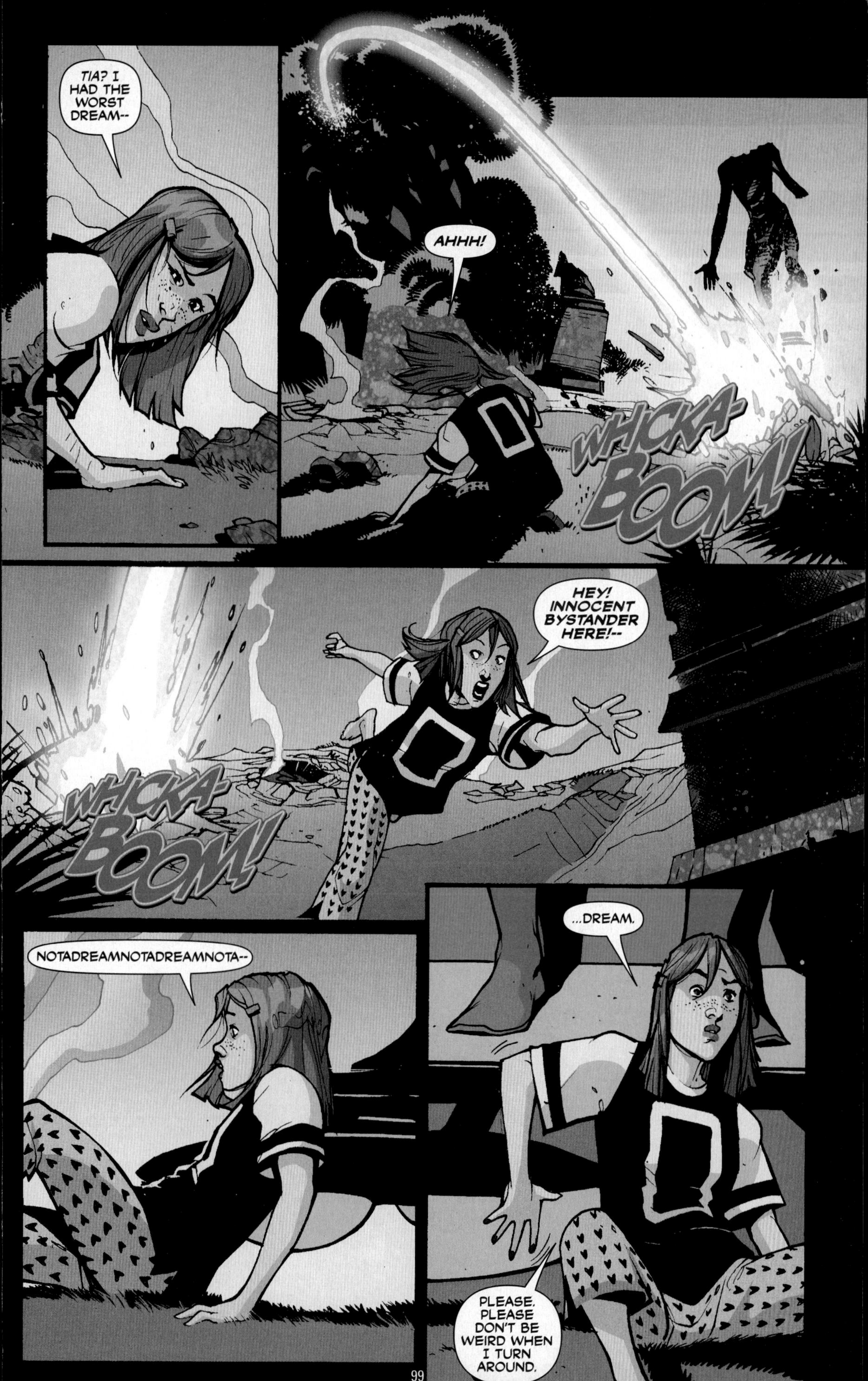
TIA? I HAD THE WORST DREAM--
AHHH!
WHICKA-BOOM!
HEY! INNOCENT BYSTANDER HERE!--
WHICKA-BOOM!
NOTADREAMNOTADREAMNOTA--
...DREAM.
PLEASE. PLEASE DON'T BE WEIRD WHEN I TURN AROUND.

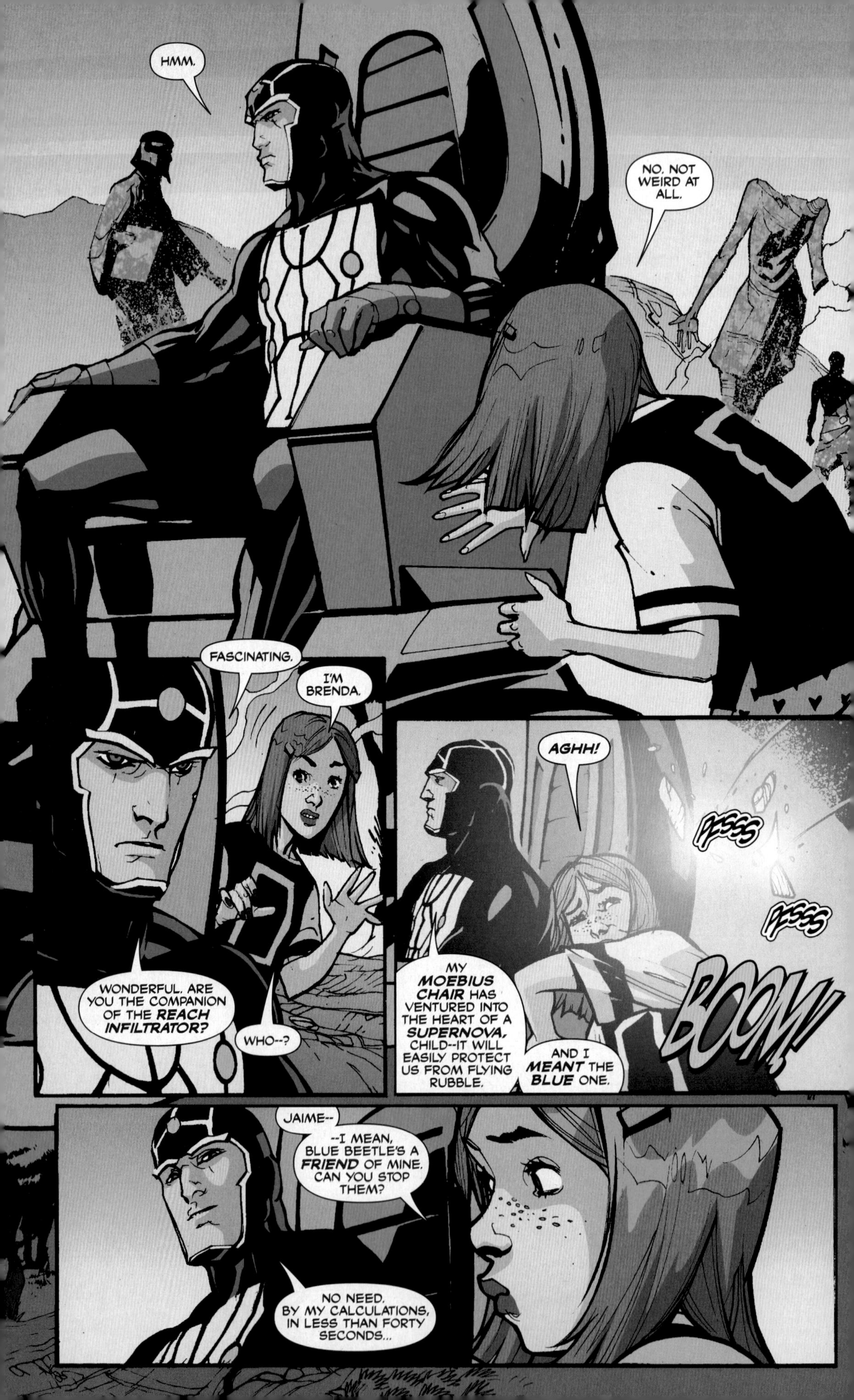
HMM.
NO. NOT WEIRD AT ALL.
FASCINATING.
I'M BRENDA.
WONDERFUL. ARE YOU THE COMPANION OF THE REACH INFILTRATOR?
WHO--?
AGHH!
PFSSS
PFSSS
MY MOEBIUS CHAIR HAS VENTURED INTO THE HEART OF A SUPERNOVA, CHILD--IT WILL EASILY PROTECT US FROM FLYING RUBBLE.
BOOM!
AND I MEANT THE BLUE ONE.
JAIME--
--I MEAN, BLUE BEETLE'S A FRIEND OF MINE. CAN YOU STOP THEM?
NO NEED. BY MY CALCULATIONS, IN LESS THAN FORTY SECONDS...

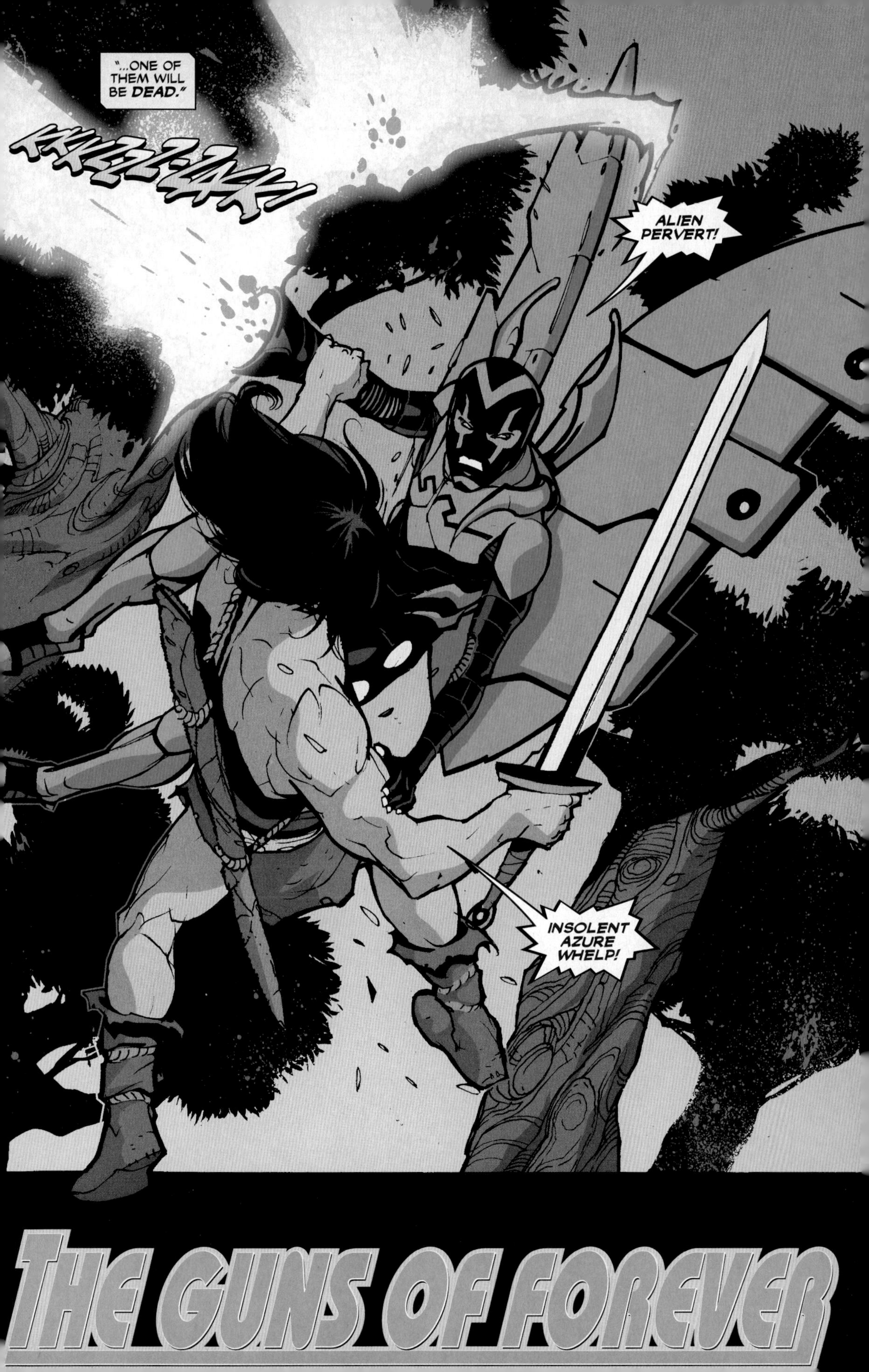
"...ONE OF THEM WILL BE *DEAD.*"
KKKLZZZ-ZACK!
ALIEN PERVERT!
INSOLENT AZURE WHELP!
THE GUNS OF FOREVER

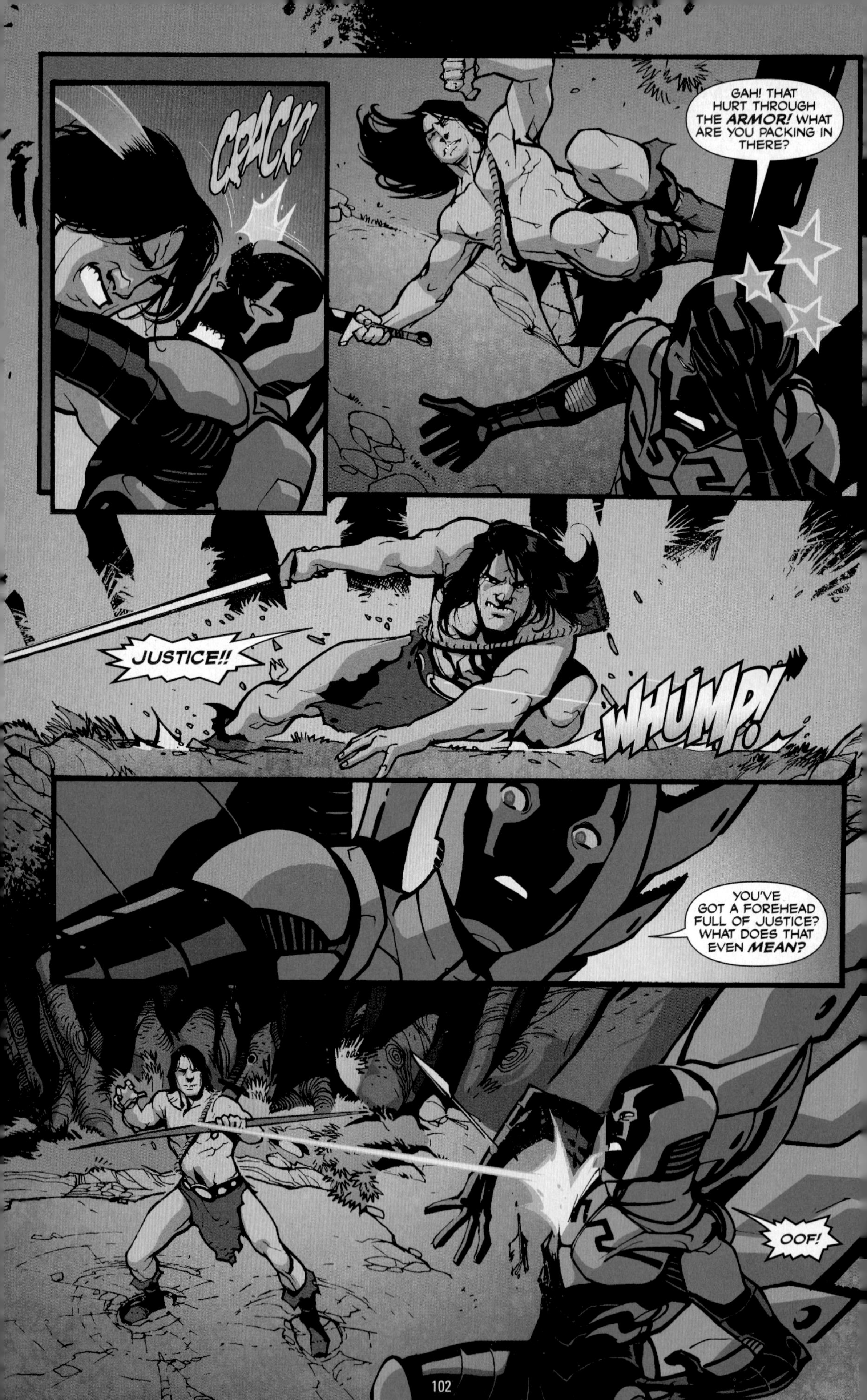
CRACK!
GAH! THAT HURT THROUGH THE ARMOR! WHAT ARE YOU PACKING IN THERE?
JUSTICE!!
WHUMP!
YOU'VE GOT A FOREHEAD FULL OF JUSTICE? WHAT DOES THAT EVEN MEAN?
OOF!

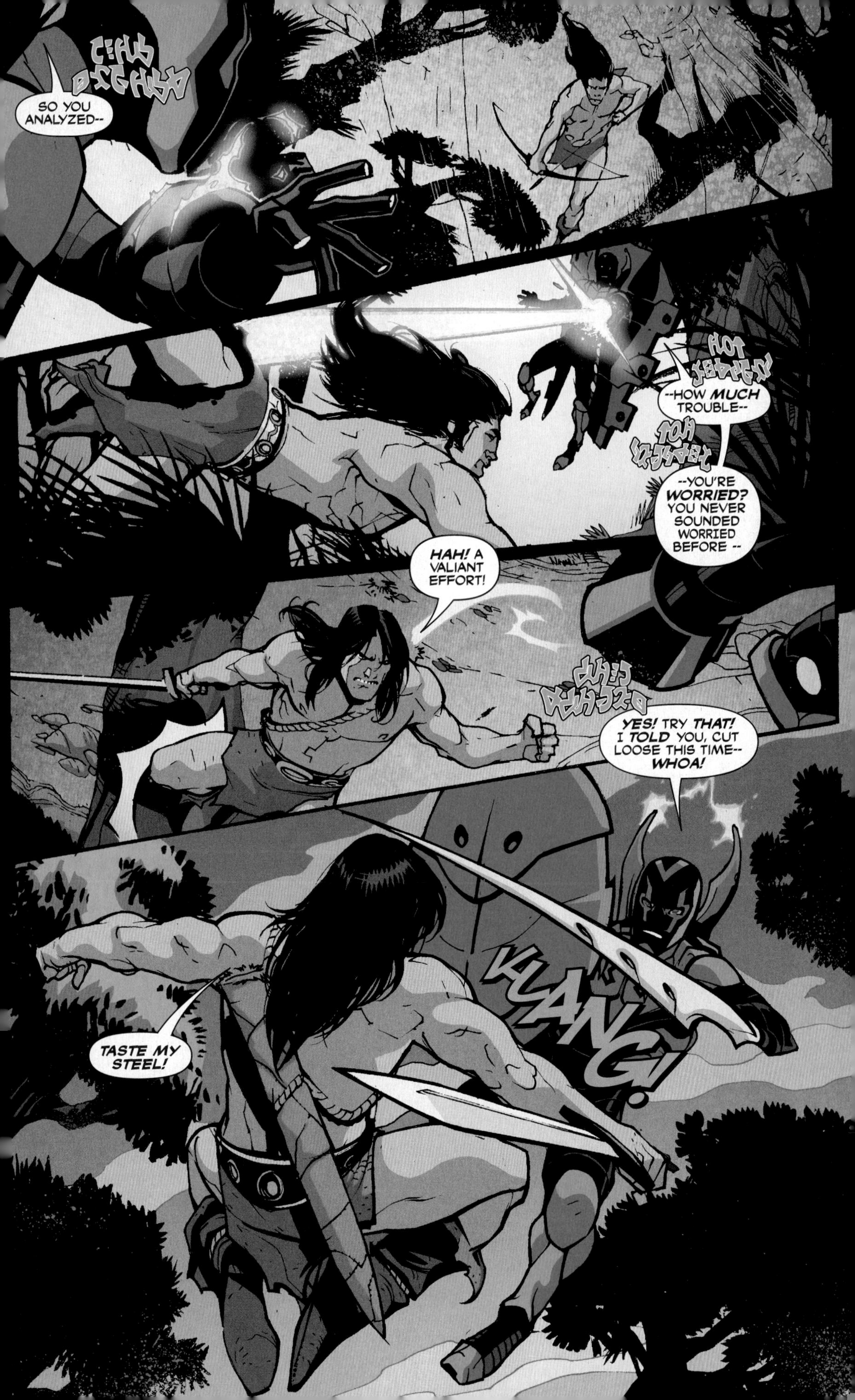
SO YOU ANALYZED--
--HOW MUCH TROUBLE--
--YOU'RE WORRIED? YOU NEVER SOUNDED WORRIED BEFORE --
HAH! A VALIANT EFFORT!
YES! TRY THAT! I TOLD YOU, CUT LOOSE THIS TIME-- WHOA!
TASTE MY STEEL!
KLANG!

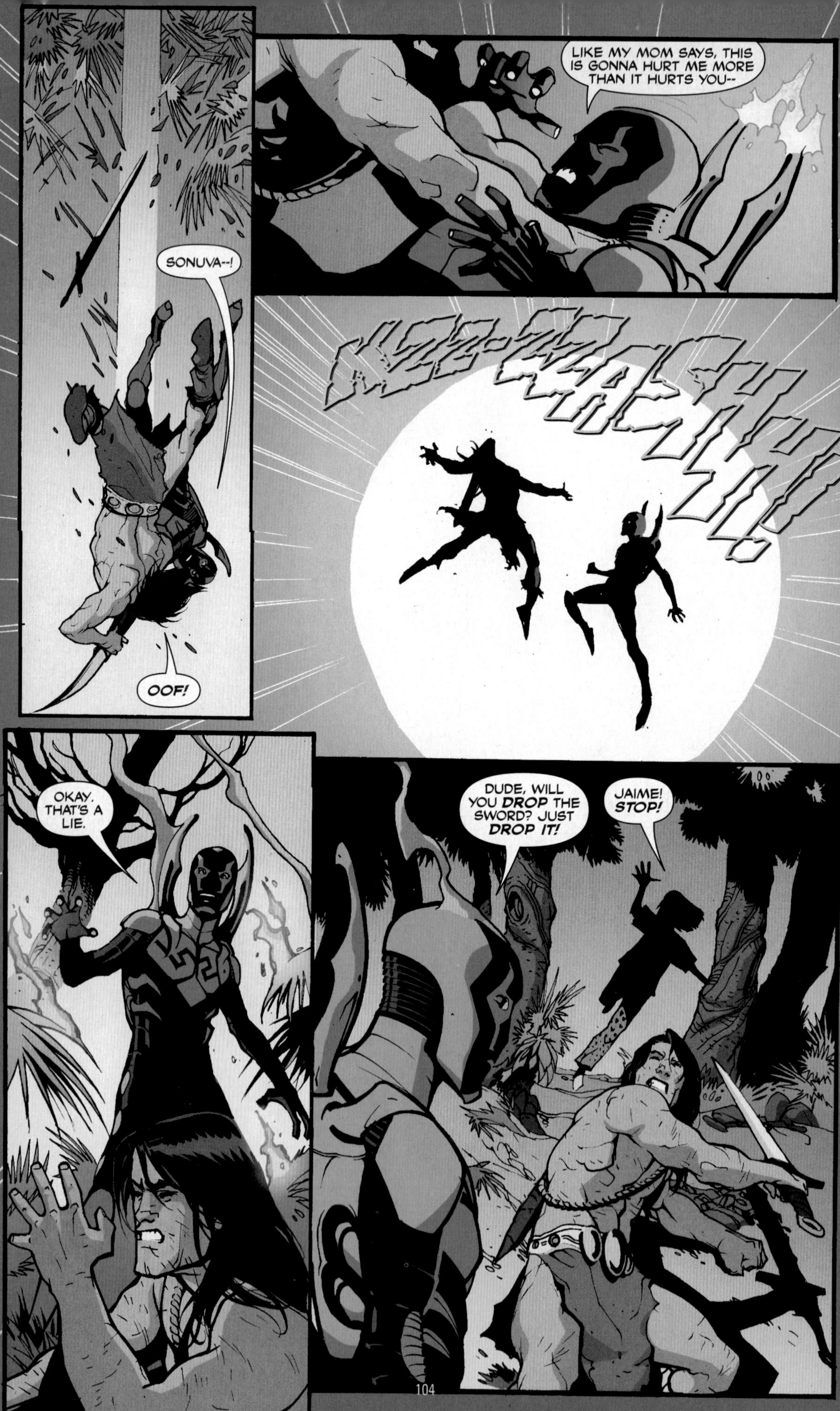
SONUVA--!
OOF!
LIKE MY MOM SAYS, THIS IS GONNA HURT ME MORE THAN IT HURTS YOU--
OKAY. THAT'S A LIE.
DUDE, WILL YOU *DROP* THE SWORD? JUST *DROP IT!*
JAIME! *STOP!*

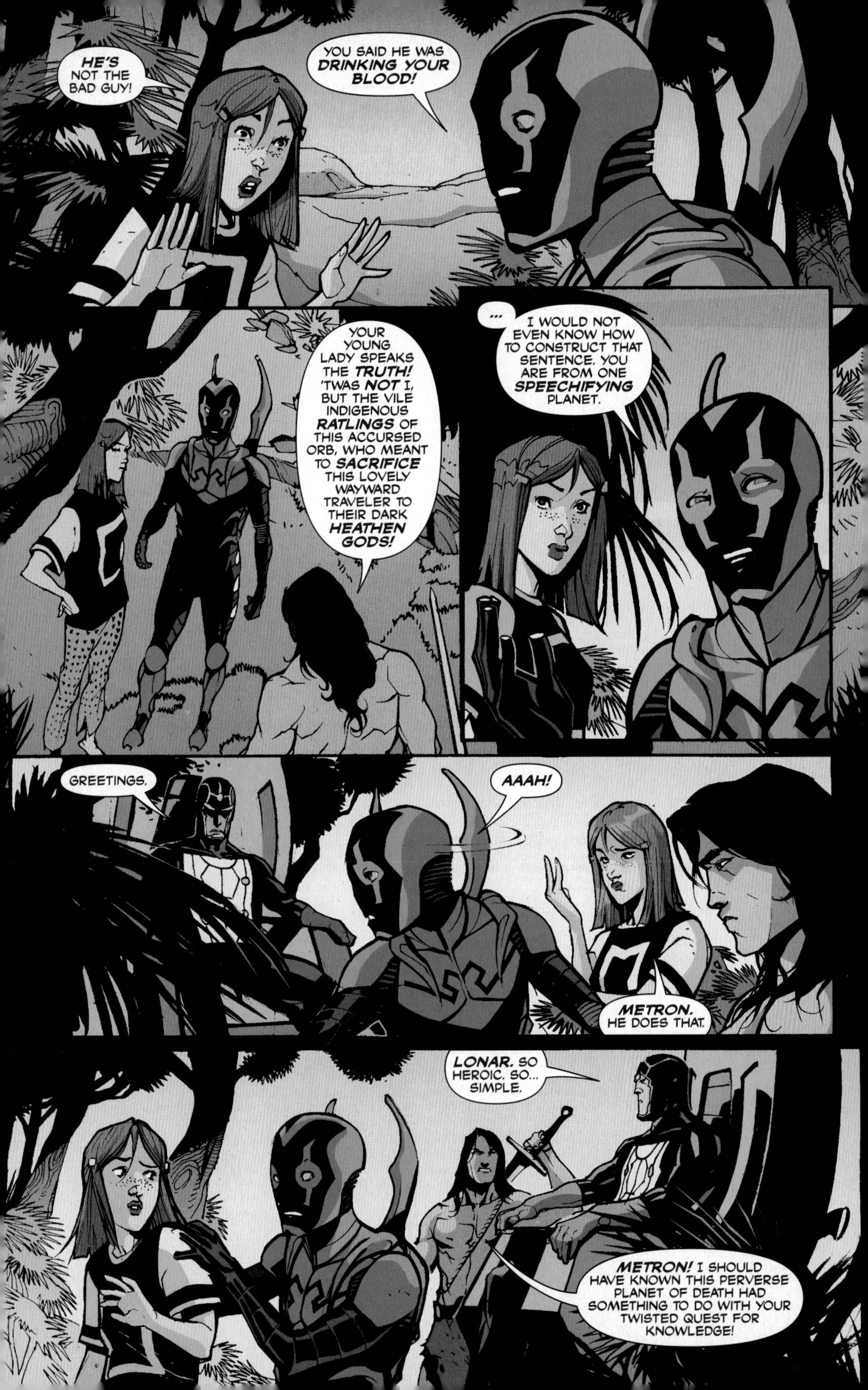
HE'S NOT THE BAD GUY!
YOU SAID HE WAS DRINKING YOUR BLOOD!
YOUR YOUNG LADY SPEAKS THE TRUTH! 'TWAS NOT I, BUT THE VILE INDIGENOUS RATLINGS OF THIS ACCURSED ORB, WHO MEANT TO SACRIFICE THIS LOVELY WAYWARD TRAVELER TO THEIR DARK HEATHEN GODS!
... I WOULD NOT EVEN KNOW HOW TO CONSTRUCT THAT SENTENCE. YOU ARE FROM ONE SPEECHIFYING PLANET.
GREETINGS.
AAAH!
METRON. HE DOES THAT.
LONAR. SO HEROIC. SO... SIMPLE.
METRON! I SHOULD HAVE KNOWN THIS PERVERSE PLANET OF DEATH HAD SOMETHING TO DO WITH YOUR TWISTED QUEST FOR KNOWLEDGE!

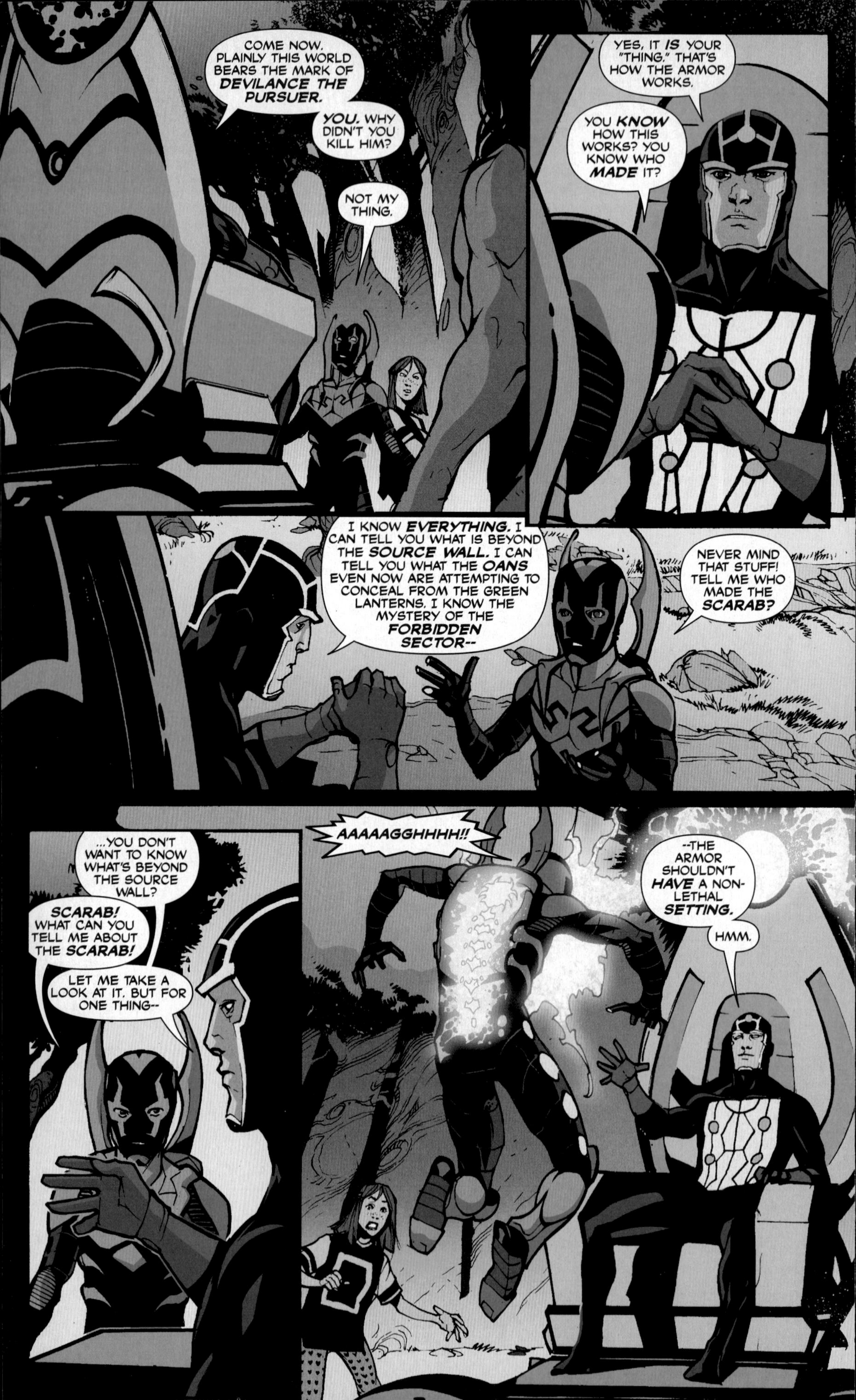
COME NOW. PLAINLY THIS WORLD BEARS THE MARK OF DEVILANCE THE PURSUER.
YOU. WHY DIDN'T YOU KILL HIM?
NOT MY THING.
YES, IT IS YOUR "THING." THAT'S HOW THE ARMOR WORKS.
YOU KNOW HOW THIS WORKS? YOU KNOW WHO MADE IT?
I KNOW EVERYTHING. I CAN TELL YOU WHAT IS BEYOND THE SOURCE WALL. I CAN TELL YOU WHAT THE OANS EVEN NOW ARE ATTEMPTING TO CONCEAL FROM THE GREEN LANTERNS. I KNOW THE MYSTERY OF THE FORBIDDEN SECTOR--
NEVER MIND THAT STUFF! TELL ME WHO MADE THE SCARAB?
...YOU DON'T WANT TO KNOW WHAT'S BEYOND THE SOURCE WALL?
SCARAB! WHAT CAN YOU TELL ME ABOUT THE SCARAB!
LET ME TAKE A LOOK AT IT. BUT FOR ONE THING--
AAAAAGGHHHH!!
--THE ARMOR SHOULDN'T HAVE A NON-LETHAL SETTING.
HMM.

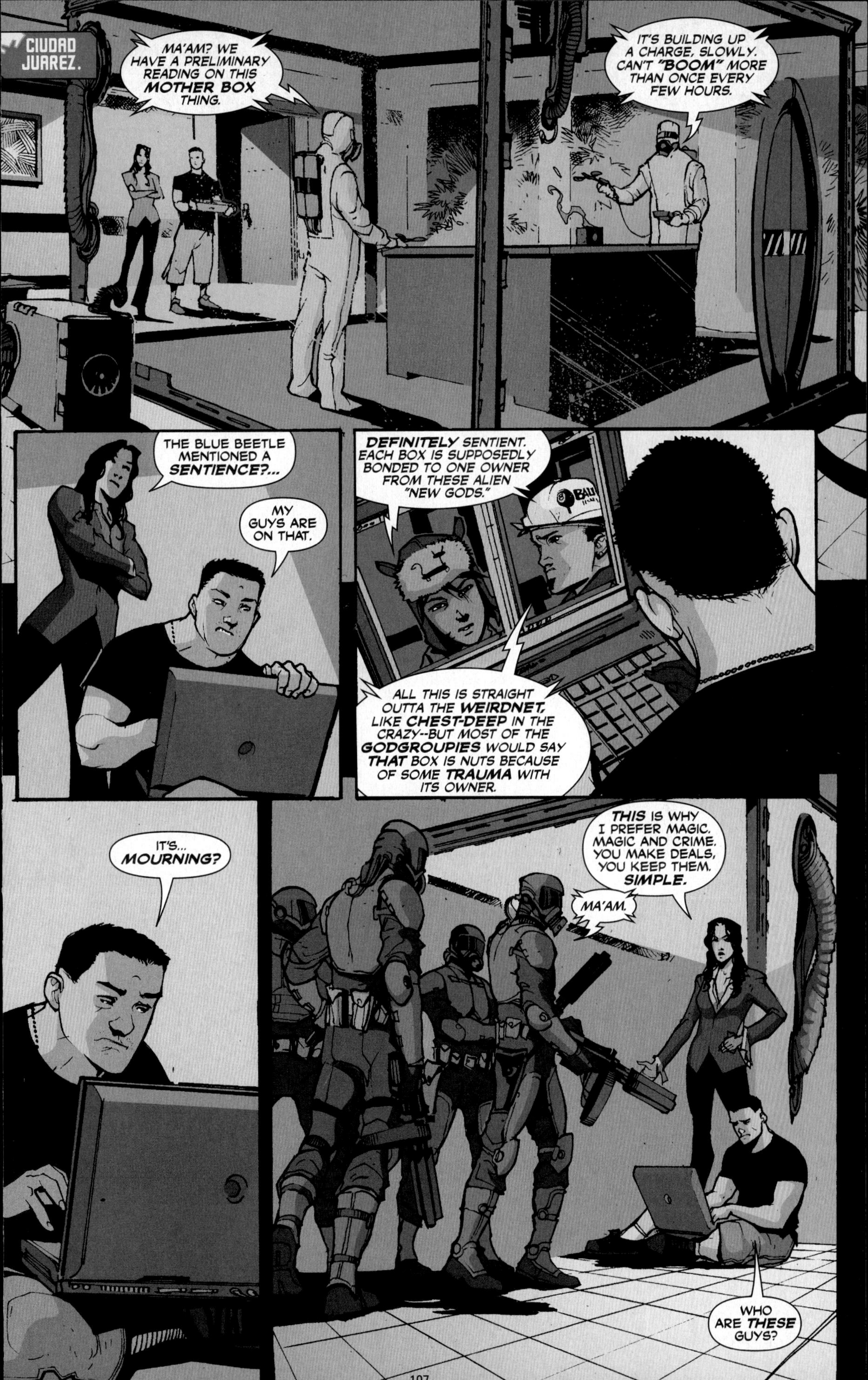
CIUDAD JUAREZ.
MA'AM? WE HAVE A PRELIMINARY READING ON THIS MOTHER BOX THING.
IT'S BUILDING UP A CHARGE, SLOWLY. CAN'T "BOOM" MORE THAN ONCE EVERY FEW HOURS.
THE BLUE BEETLE MENTIONED A SENTIENCE?...
MY GUYS ARE ON THAT.
DEFINITELY SENTIENT. EACH BOX IS SUPPOSEDLY BONDED TO ONE OWNER FROM THESE ALIEN "NEW GODS."
ALL THIS IS STRAIGHT OUTTA THE WEIRDNET, LIKE CHEST-DEEP IN THE CRAZY--BUT MOST OF THE GODGROUPIES WOULD SAY THAT BOX IS NUTS BECAUSE OF SOME TRAUMA WITH ITS OWNER.
IT'S... MOURNING?
THIS IS WHY I PREFER MAGIC. MAGIC AND CRIME. YOU MAKE DEALS, YOU KEEP THEM. SIMPLE.
MA'AM.
WHO ARE THESE GUYS?

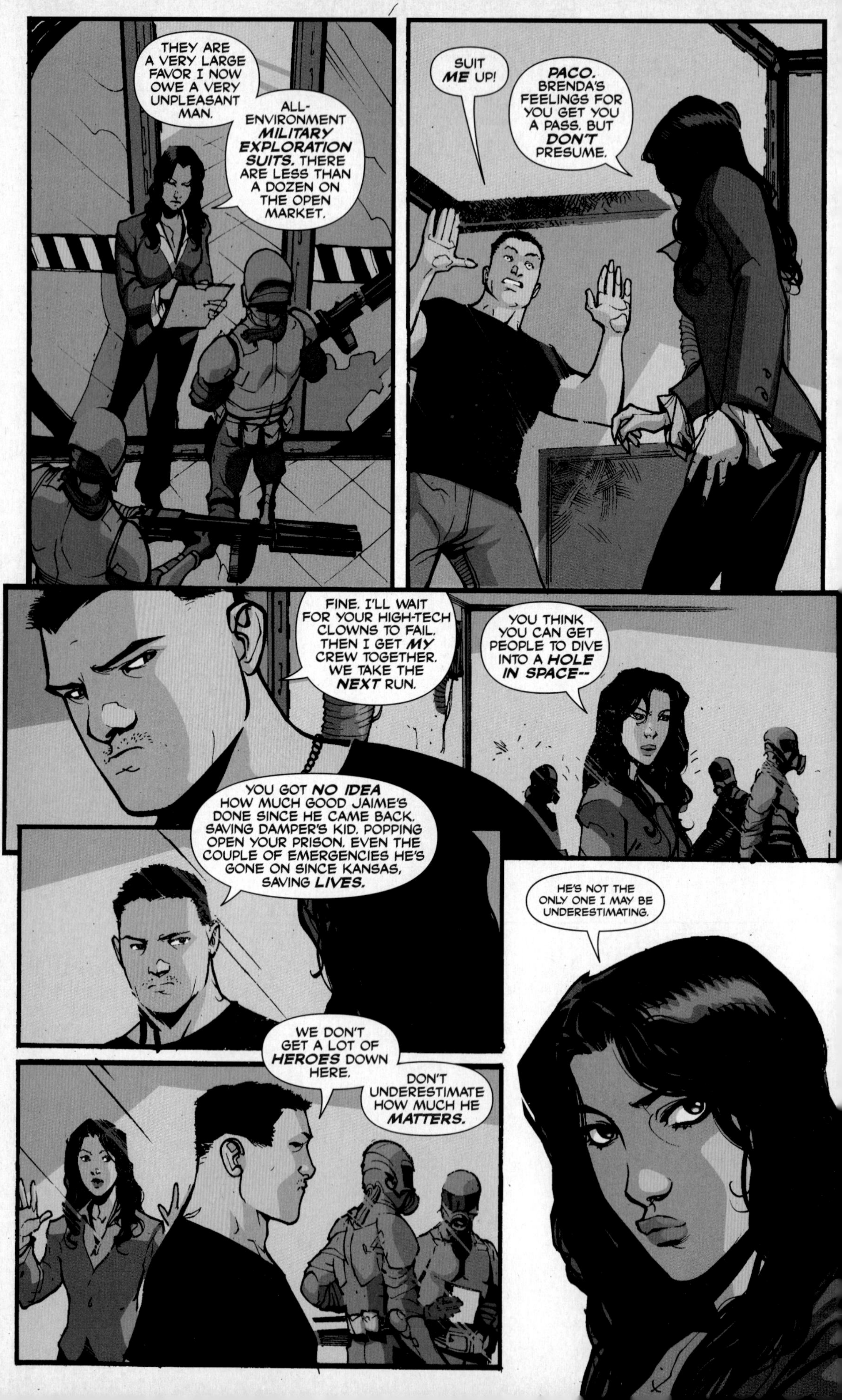
THEY ARE A VERY LARGE FAVOR I NOW OWE A VERY UNPLEASANT MAN.
ALL-ENVIRONMENT MILITARY EXPLORATION SUITS. THERE ARE LESS THAN A DOZEN ON THE OPEN MARKET.
SUIT ME UP!
PACO. BRENDA'S FEELINGS FOR YOU GET YOU A PASS. BUT DON'T PRESUME.
FINE. I'LL WAIT FOR YOUR HIGH-TECH CLOWNS TO FAIL. THEN I GET MY CREW TOGETHER. WE TAKE THE NEXT RUN.
YOU THINK YOU CAN GET PEOPLE TO DIVE INTO A HOLE IN SPACE--
YOU GOT NO IDEA HOW MUCH GOOD JAIME'S DONE SINCE HE CAME BACK. SAVING DAMPER'S KID, POPPING OPEN YOUR PRISON, EVEN THE COUPLE OF EMERGENCIES HE'S GONE ON SINCE KANSAS, SAVING LIVES.
WE DON'T GET A LOT OF HEROES DOWN HERE.
DON'T UNDERESTIMATE HOW MUCH HE MATTERS.
HE'S NOT THE ONLY ONE I MAY BE UNDERESTIMATING.

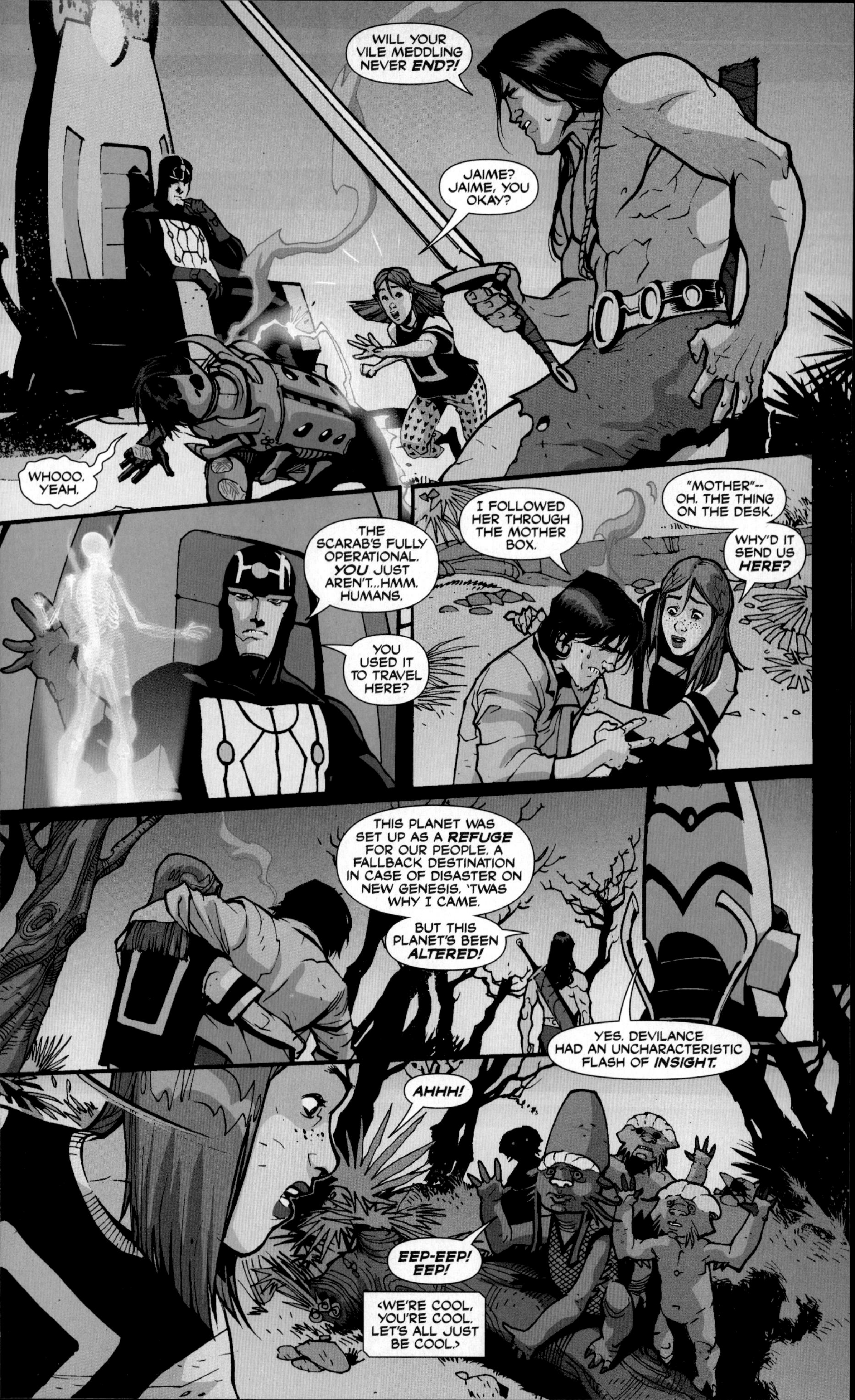
WILL YOUR VILE MEDDLING NEVER END?!
JAIME? JAIME, YOU OKAY?
WHOOO, YEAH.
THE SCARAB'S FULLY OPERATIONAL. YOU JUST AREN'T...HMM. HUMANS.
YOU USED IT TO TRAVEL HERE?
I FOLLOWED HER THROUGH THE MOTHER BOX.
"MOTHER"-- OH. THE THING ON THE DESK.
WHY'D IT SEND US HERE?
THIS PLANET WAS SET UP AS A REFUGE FOR OUR PEOPLE. A FALLBACK DESTINATION IN CASE OF DISASTER ON NEW GENESIS. 'TWAS WHY I CAME.
BUT THIS PLANET'S BEEN ALTERED!
YES. DEVILANCE HAD AN UNCHARACTERISTIC FLASH OF INSIGHT.
AHHH!
EEP-EEP! EEP!
‹WE'RE COOL, YOU'RE COOL. LET'S ALL JUST BE COOL.›

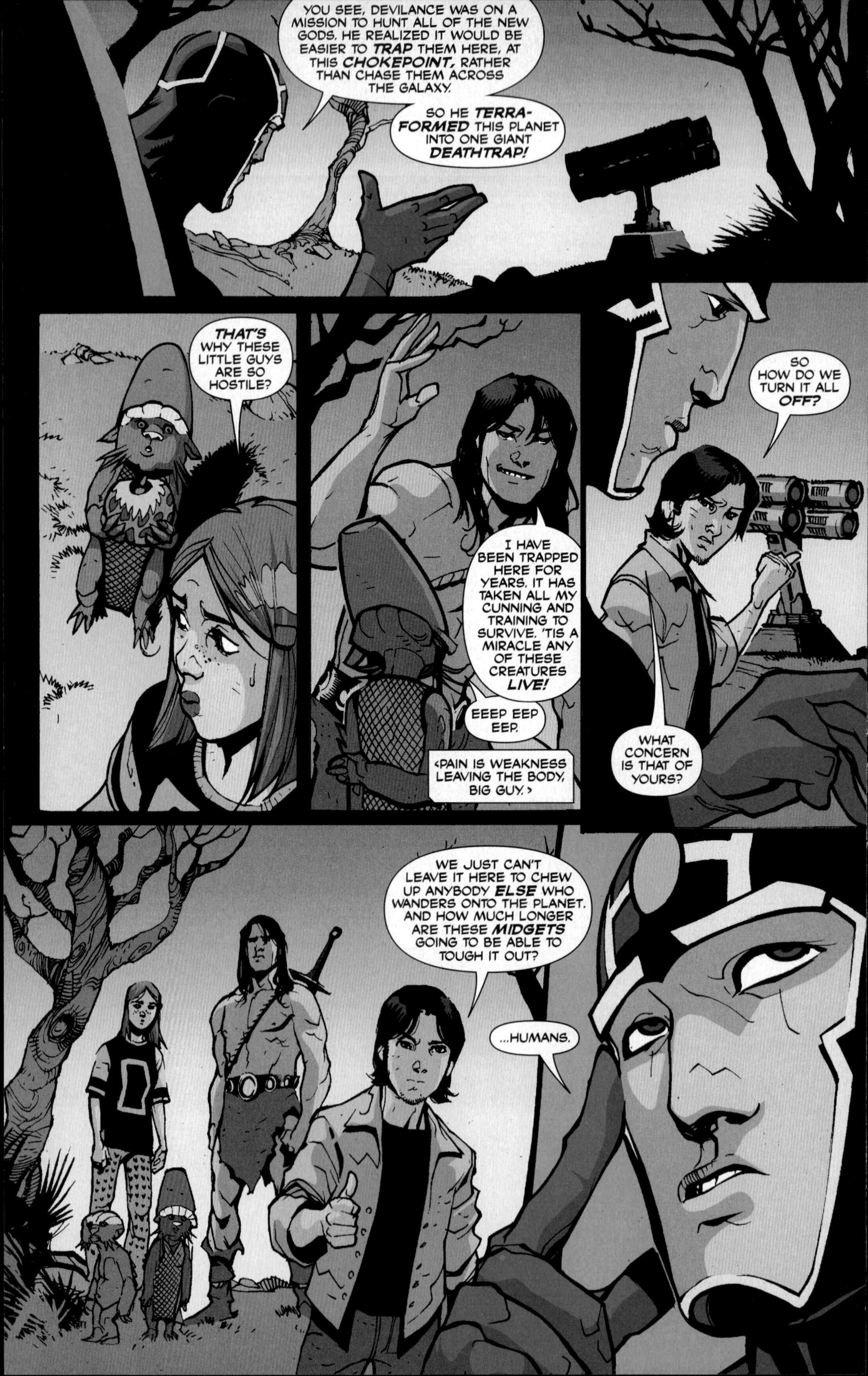
YOU SEE, DEVILANCE WAS ON A MISSION TO HUNT ALL OF THE NEW GODS. HE REALIZED IT WOULD BE EASIER TO TRAP THEM HERE, AT THIS CHOKEPOINT, RATHER THAN CHASE THEM ACROSS THE GALAXY.
SO HE TERRA-FORMED THIS PLANET INTO ONE GIANT DEATHTRAP!
THAT'S WHY THESE LITTLE GUYS ARE SO HOSTILE?
I HAVE BEEN TRAPPED HERE FOR YEARS. IT HAS TAKEN ALL MY CUNNING AND TRAINING TO SURVIVE. 'TIS A MIRACLE ANY OF THESE CREATURES LIVE!
EEEP EEP EEP.
<PAIN IS WEAKNESS LEAVING THE BODY, BIG GUY.>
SO HOW DO WE TURN IT ALL OFF?
WHAT CONCERN IS THAT OF YOURS?
WE JUST CAN'T LEAVE IT HERE TO CHEW UP ANYBODY ELSE WHO WANDERS ONTO THE PLANET. AND HOW MUCH LONGER ARE THESE MIDGETS GOING TO BE ABLE TO TOUGH IT OUT?
...HUMANS.

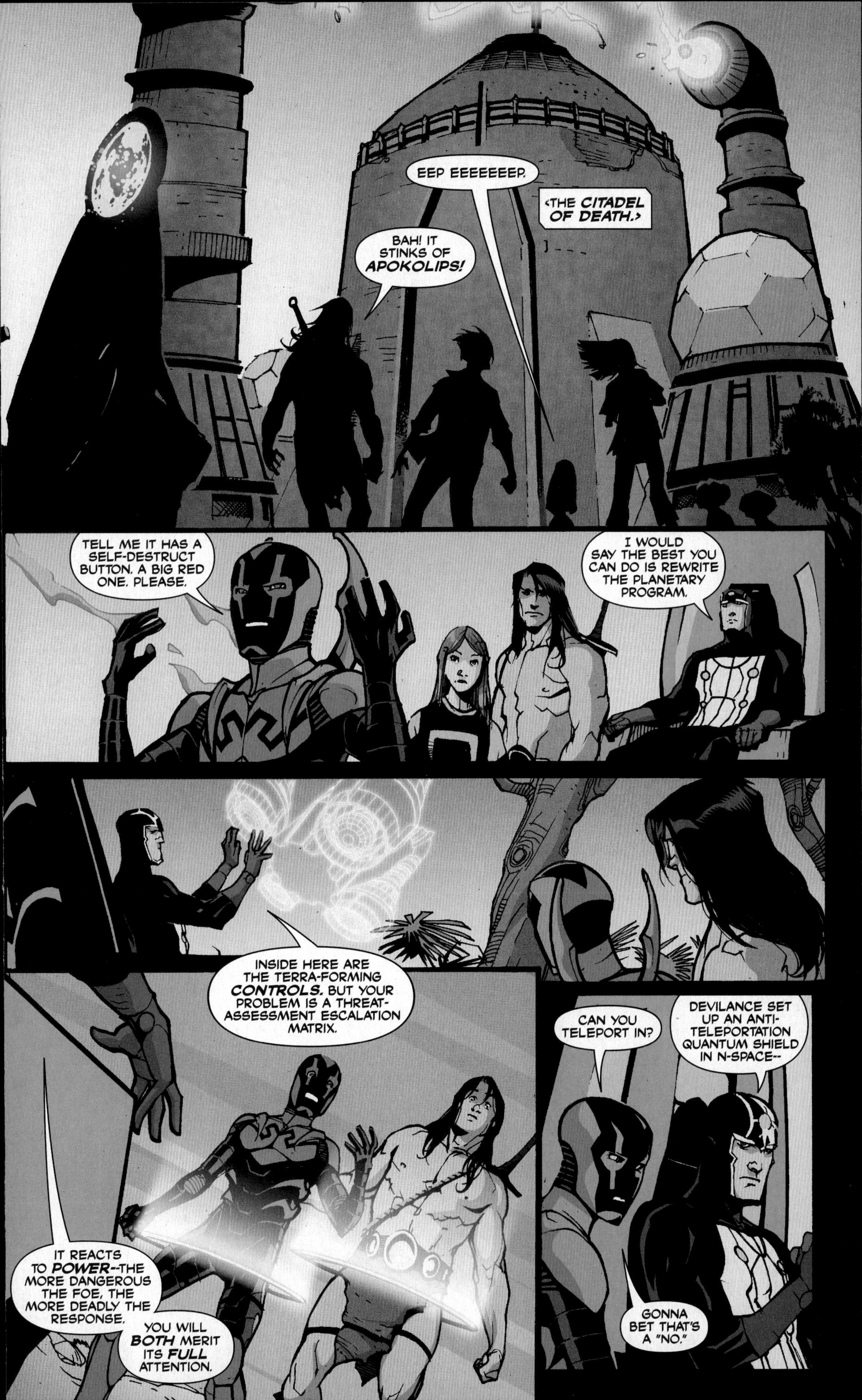

EEP EEEEEEEP.
‹THE CITADEL OF DEATH.›
BAH! IT STINKS OF APOKOLIPS!
TELL ME IT HAS A SELF-DESTRUCT BUTTON. A BIG RED ONE. PLEASE.
I WOULD SAY THE BEST YOU CAN DO IS REWRITE THE PLANETARY PROGRAM.
INSIDE HERE ARE THE TERRA-FORMING CONTROLS. BUT YOUR PROBLEM IS A THREAT-ASSESSMENT ESCALATION MATRIX.
IT REACTS TO POWER--THE MORE DANGEROUS THE FOE, THE MORE DEADLY THE RESPONSE.
YOU WILL BOTH MERIT ITS FULL ATTENTION.
CAN YOU TELEPORT IN?
DEVILANCE SET UP AN ANTI-TELEPORTATION QUANTUM SHIELD IN N-SPACE--
GONNA BET THAT'S A "NO."

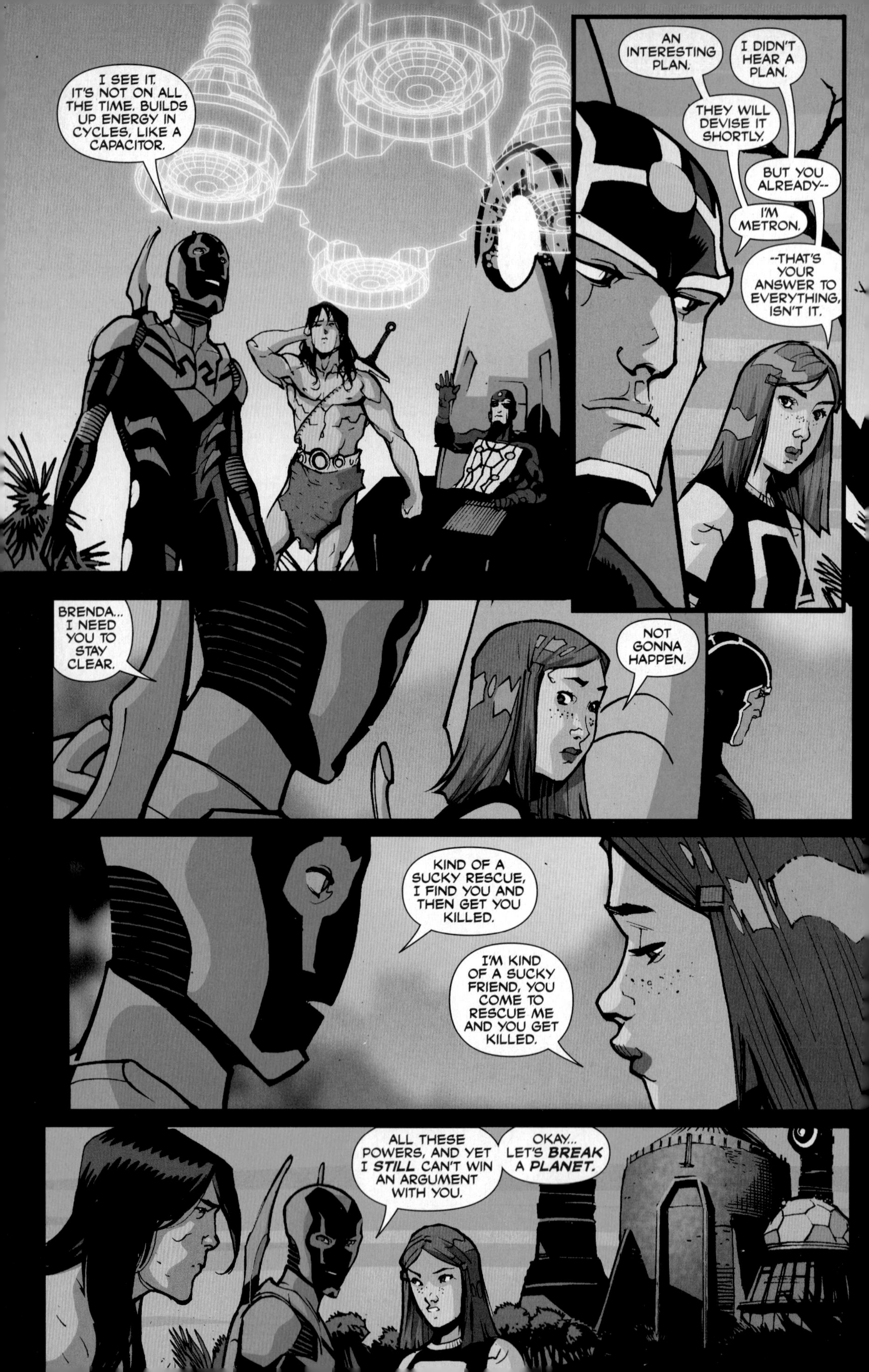
I SEE IT. IT'S NOT ON ALL THE TIME. BUILDS UP ENERGY IN CYCLES, LIKE A CAPACITOR.
AN INTERESTING PLAN.
I DIDN'T HEAR A PLAN.
THEY WILL DEVISE IT SHORTLY.
BUT YOU ALREADY--
I'M METRON.
--THAT'S YOUR ANSWER TO EVERYTHING, ISN'T IT.
BRENDA... I NEED YOU TO STAY CLEAR.
NOT GONNA HAPPEN.
KIND OF A SUCKY RESCUE, I FIND YOU AND THEN GET YOU KILLED.
I'M KIND OF A SUCKY FRIEND, YOU COME TO RESCUE ME AND YOU GET KILLED.
ALL THESE POWERS, AND YET I STILL CAN'T WIN AN ARGUMENT WITH YOU.
OKAY... LET'S BREAK A PLANET.

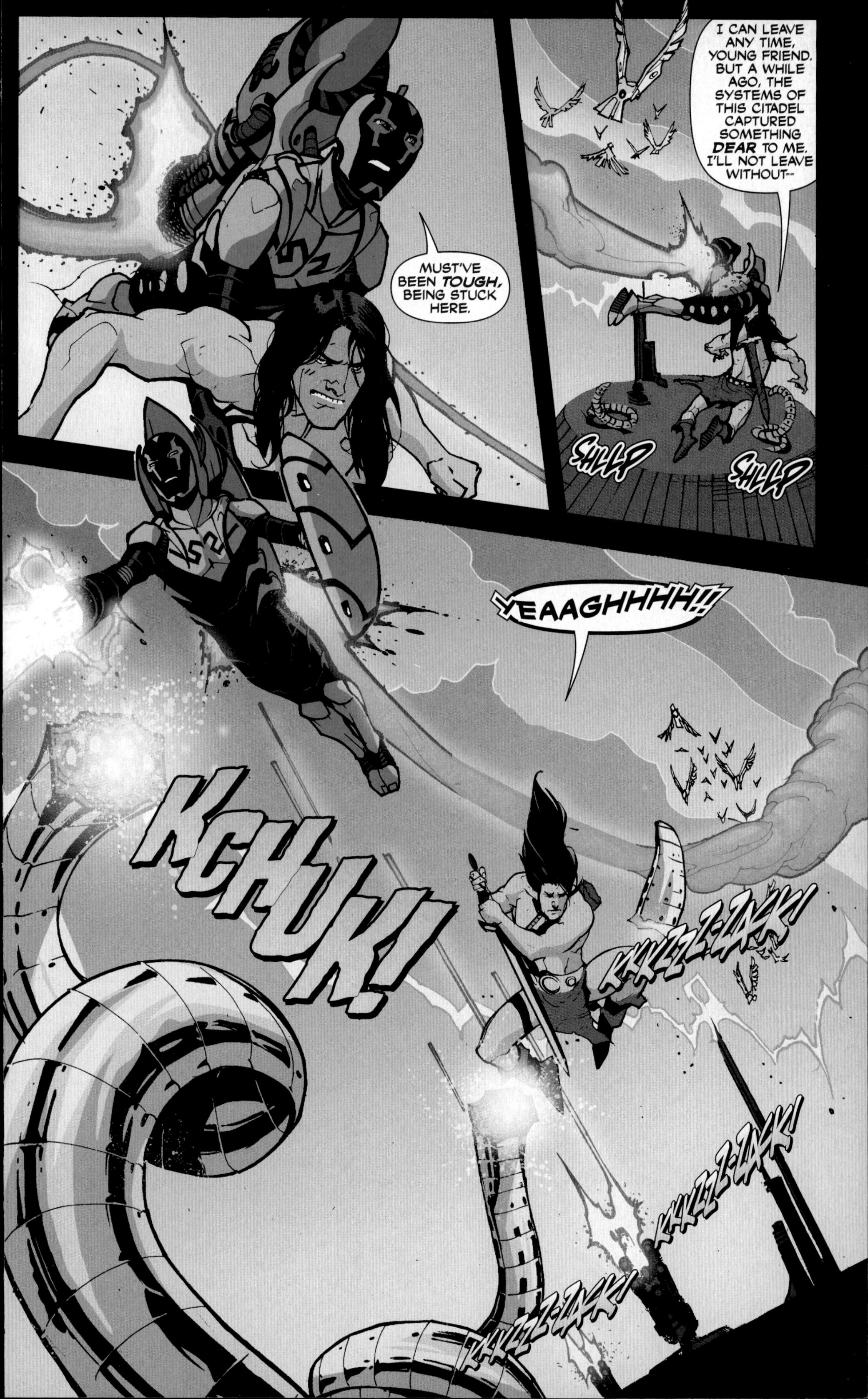
MUST'VE BEEN TOUGH, BEING STUCK HERE.
I CAN LEAVE ANY TIME, YOUNG FRIEND. BUT A WHILE AGO, THE SYSTEMS OF THIS CITADEL CAPTURED SOMETHING DEAR TO ME. I'LL NOT LEAVE WITHOUT--
SHLLP
SHLLP
YEAAGHHHH!!
KCHUK!
KAKZZZ-ZAK!
KAKZZZ-ZAK!
KAKZZZ-ZAK!

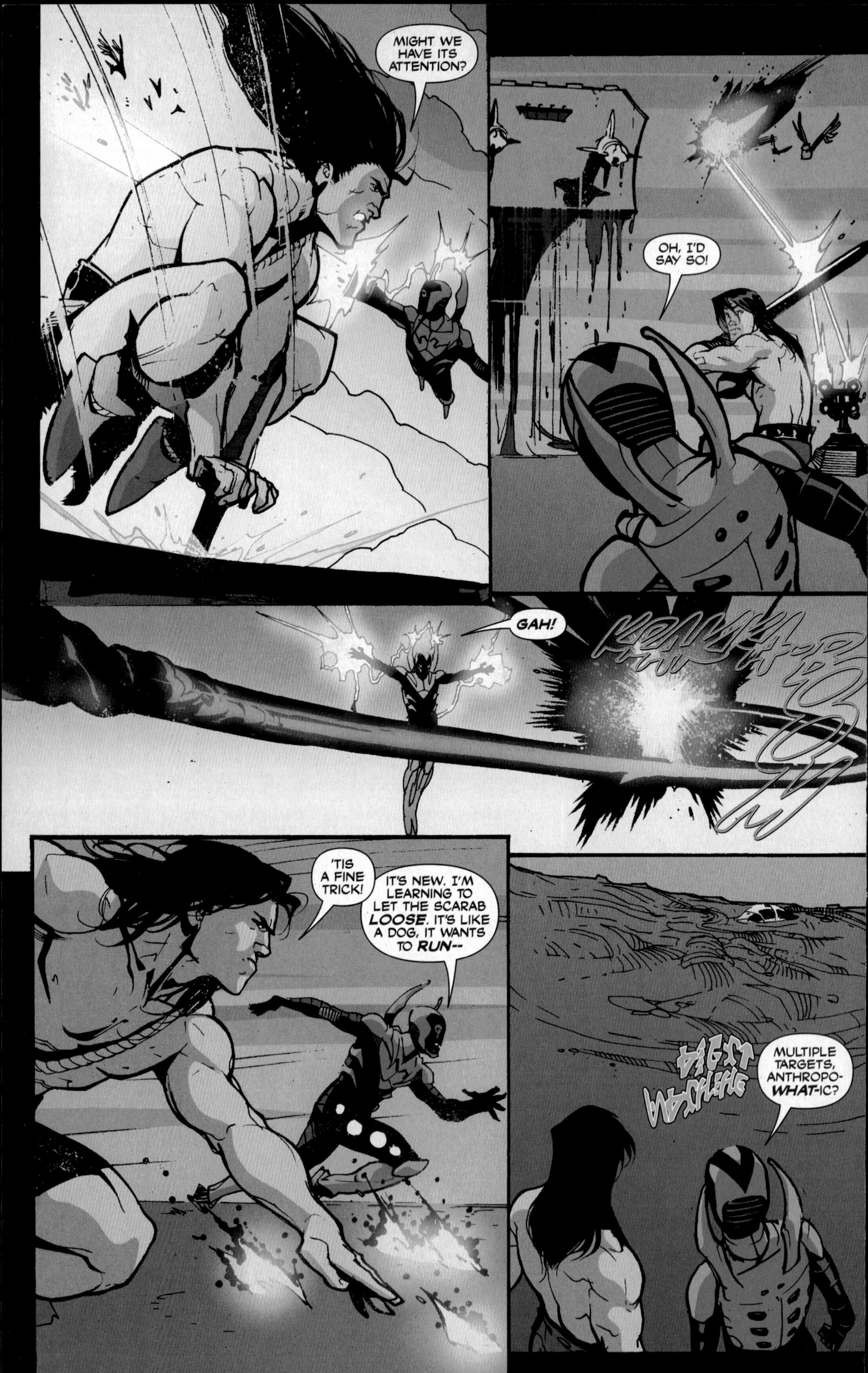
MIGHT WE HAVE ITS ATTENTION?
OH, I'D SAY SO!
GAH!
'TIS A FINE TRICK!
IT'S NEW. I'M LEARNING TO LET THE SCARAB LOOSE. IT'S LIKE A DOG, IT WANTS TO RUN--
MULTIPLE TARGETS, ANTHROPO-WHAT-IC?

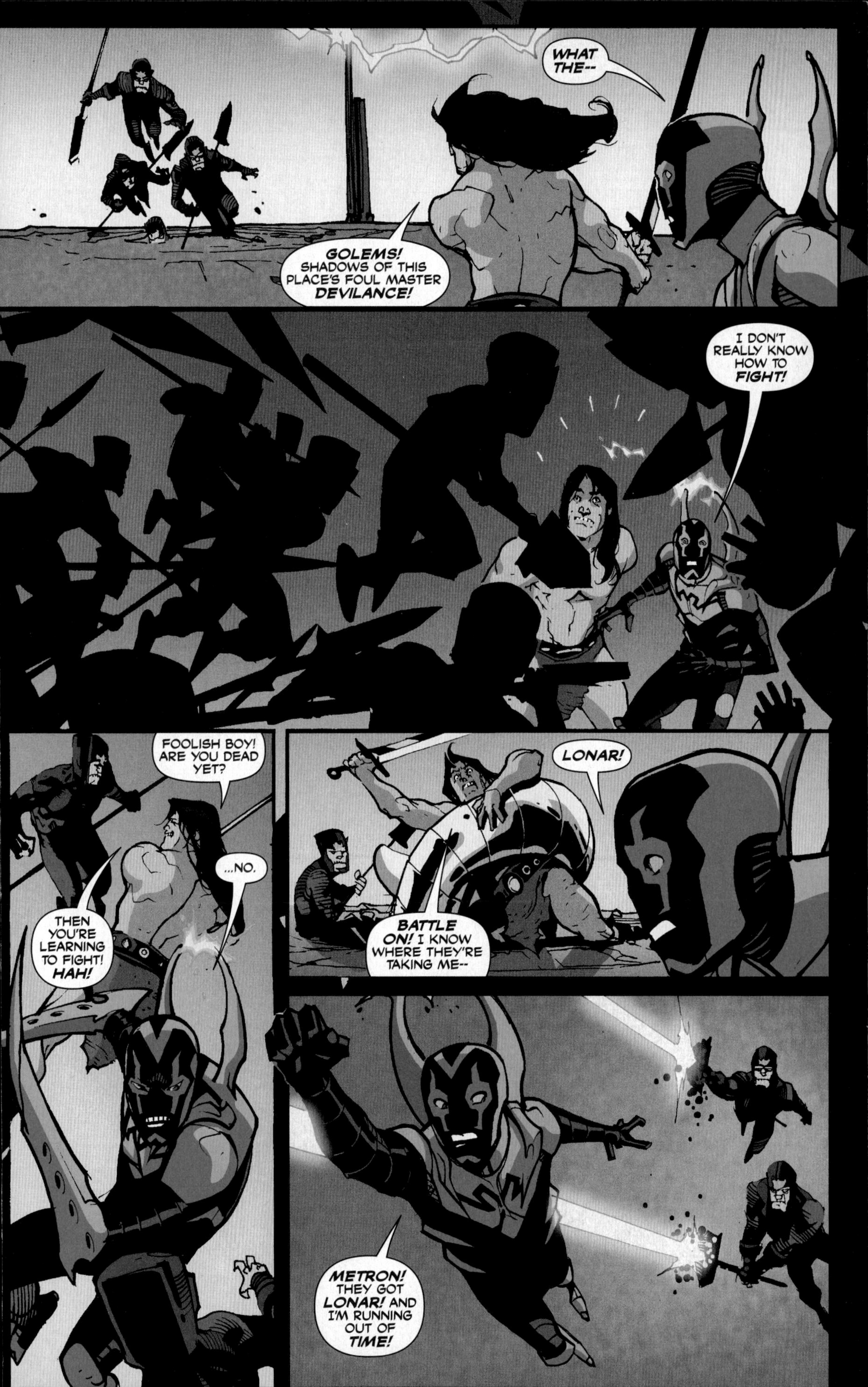
WHAT THE--
GOLEMS! SHADOWS OF THIS PLACE'S FOUL MASTER DEVILANCE!
I DON'T REALLY KNOW HOW TO FIGHT!
FOOLISH BOY! ARE YOU DEAD YET?
...NO.
THEN YOU'RE LEARNING TO FIGHT! HAH!
LONAR!
BATTLE ON! I KNOW WHERE THEY'RE TAKING ME--
METRON! THEY GOT LONAR! AND I'M RUNNING OUT OF TIME!

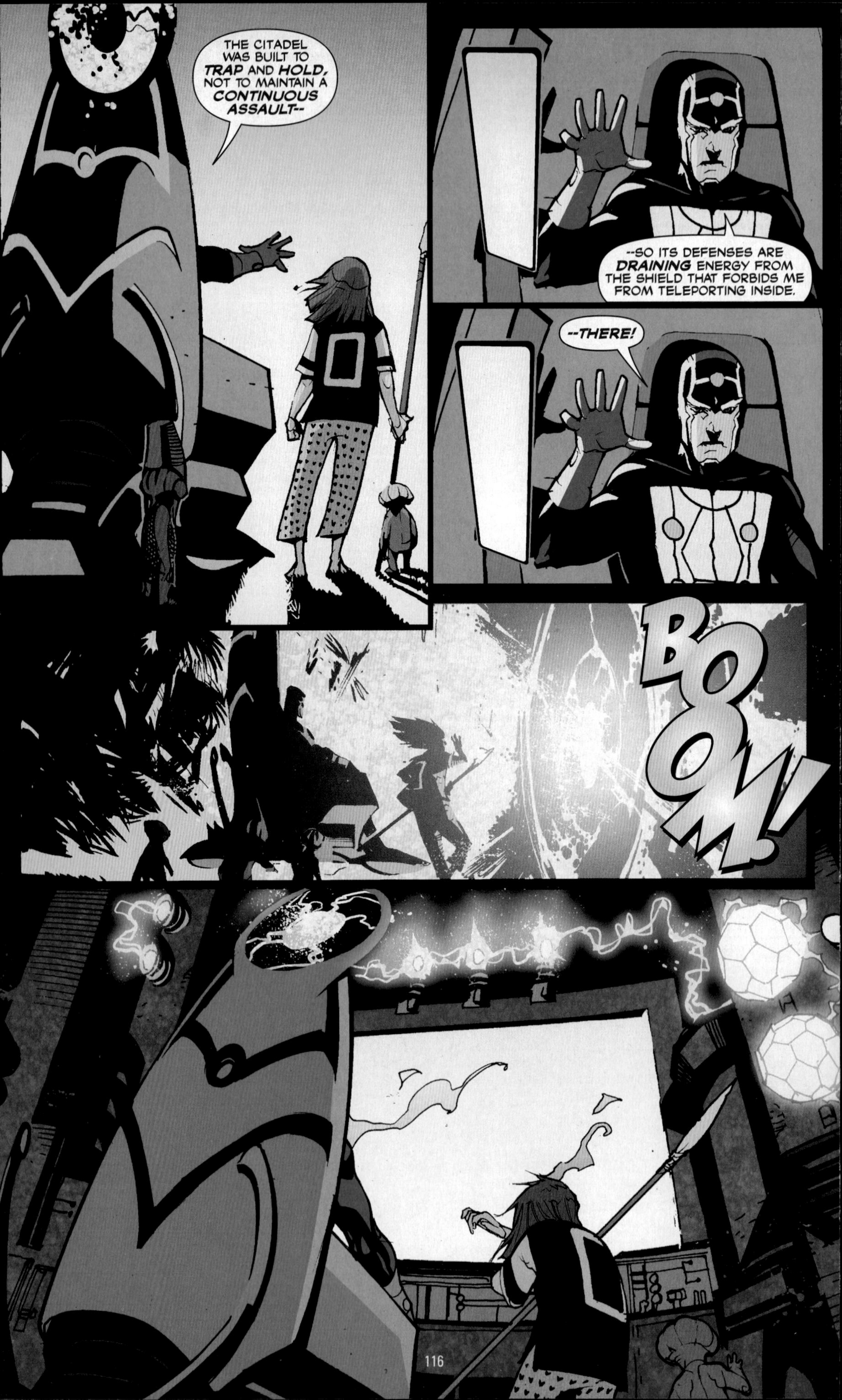
THE CITADEL WAS BUILT TO TRAP AND HOLD, NOT TO MAINTAIN A CONTINUOUS ASSAULT--
--SO ITS DEFENSES ARE DRAINING ENERGY FROM THE SHIELD THAT FORBIDS ME FROM TELEPORTING INSIDE.
--THERE!
BOOOM!

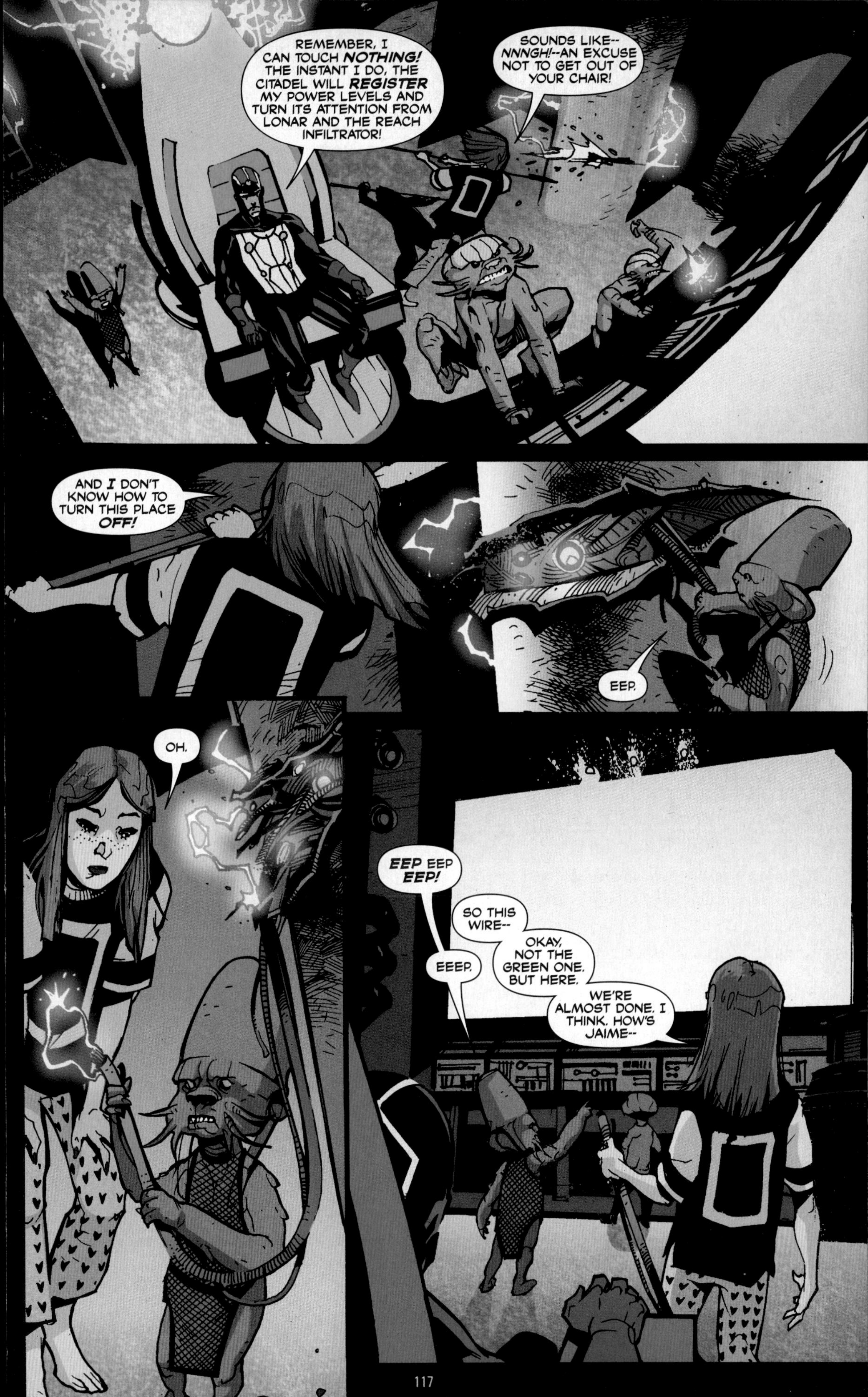
REMEMBER, I CAN TOUCH NOTHING! THE INSTANT I DO, THE CITADEL WILL REGISTER MY POWER LEVELS AND TURN ITS ATTENTION FROM LONAR AND THE REACH INFILTRATOR!
SOUNDS LIKE-- NNNGH!--AN EXCUSE NOT TO GET OUT OF YOUR CHAIR!
AND I DON'T KNOW HOW TO TURN THIS PLACE OFF!
EEP.
OH.
EEP EEP EEP!
SO THIS WIRE--
EEEP.
OKAY, NOT THE GREEN ONE. BUT HERE.
WE'RE ALMOST DONE. I THINK. HOW'S JAIME--

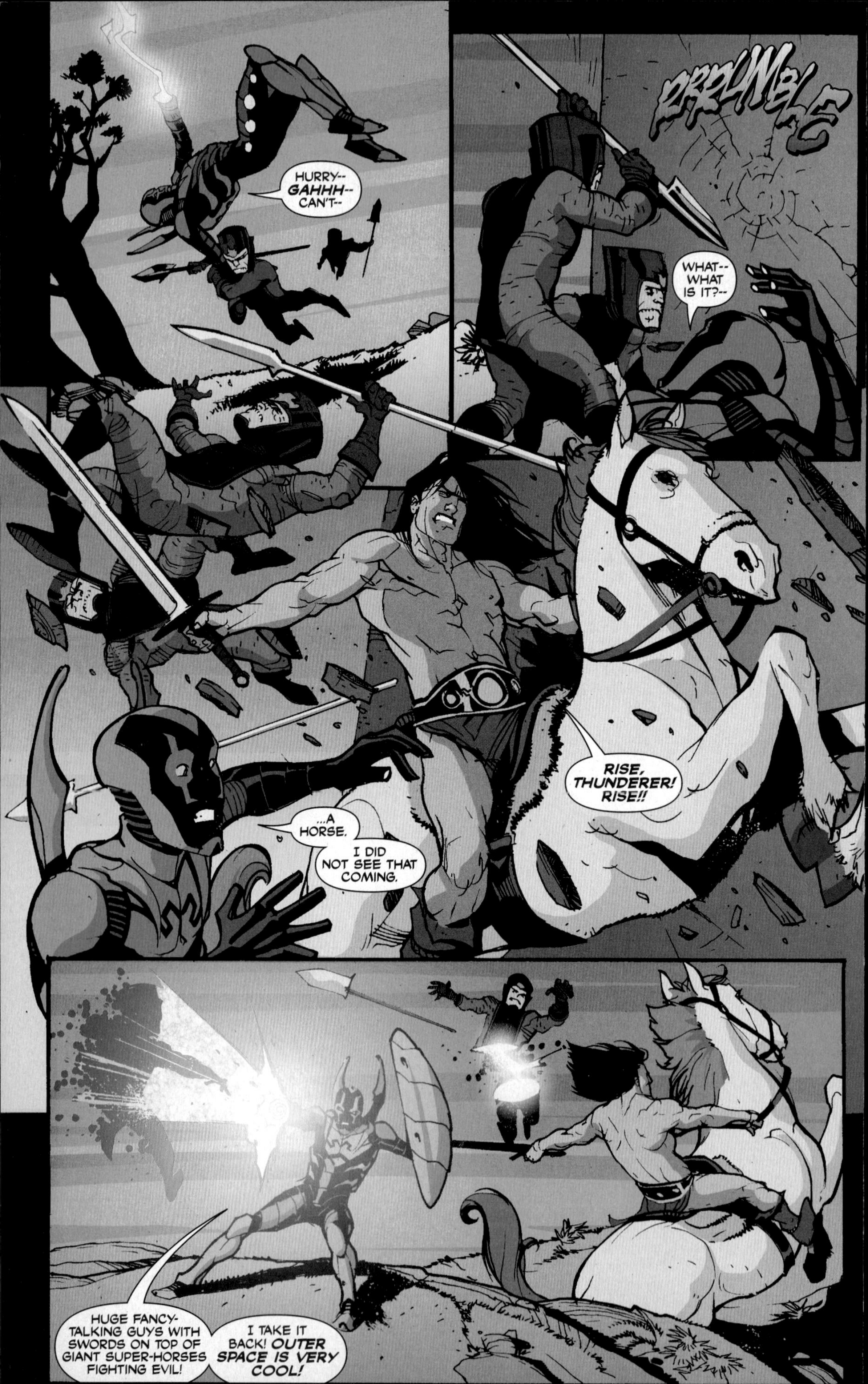
HURRY-- GAHHH-- CAN'T--
BRRUMBLE
WHAT-- WHAT IS IT?--
RISE, THUNDERER! RISE!!
...A HORSE.
I DID NOT SEE THAT COMING.
HUGE FANCY-TALKING GUYS WITH SWORDS ON TOP OF GIANT SUPER-HORSES FIGHTING EVIL!
I TAKE IT BACK! OUTER SPACE IS VERY COOL!

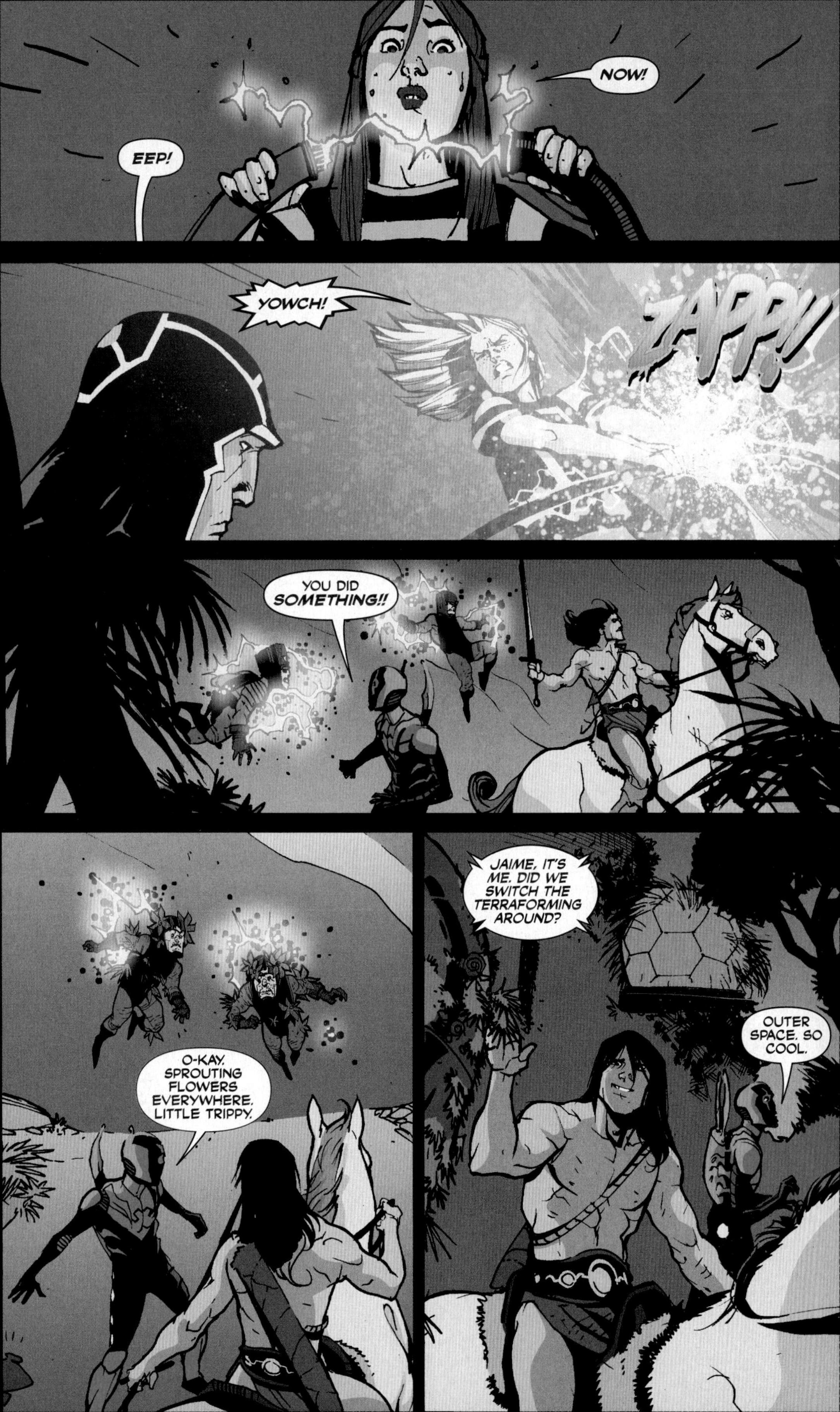
NOW!
EEP!
YOWCH!
ZAPP!!
YOU DID SOMETHING!!
O-KAY. SPROUTING FLOWERS EVERYWHERE. LITTLE TRIPPY.
JAIME, IT'S ME. DID WE SWITCH THE TERRAFORMING AROUND?
OUTER SPACE. SO COOL.

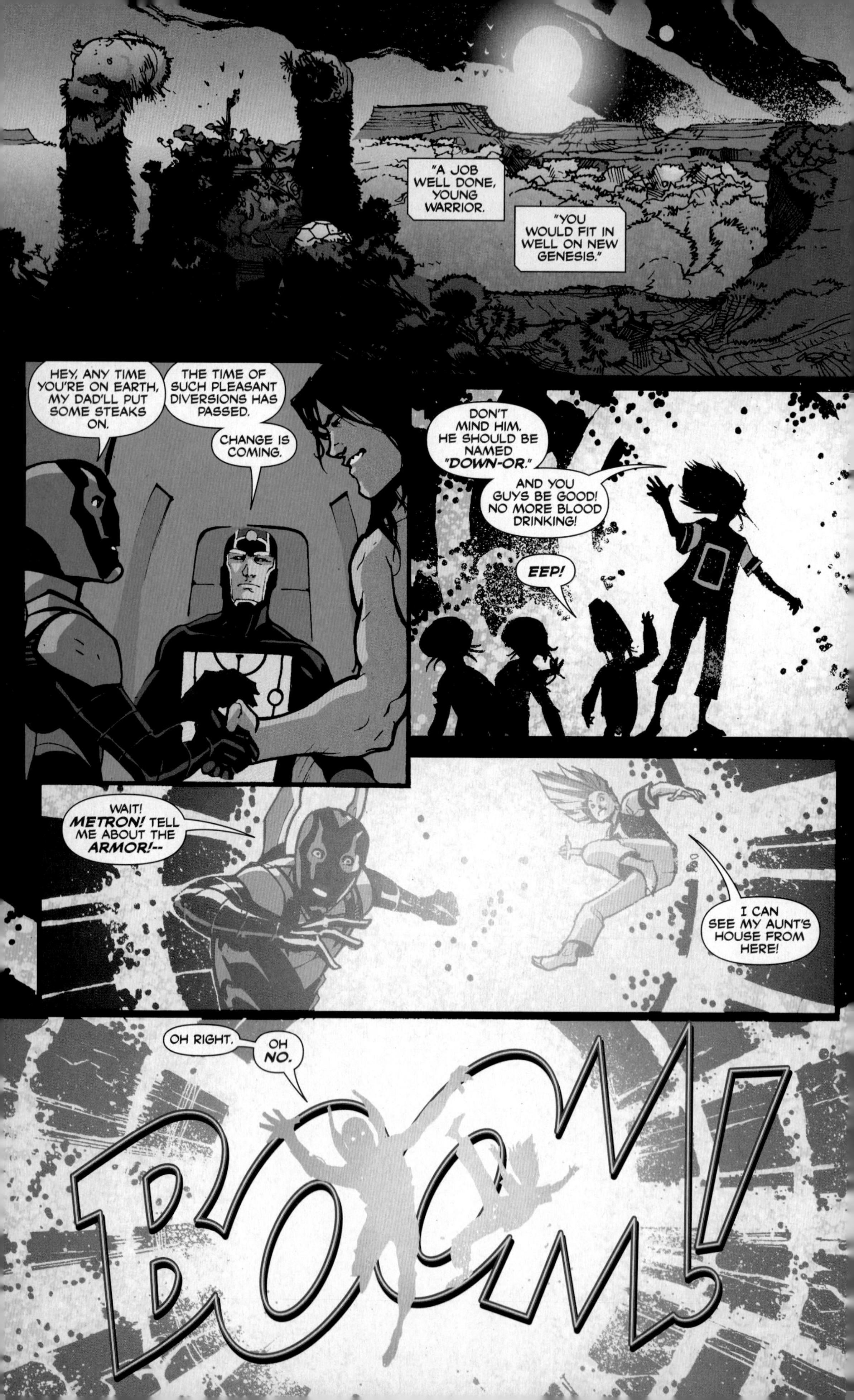
"A JOB WELL DONE, YOUNG WARRIOR.
"YOU WOULD FIT IN WELL ON NEW GENESIS."
HEY, ANY TIME YOU'RE ON EARTH, MY DAD'LL PUT SOME STEAKS ON.
THE TIME OF SUCH PLEASANT DIVERSIONS HAS PASSED.
CHANGE IS COMING.
DON'T MIND HIM. HE SHOULD BE NAMED "DOWN-OR."
AND YOU GUYS BE GOOD! NO MORE BLOOD DRINKING!
EEP!
WAIT! METRON! TELL ME ABOUT THE ARMOR!--
I CAN SEE MY AUNT'S HOUSE FROM HERE!
OH RIGHT.
OH NO.
BOOM!

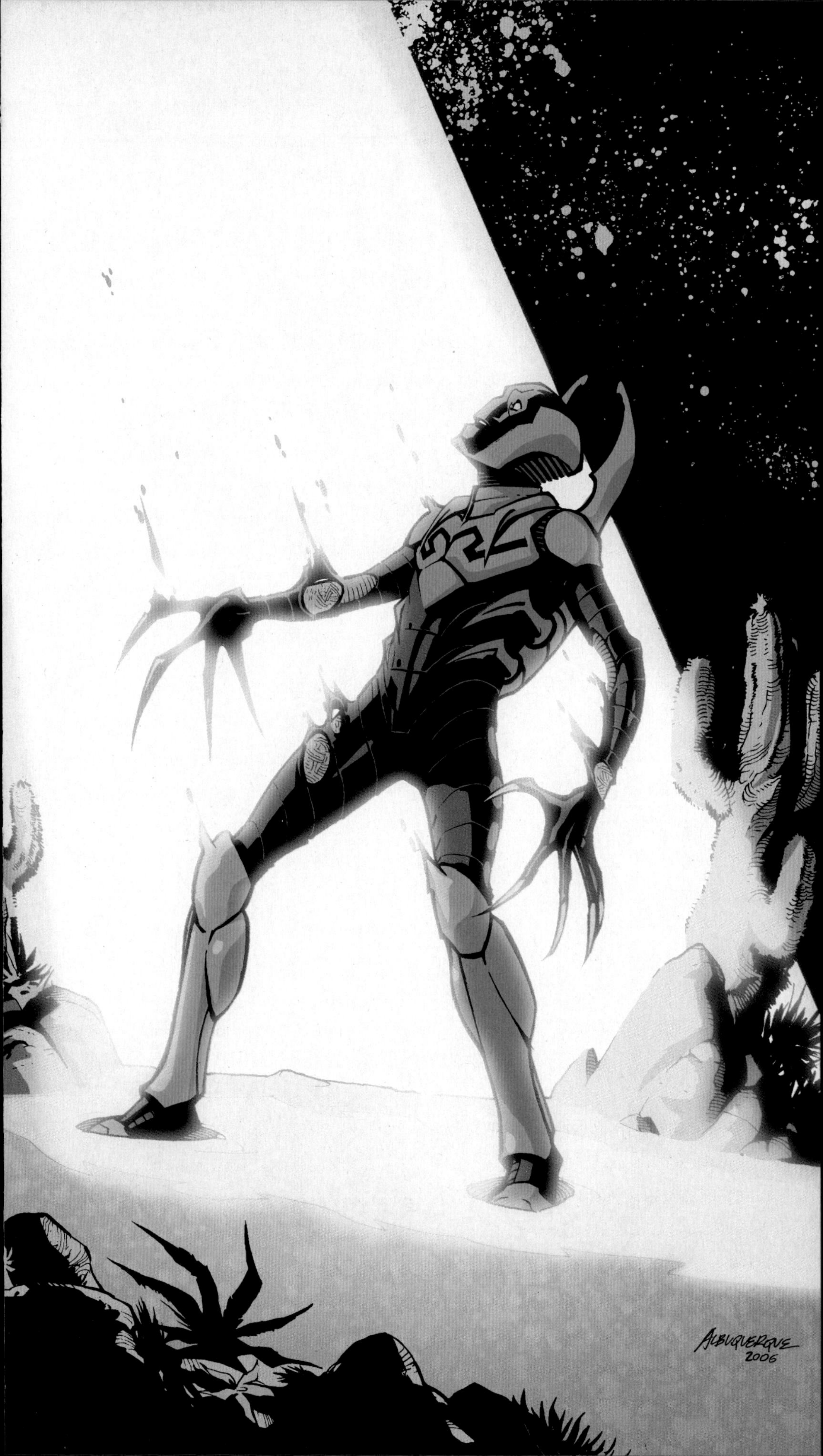
ALBUQUERQUE
2006

BLUE BEETLE #12 Written by John Rogers Cover and interior art by Rafael Albuquerque

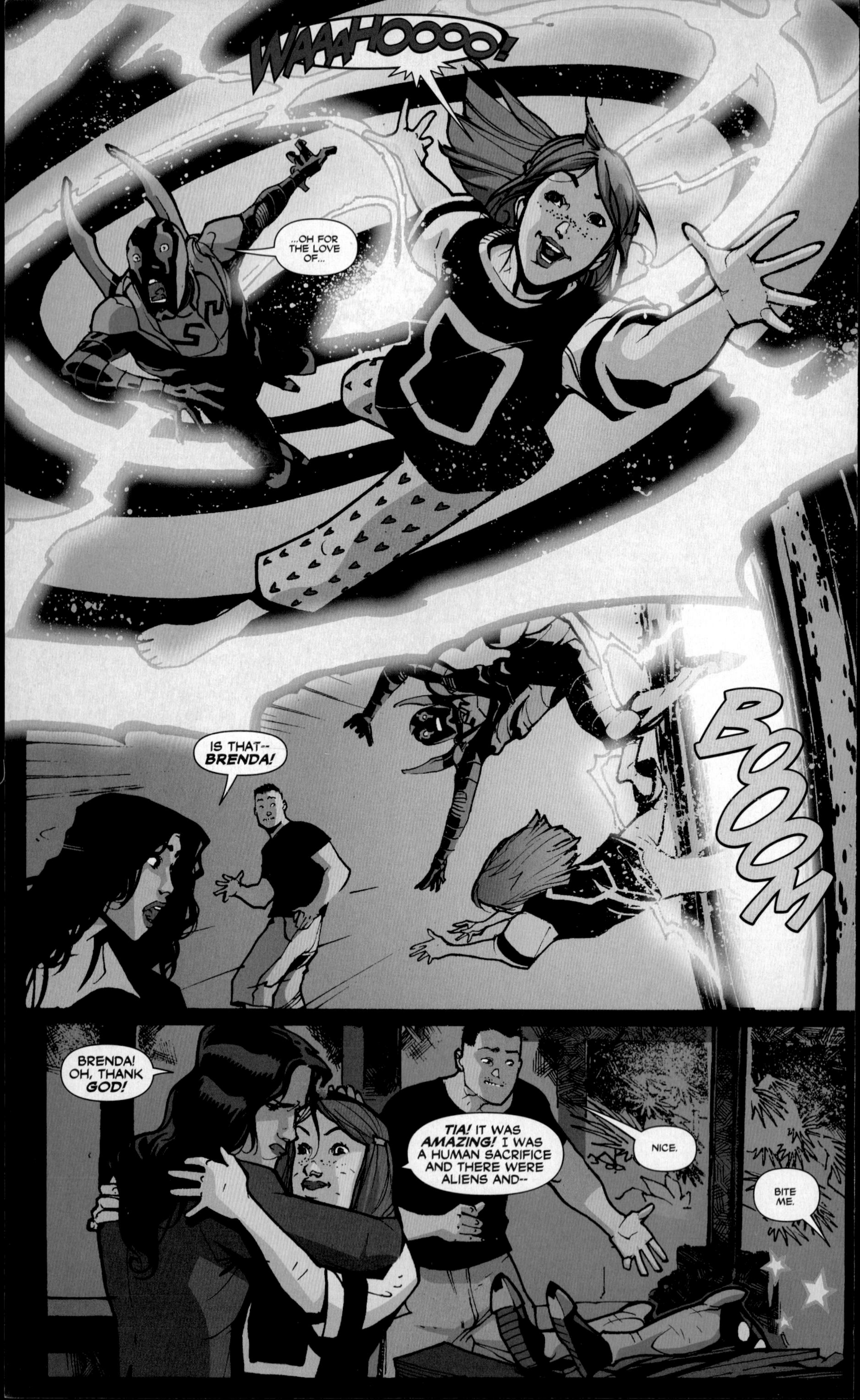
WAAAHOOOO!
...OH FOR THE LOVE OF...
IS THAT-- BRENDA!
BOOOM
BRENDA! OH, THANK GOD!
TIA! IT WAS AMAZING! I WAS A HUMAN SACRIFICE AND THERE WERE ALIENS AND--
NICE.
BITE ME.

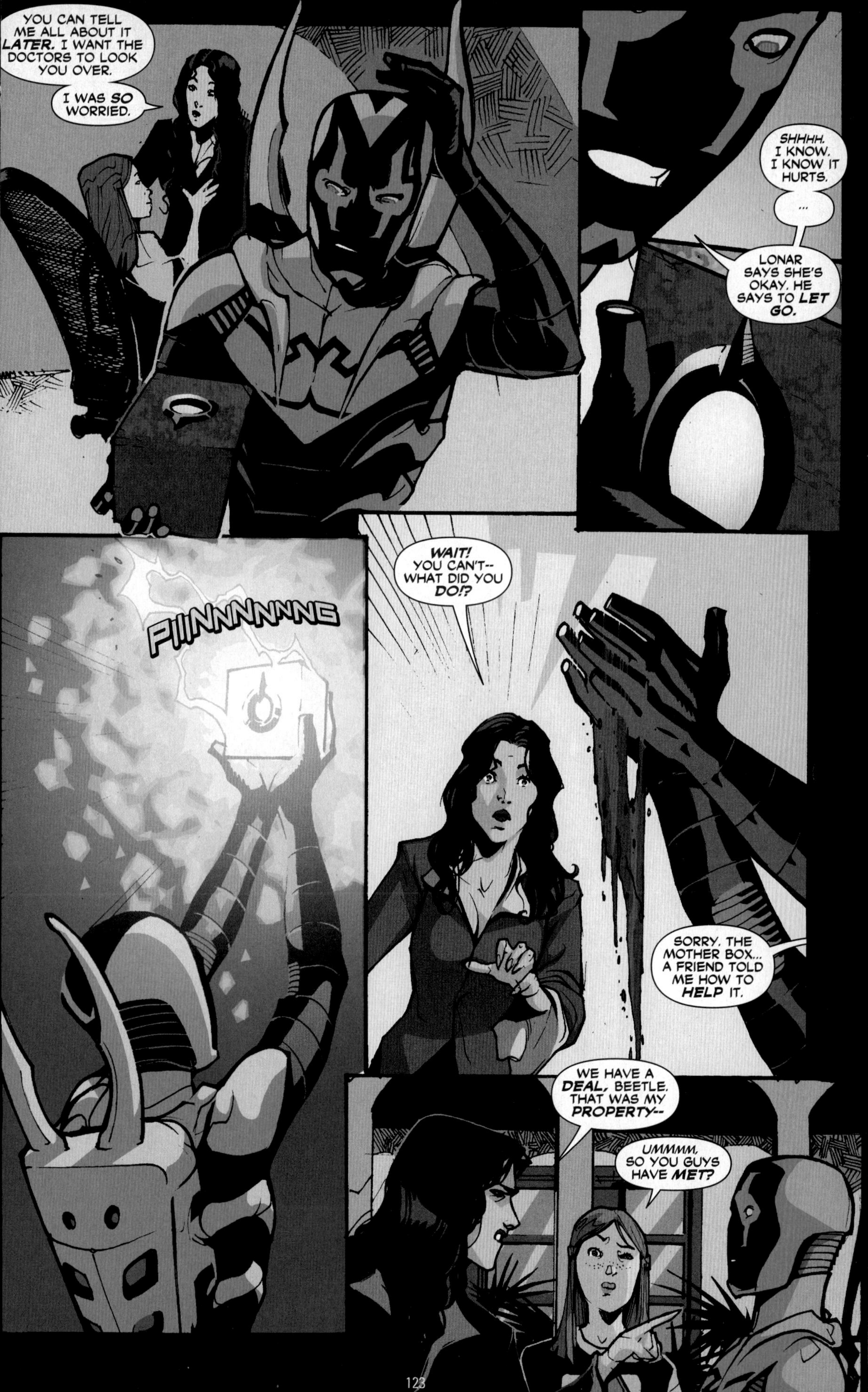
YOU CAN TELL ME ALL ABOUT IT LATER. I WANT THE DOCTORS TO LOOK YOU OVER.
I WAS SO WORRIED.
SHHHH. I KNOW. I KNOW IT HURTS.
...
LONAR SAYS SHE'S OKAY. HE SAYS TO LET GO.
PIIINNNNNNG
WAIT! YOU CAN'T-- WHAT DID YOU DO!?
SORRY. THE MOTHER BOX... A FRIEND TOLD ME HOW TO HELP IT.
WE HAVE A DEAL, BEETLE. THAT WAS MY PROPERTY--
UMMMM, SO YOU GUYS HAVE MET?

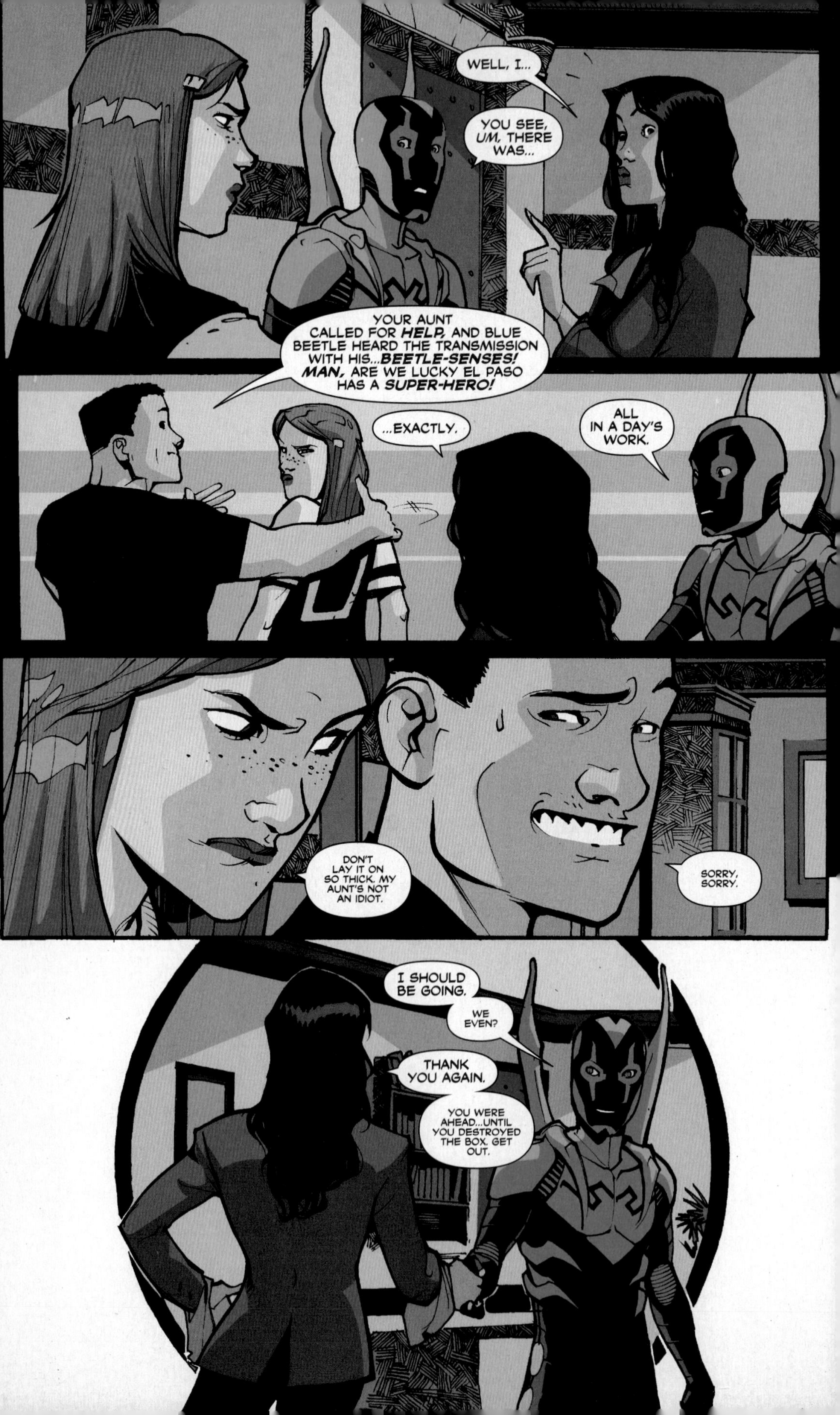
WELL, I...
YOU SEE, UM, THERE WAS...
YOUR AUNT CALLED FOR HELP, AND BLUE BEETLE HEARD THE TRANSMISSION WITH HIS...BEETLE-SENSES! MAN, ARE WE LUCKY EL PASO HAS A SUPER-HERO!
...EXACTLY.
ALL IN A DAY'S WORK.
DON'T LAY IT ON SO THICK. MY AUNT'S NOT AN IDIOT.
SORRY, SORRY.
I SHOULD BE GOING.
WE EVEN?
THANK YOU AGAIN.
YOU WERE AHEAD...UNTIL YOU DESTROYED THE BOX. GET OUT.

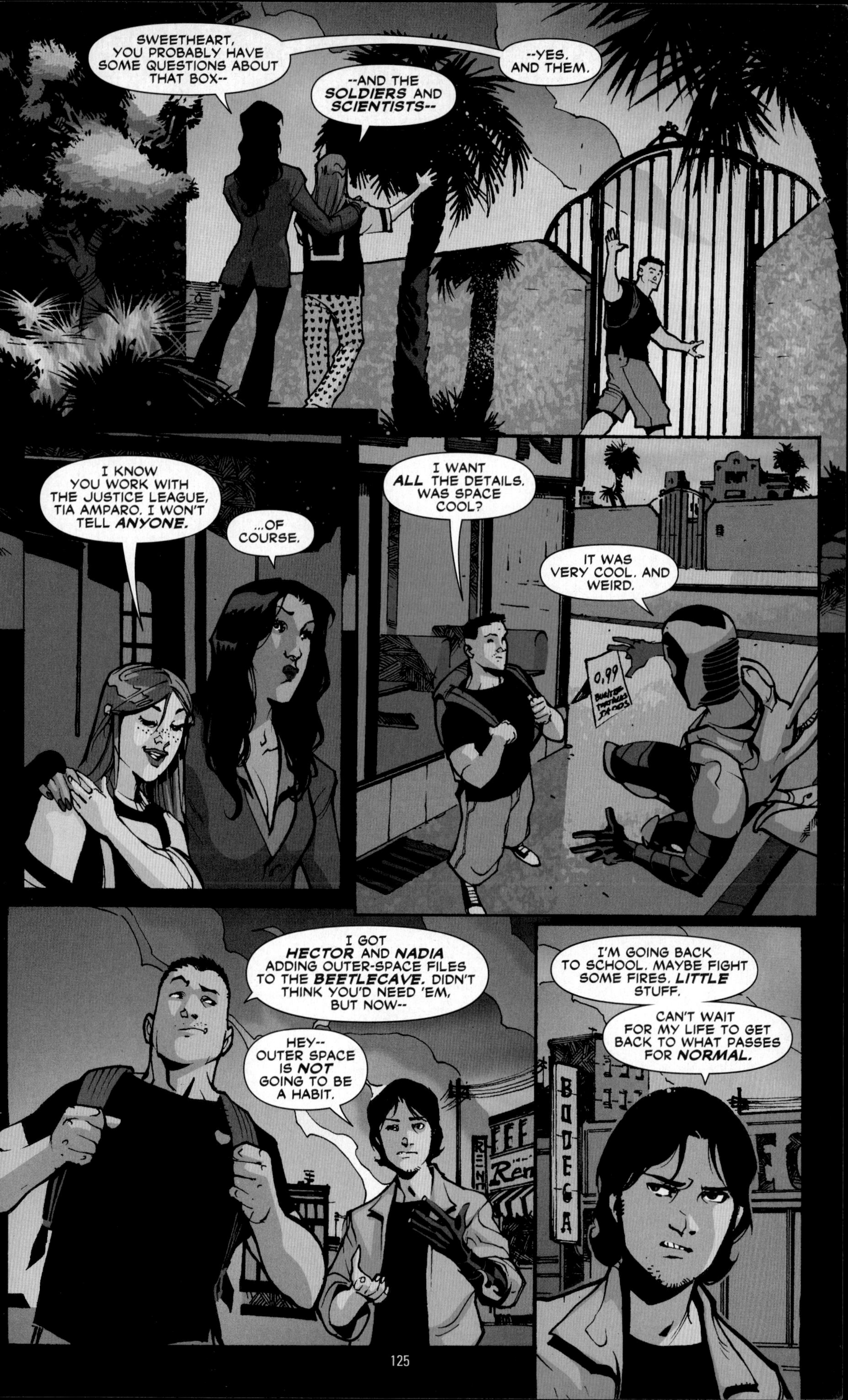
SWEETHEART, YOU PROBABLY HAVE SOME QUESTIONS ABOUT THAT BOX--
--AND THE SOLDIERS AND SCIENTISTS--
--YES. AND THEM.
I KNOW YOU WORK WITH THE JUSTICE LEAGUE, TIA AMPARO. I WON'T TELL ANYONE.
...OF COURSE.
I WANT ALL THE DETAILS. WAS SPACE COOL?
IT WAS VERY COOL. AND WEIRD.
0,99
I GOT HECTOR AND NADIA ADDING OUTER-SPACE FILES TO THE BEETLECAVE. DIDN'T THINK YOU'D NEED 'EM, BUT NOW--
HEY-- OUTER SPACE IS NOT GOING TO BE A HABIT.
I'M GOING BACK TO SCHOOL. MAYBE FIGHT SOME FIRES. LITTLE STUFF.
CAN'T WAIT FOR MY LIFE TO GET BACK TO WHAT PASSES FOR NORMAL.
BODEGA

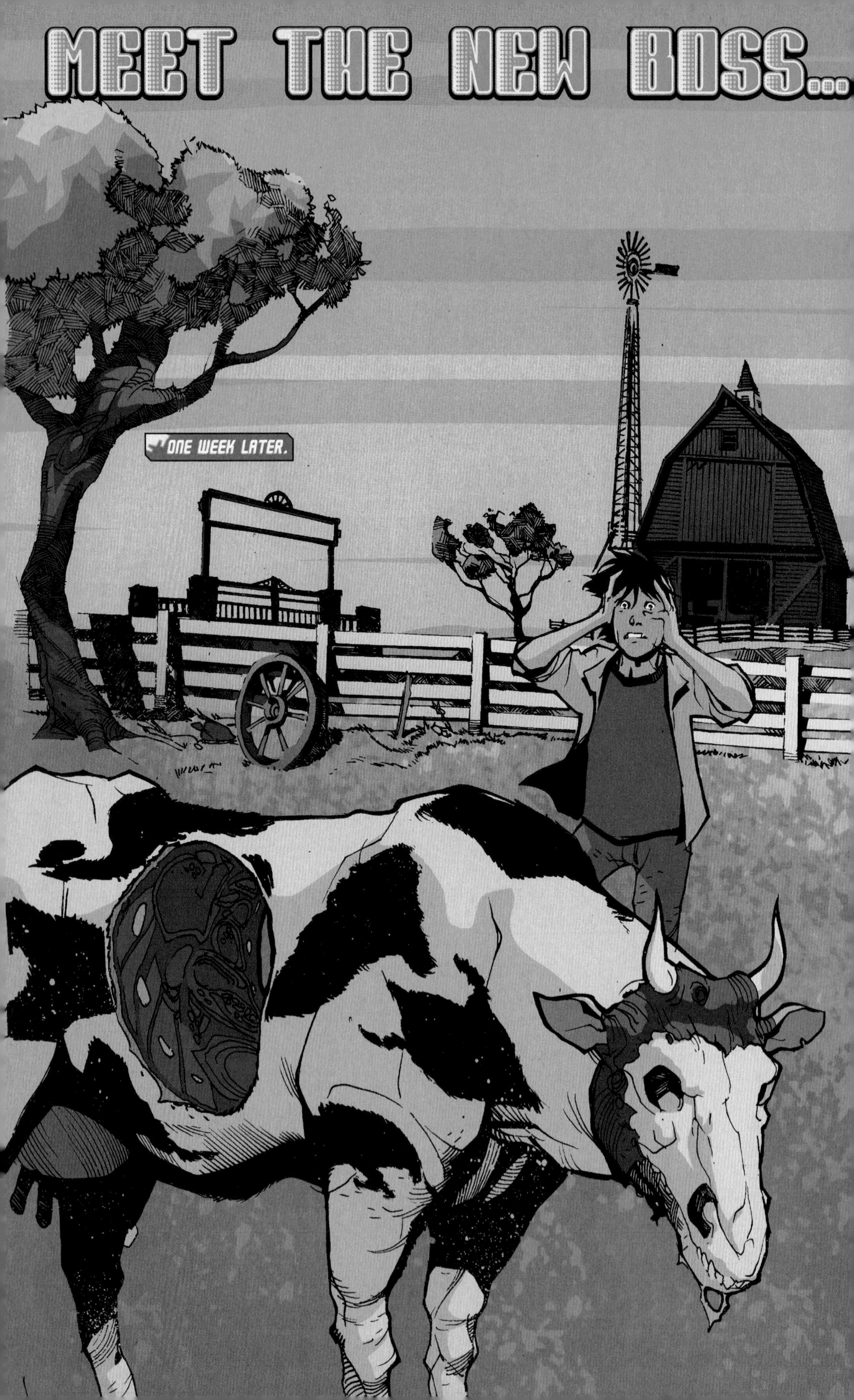
MEET THE NEW BOSS...
ONE WEEK LATER.

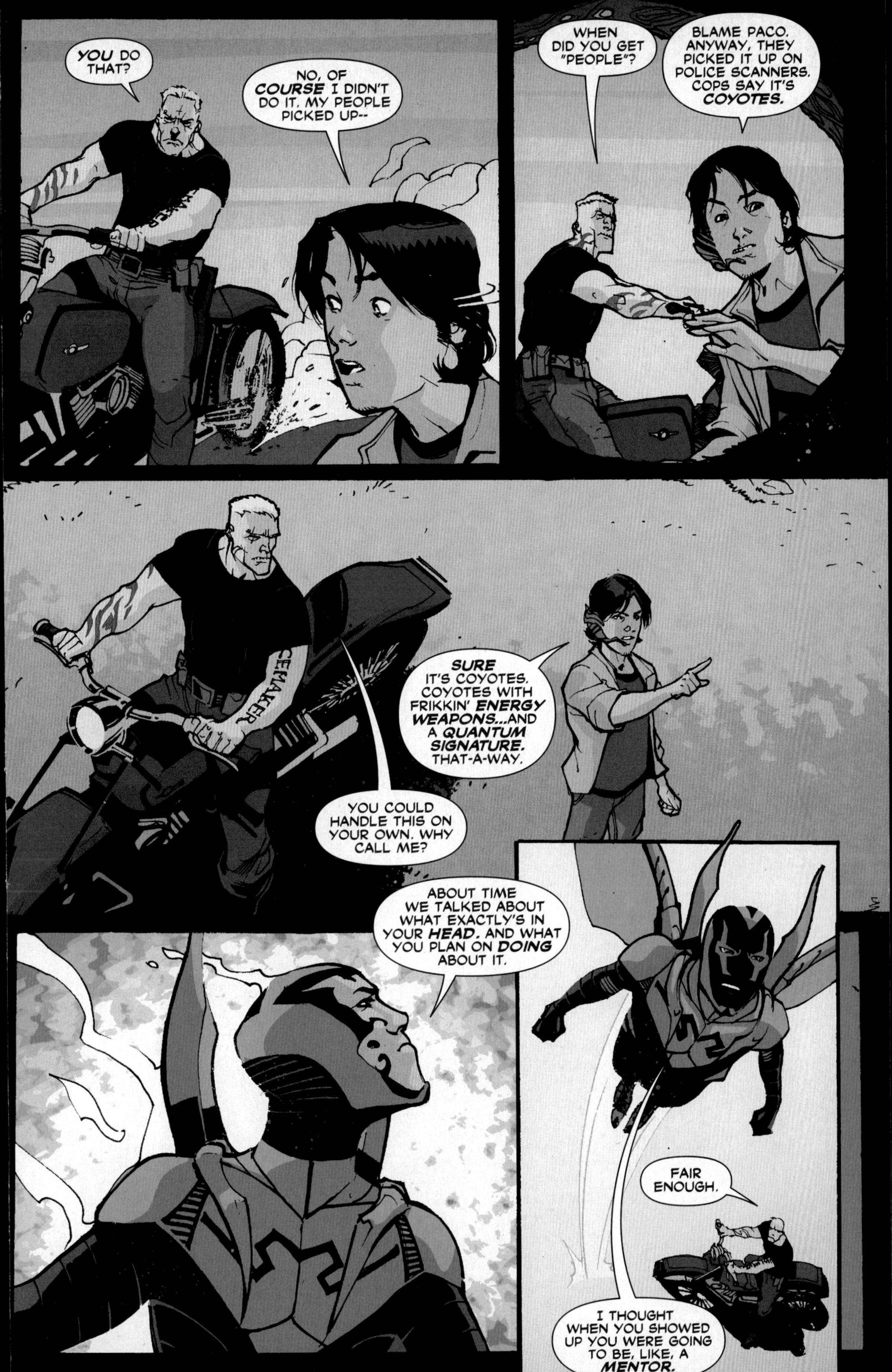
YOU DO THAT?
NO, OF COURSE I DIDN'T DO IT. MY PEOPLE PICKED UP--
WHEN DID YOU GET "PEOPLE"?
BLAME PACO. ANYWAY, THEY PICKED IT UP ON POLICE SCANNERS. COPS SAY IT'S COYOTES.
SURE IT'S COYOTES. COYOTES WITH FRIKKIN' ENERGY WEAPONS...AND A QUANTUM SIGNATURE. THAT-A-WAY.
YOU COULD HANDLE THIS ON YOUR OWN. WHY CALL ME?
ABOUT TIME WE TALKED ABOUT WHAT EXACTLY'S IN YOUR HEAD. AND WHAT YOU PLAN ON DOING ABOUT IT.
FAIR ENOUGH.
I THOUGHT WHEN YOU SHOWED UP YOU WERE GOING TO BE, LIKE, A MENTOR.

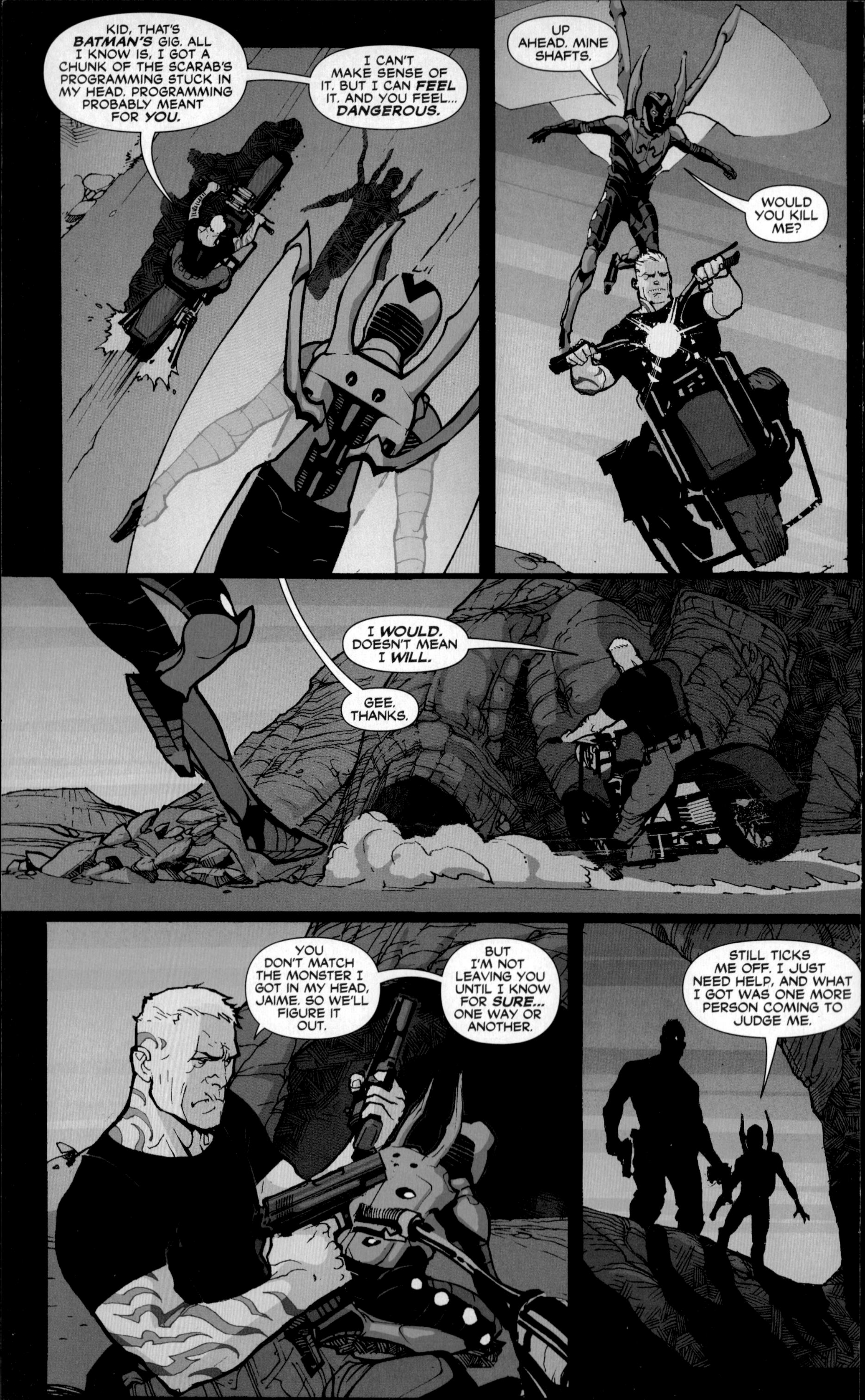
KID, THAT'S BATMAN'S GIG. ALL I KNOW IS, I GOT A CHUNK OF THE SCARAB'S PROGRAMMING STUCK IN MY HEAD. PROGRAMMING PROBABLY MEANT FOR YOU.
I CAN'T MAKE SENSE OF IT. BUT I CAN FEEL IT. AND YOU FEEL... DANGEROUS.
UP AHEAD. MINE SHAFTS.
WOULD YOU KILL ME?
I WOULD. DOESN'T MEAN I WILL.
GEE. THANKS.
YOU DON'T MATCH THE MONSTER I GOT IN MY HEAD, JAIME. SO WE'LL FIGURE IT OUT.
BUT I'M NOT LEAVING YOU UNTIL I KNOW FOR SURE... ONE WAY OR ANOTHER.
STILL TICKS ME OFF. I JUST NEED HELP, AND WHAT I GOT WAS ONE MORE PERSON COMING TO JUDGE ME.

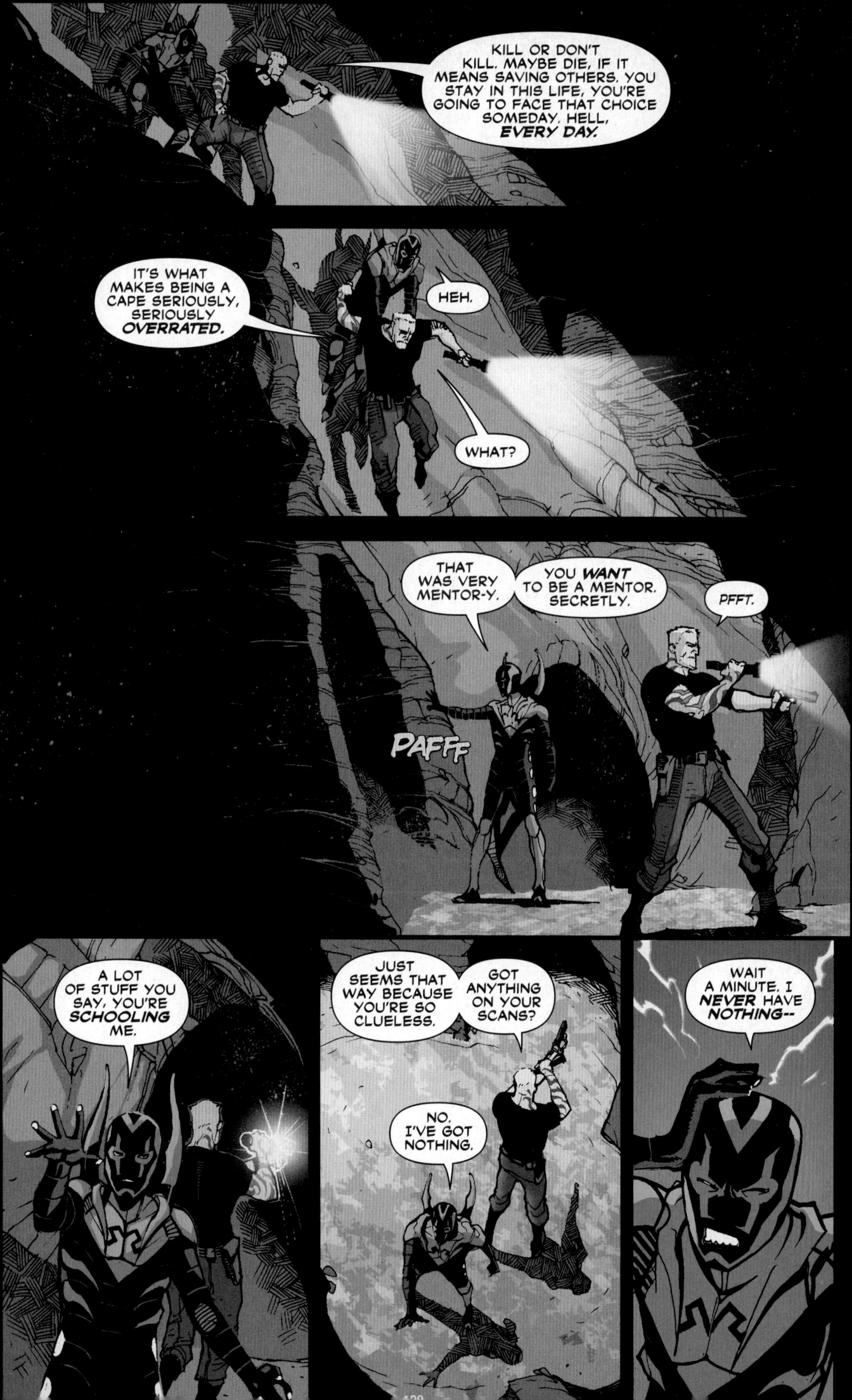
KILL OR DON'T KILL. MAYBE DIE, IF IT MEANS SAVING OTHERS. YOU STAY IN THIS LIFE, YOU'RE GOING TO FACE THAT CHOICE SOMEDAY. HELL, ***EVERY DAY.***
IT'S WHAT MAKES BEING A CAPE SERIOUSLY, SERIOUSLY ***OVERRATED.***
HEH.
WHAT?
THAT WAS VERY MENTOR-Y.
YOU **WANT** TO BE A MENTOR. SECRETLY.
PFFT.
PAFFF
A LOT OF STUFF YOU SAY, YOU'RE **SCHOOLING** ME.
JUST SEEMS THAT WAY BECAUSE YOU'RE SO CLUELESS.
GOT ANYTHING ON YOUR SCANS?
NO. I'VE GOT NOTHING.
WAIT A MINUTE. I ***NEVER*** HAVE ***NOTHING--***

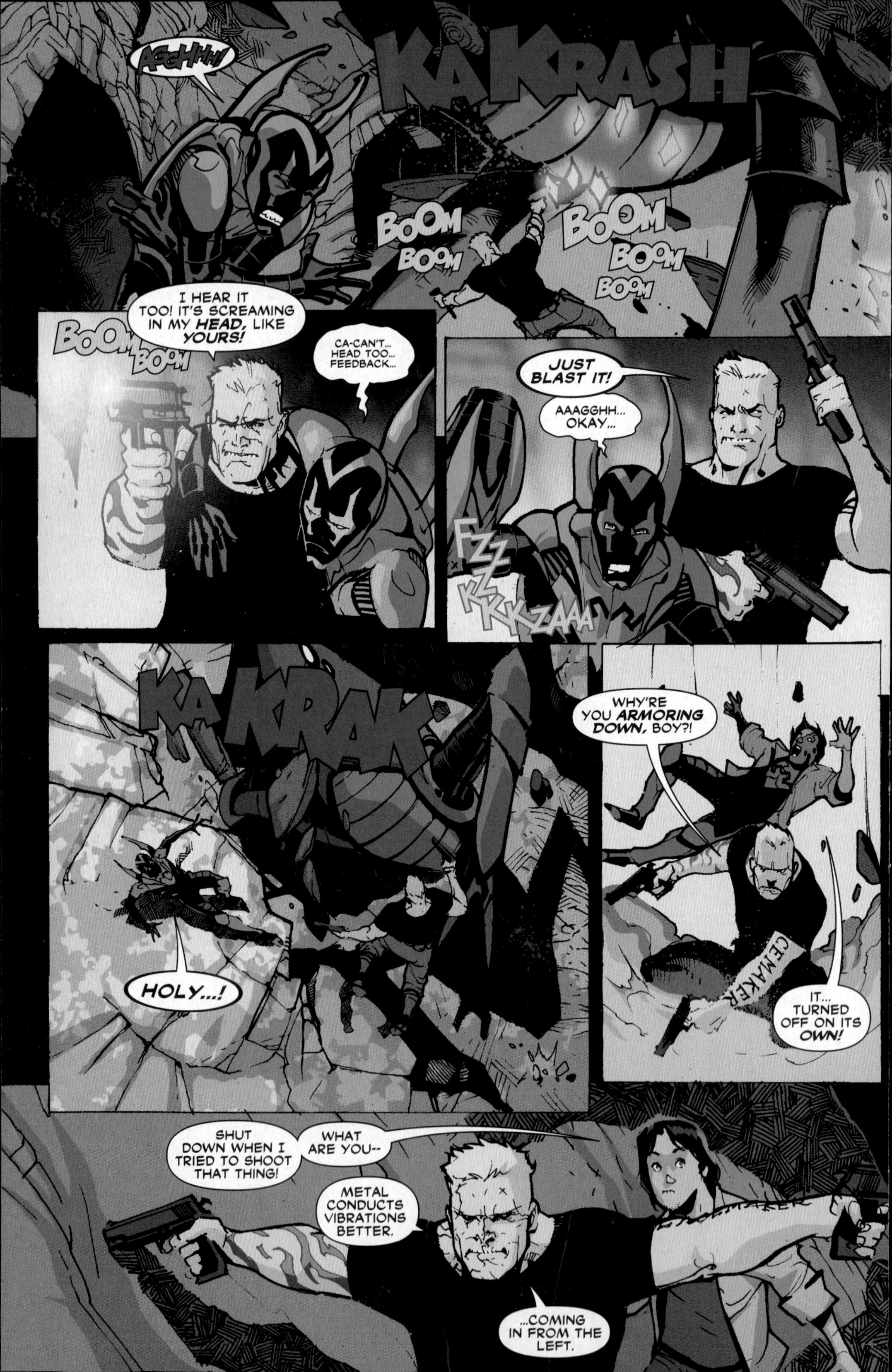

AGGHHH!
KA KRASH
BOOM
BOOM
BOOM
BOOM
BOOM
BOOM BOOM
I HEAR IT TOO! IT'S SCREAMING IN MY HEAD, LIKE YOURS!
CA-CAN'T... HEAD TOO... FEEDBACK...
JUST BLAST IT!
AAAGGHH... OKAY...
FZZZKKKKZAAA
KA KRAK
HOLY...!
WHY'RE YOU ARMORING DOWN, BOY?!
IT... TURNED OFF ON ITS OWN!
SHUT DOWN WHEN I TRIED TO SHOOT THAT THING!
WHAT ARE YOU--
METAL CONDUCTS VIBRATIONS BETTER.
...COMING IN FROM THE LEFT.

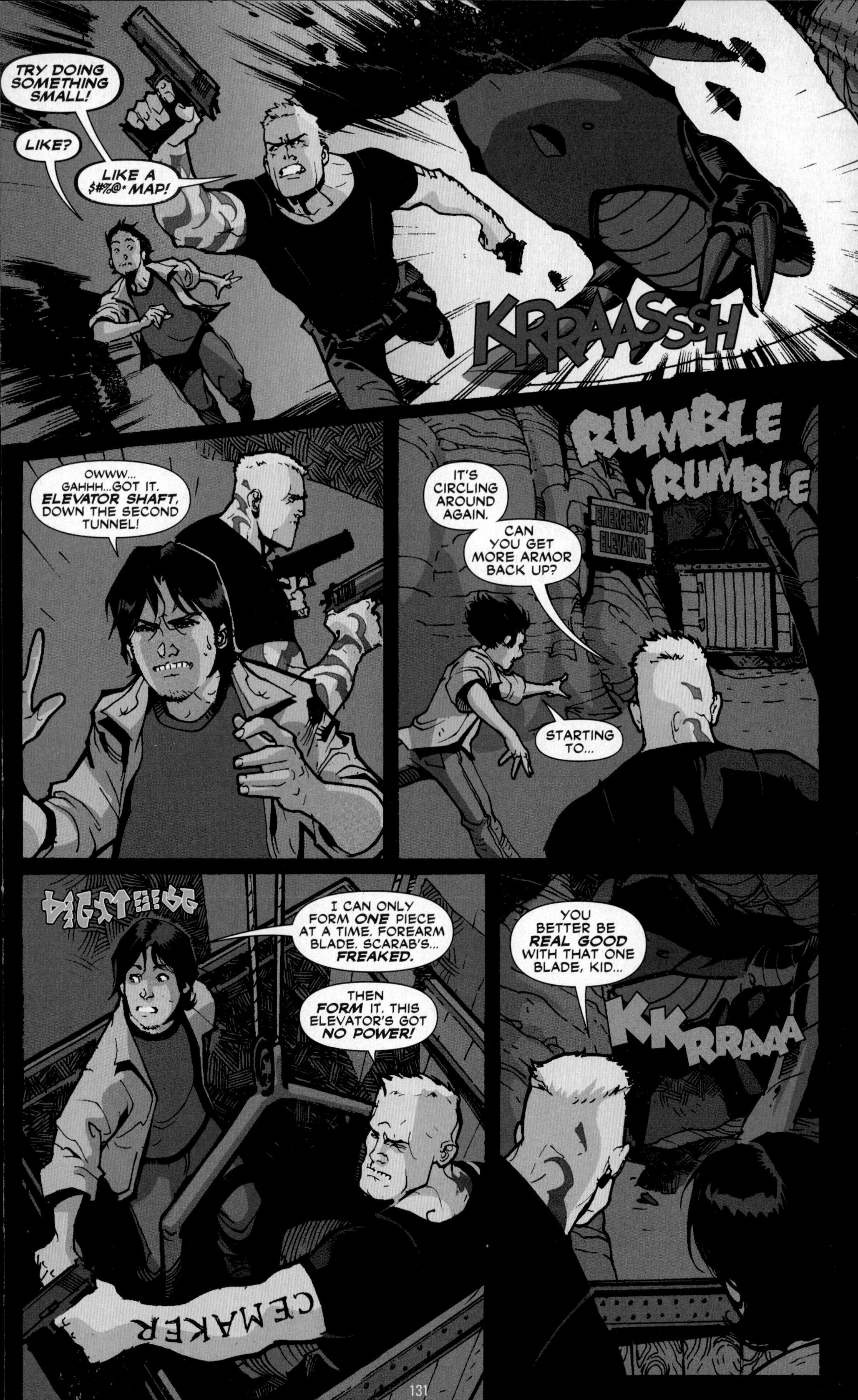

TRY DOING SOMETHING SMALL!
LIKE?
LIKE A $#%@* MAP!
KRRAASSSH
OWWW... GAHHH...GOT IT. ELEVATOR SHAFT, DOWN THE SECOND TUNNEL!
RUMBLE
RUMBLE
EMERGENCY ELEVATOR
IT'S CIRCLING AROUND AGAIN.
CAN YOU GET MORE ARMOR BACK UP?
STARTING TO...
I CAN ONLY FORM ONE PIECE AT A TIME. FOREARM BLADE. SCARAB'S... FREAKED.
THEN FORM IT. THIS ELEVATOR'S GOT NO POWER!
CEMAKER
YOU BETTER BE REAL GOOD WITH THAT ONE BLADE, KID...
KKRRAAA

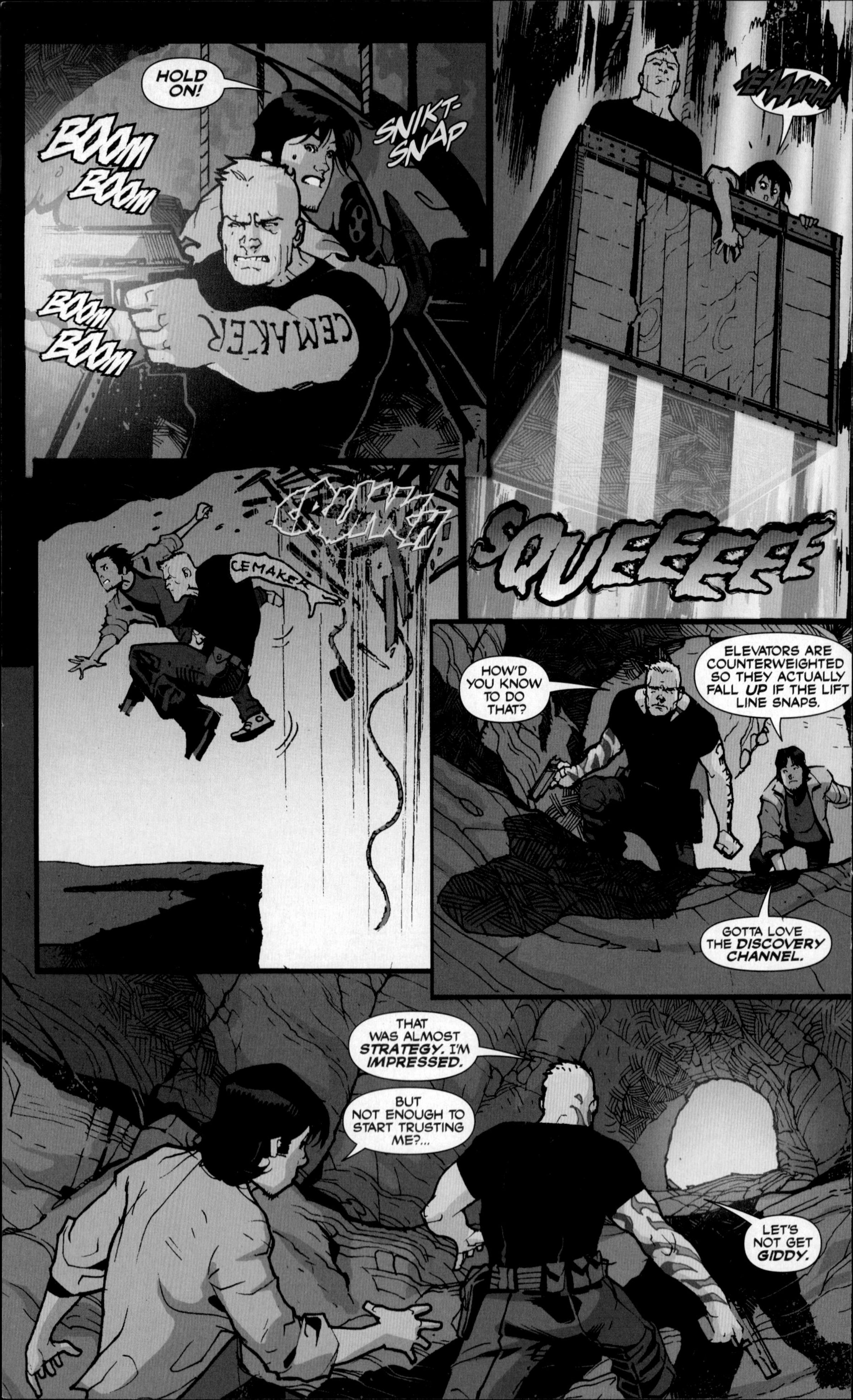
HOLD ON!
BOOM BOOM
BOOM BOOM
SNIKT-SNAP
CEMAKER
YEAAAHH!
CLUNK
CEMAKER
SQUEEEEEE
HOW'D YOU KNOW TO DO THAT?
ELEVATORS ARE COUNTERWEIGHTED SO THEY ACTUALLY FALL UP IF THE LIFT LINE SNAPS.
GOTTA LOVE THE DISCOVERY CHANNEL.
THAT WAS ALMOST STRATEGY. I'M IMPRESSED.
BUT NOT ENOUGH TO START TRUSTING ME?...
LET'S NOT GET GIDDY.

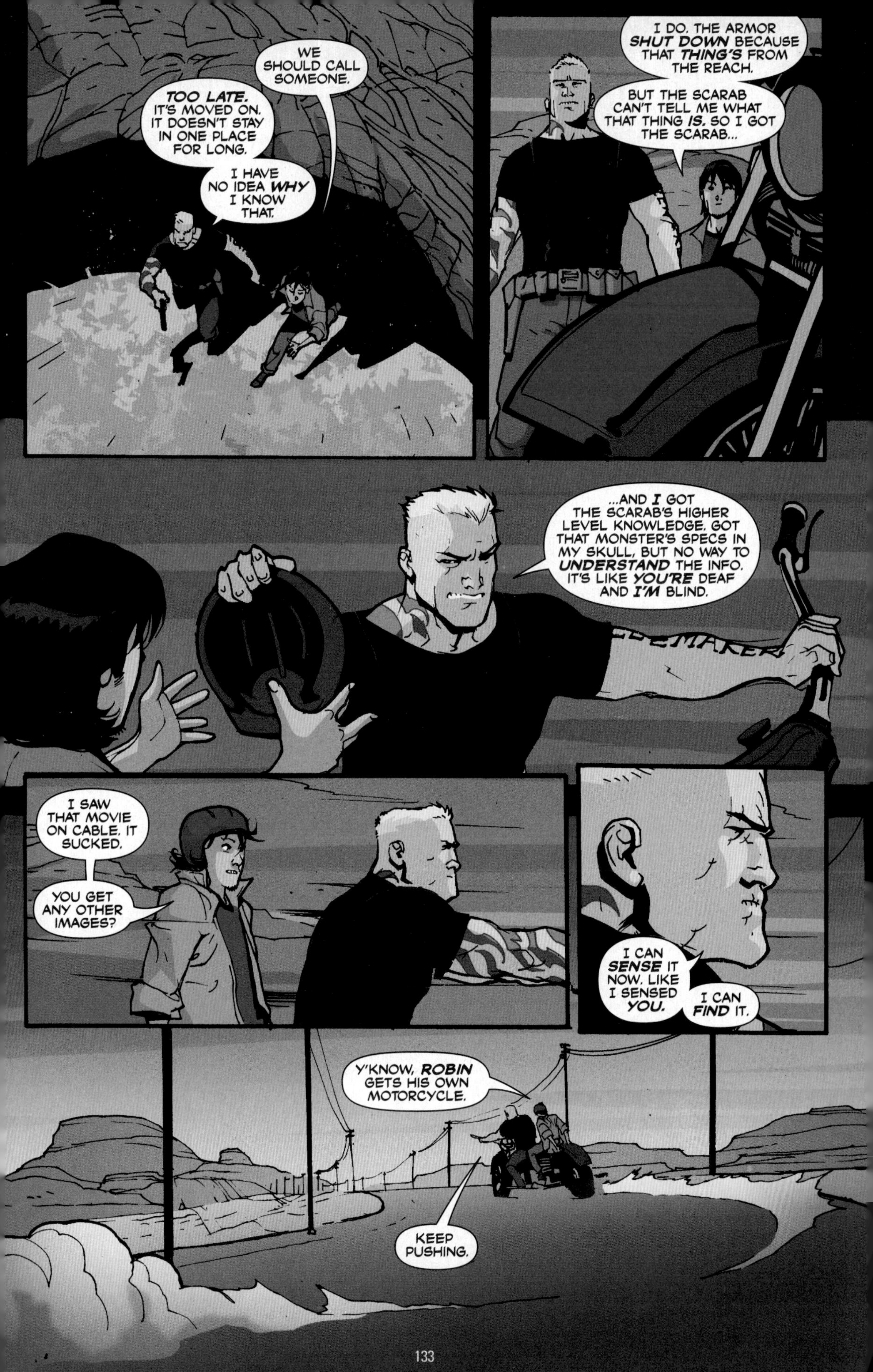
WE SHOULD CALL SOMEONE.
TOO LATE. IT'S MOVED ON. IT DOESN'T STAY IN ONE PLACE FOR LONG.
I HAVE NO IDEA WHY I KNOW THAT.
I DO. THE ARMOR SHUT DOWN BECAUSE THAT THING'S FROM THE REACH.
BUT THE SCARAB CAN'T TELL ME WHAT THAT THING IS. SO I GOT THE SCARAB...
...AND I GOT THE SCARAB'S HIGHER LEVEL KNOWLEDGE. GOT THAT MONSTER'S SPECS IN MY SKULL, BUT NO WAY TO UNDERSTAND THE INFO. IT'S LIKE YOU'RE DEAF AND I'M BLIND.
I SAW THAT MOVIE ON CABLE. IT SUCKED.
YOU GET ANY OTHER IMAGES?
I CAN SENSE IT NOW. LIKE I SENSED YOU.
I CAN FIND IT.
Y'KNOW, ROBIN GETS HIS OWN MOTORCYCLE.
KEEP PUSHING.

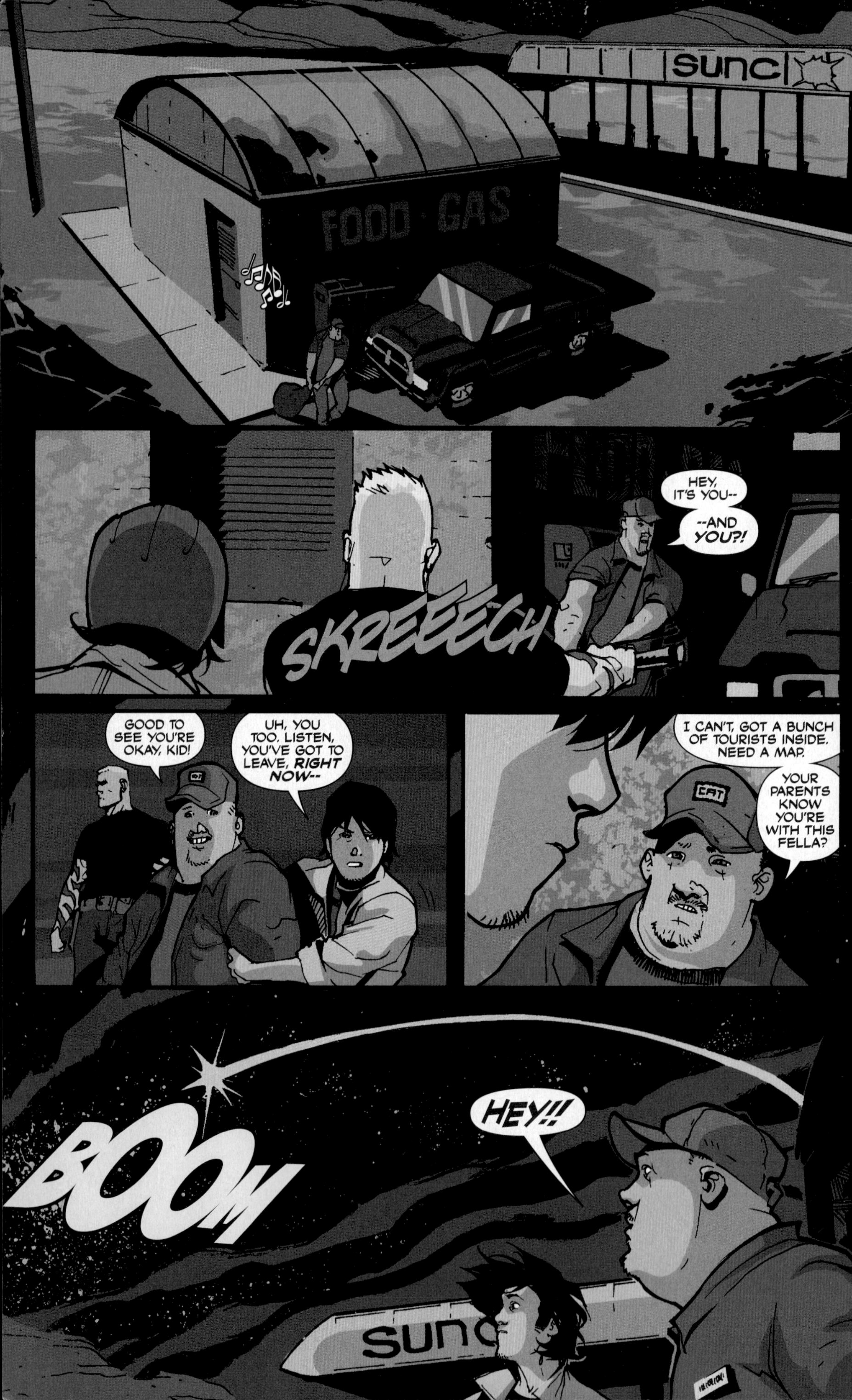
SUNO
FOOD · GAS
HEY, IT'S YOU--
--AND YOU?!
SKREEECH
GOOD TO SEE YOU'RE OKAY, KID!
UH, YOU TOO. LISTEN, YOU'VE GOT TO LEAVE, RIGHT NOW--
I CAN'T, GOT A BUNCH OF TOURISTS INSIDE. NEED A MAP.
YOUR PARENTS KNOW YOU'RE WITH THIS FELLA?
BOOM
HEY!!

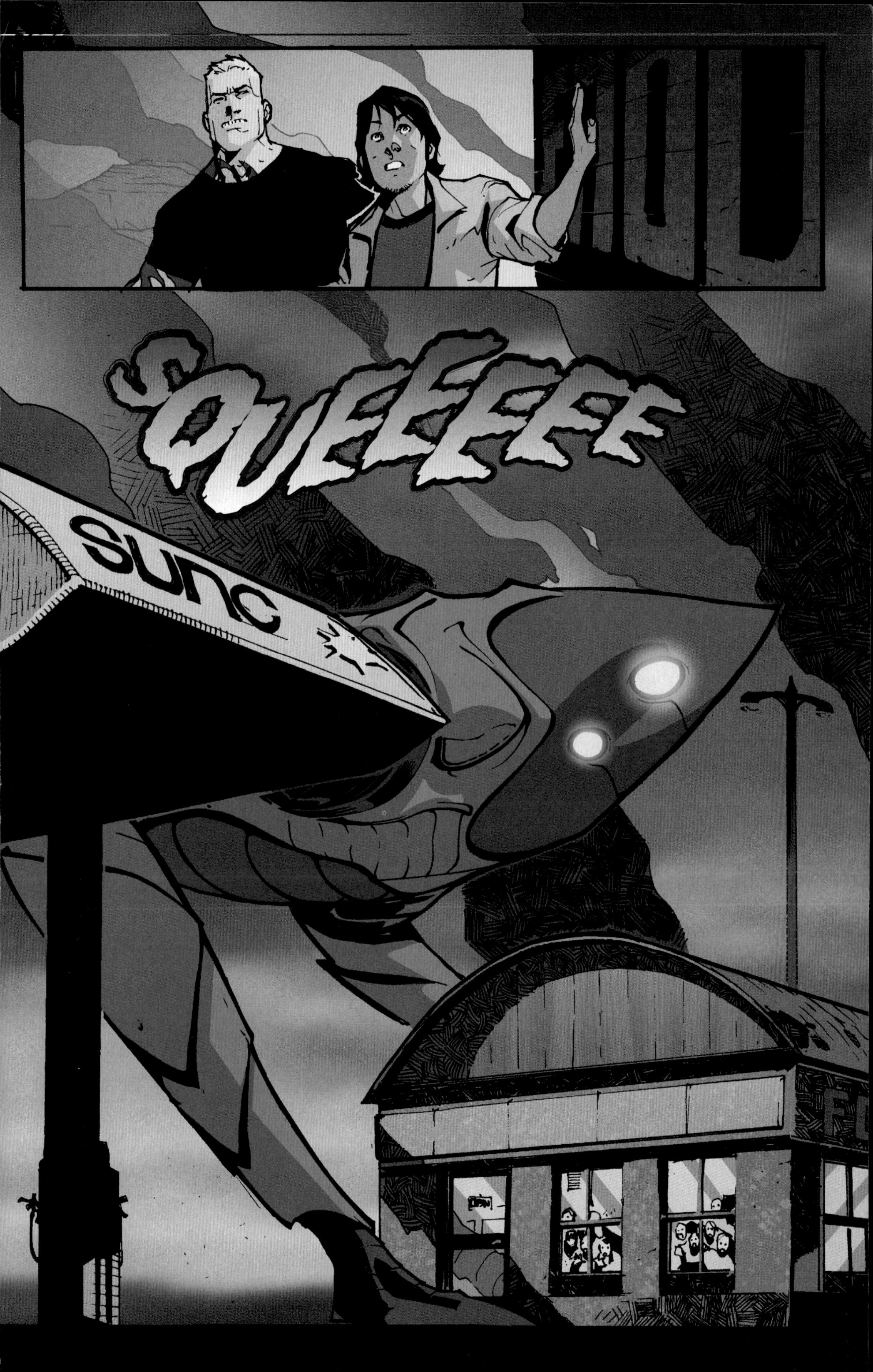
SQUEEEEE

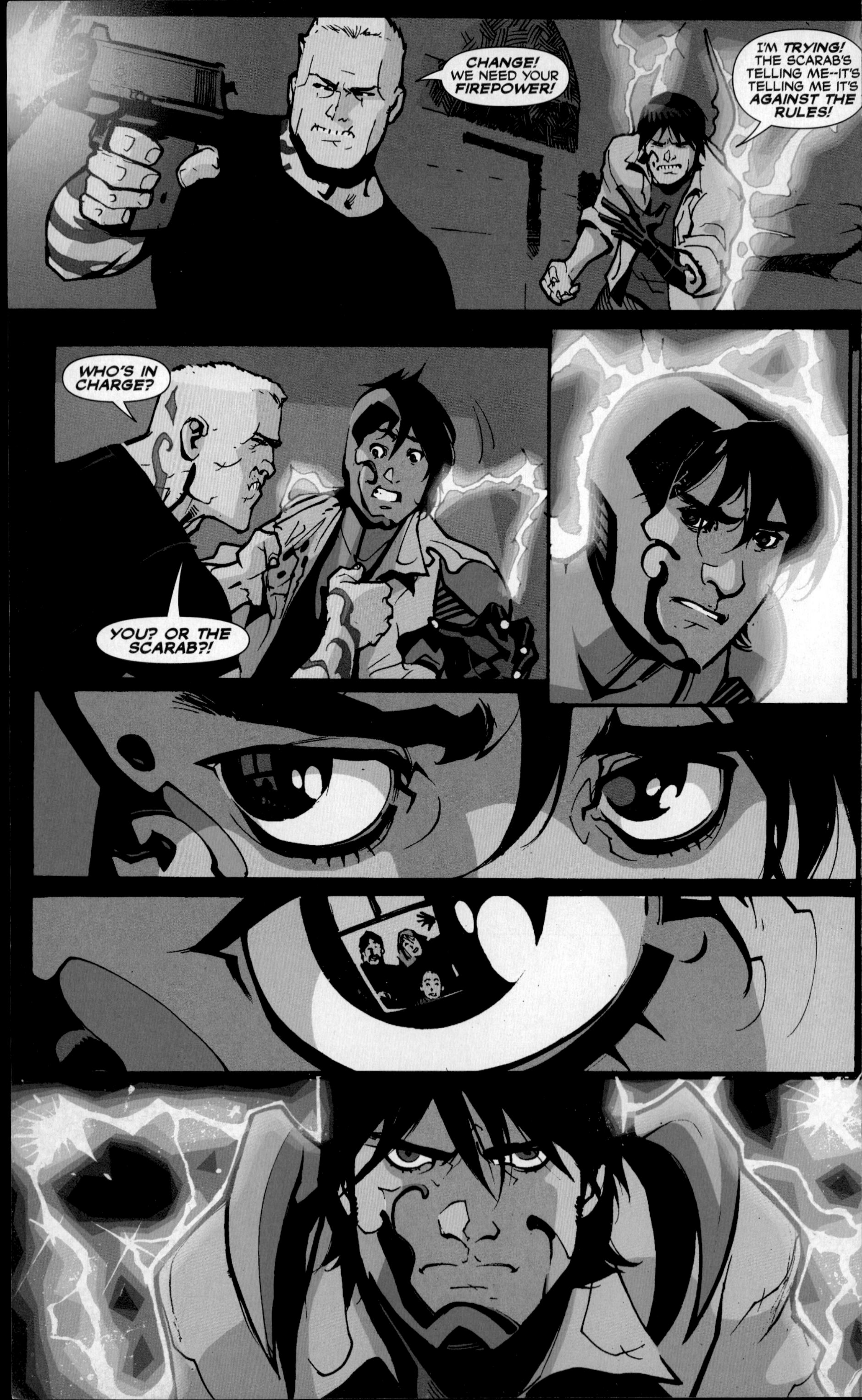
CHANGE! WE NEED YOUR FIREPOWER!
I'M TRYING! THE SCARAB'S TELLING ME--IT'S TELLING ME IT'S AGAINST THE RULES!
WHO'S IN CHARGE?
YOU? OR THE SCARAB?!

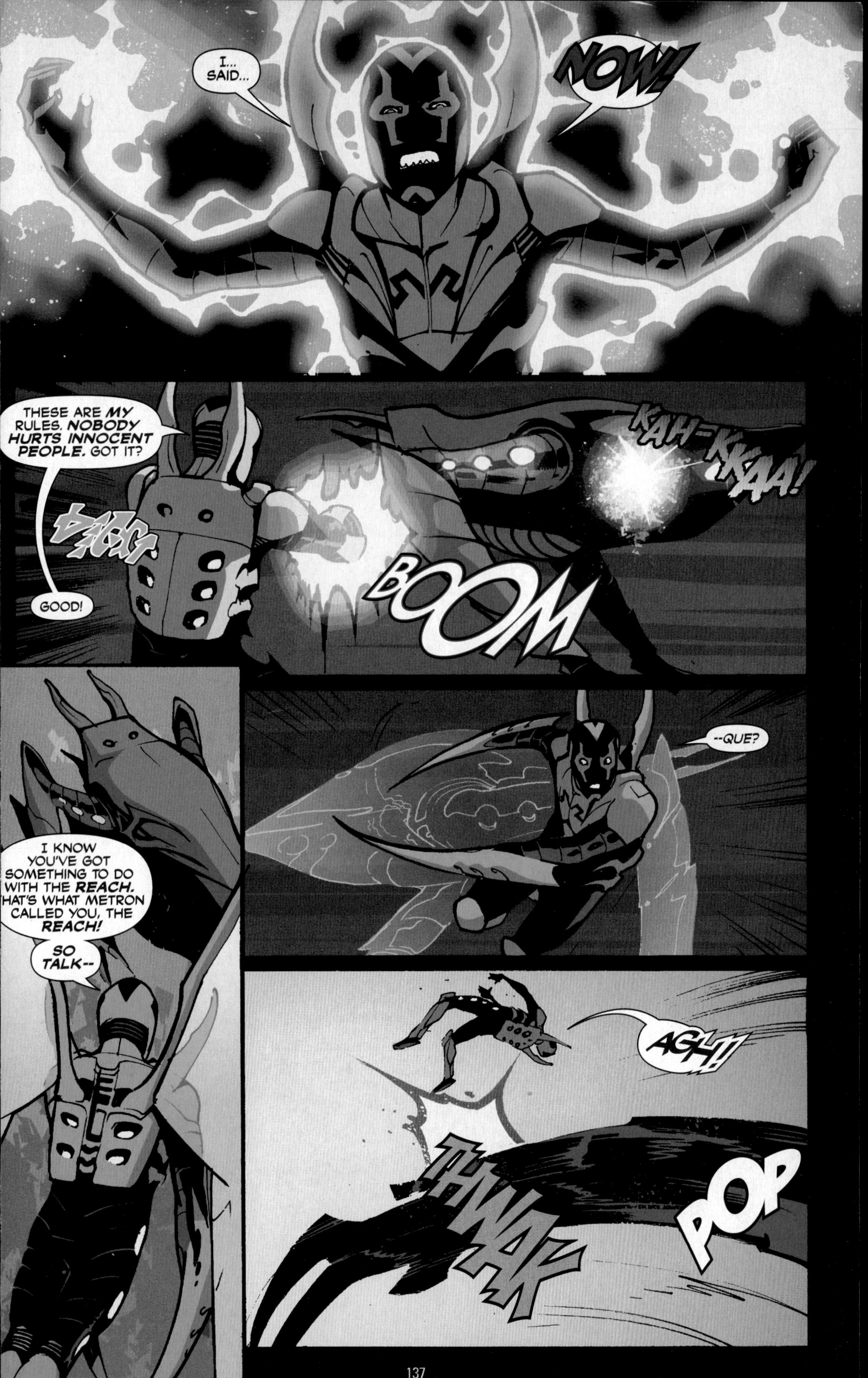
I... SAID...
NOW!
THESE ARE MY RULES. NOBODY HURTS INNOCENT PEOPLE. GOT IT?
GOOD!
KAH-KKAA!
BOOM
--QUE?
I KNOW YOU'VE GOT SOMETHING TO DO WITH THE REACH. HAT'S WHAT METRON CALLED YOU, THE REACH!
SO TALK--
AGH!!
THWAK
POP

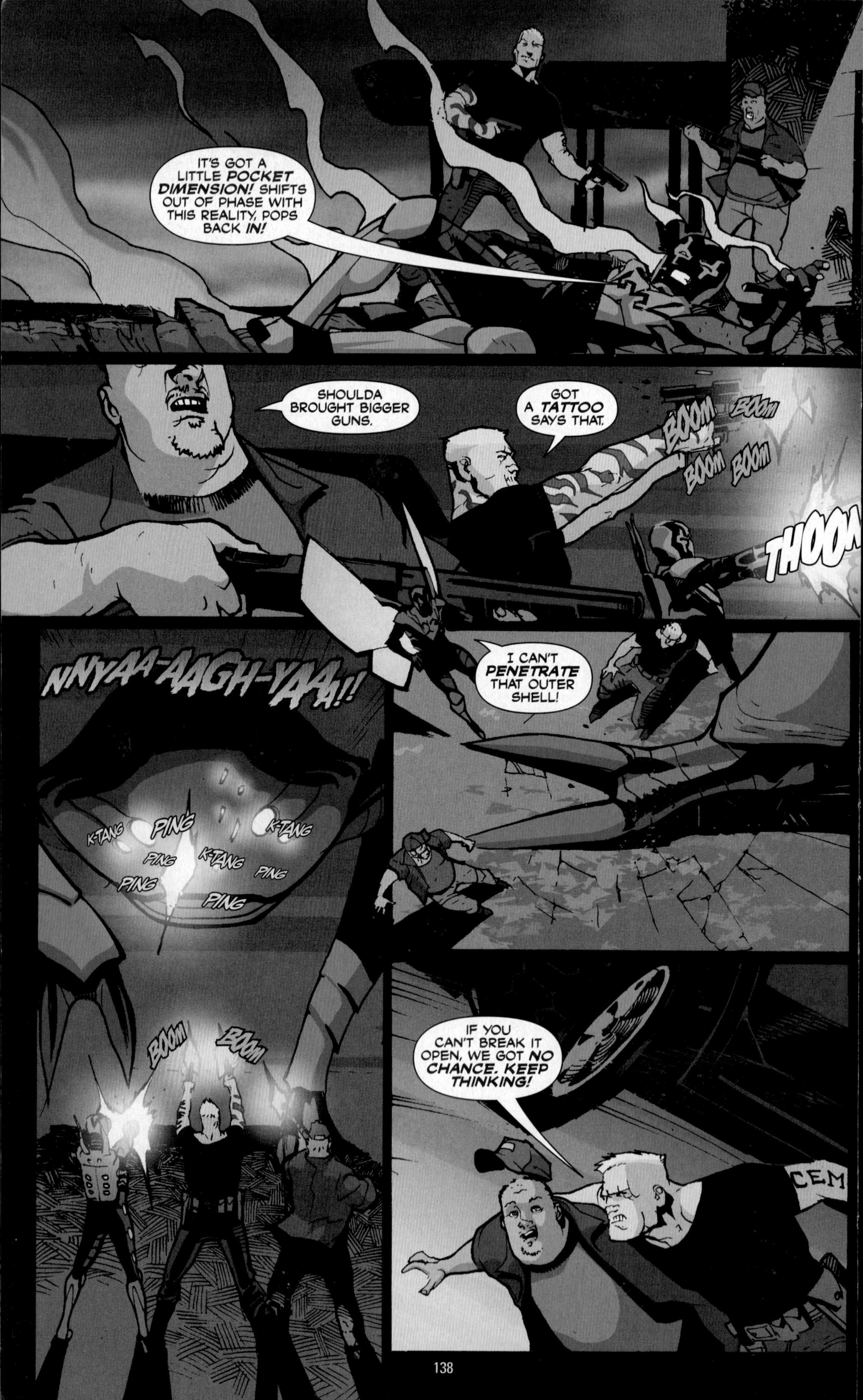

IT'S GOT A LITTLE POCKET DIMENSION! SHIFTS OUT OF PHASE WITH THIS REALITY, POPS BACK IN!
SHOULDA BROUGHT BIGGER GUNS.
GOT A TATTOO SAYS THAT.
BOOM BOOM BOOM BOOM
THOOM
NNYAA-AAGH-YAAA!!
I CAN'T PENETRATE THAT OUTER SHELL!
K-TANG PING K-TANG PING K-TANG PING PING PING
BOOM BOOM
IF YOU CAN'T BREAK IT OPEN, WE GOT NO CHANCE. KEEP THINKING!
CEM

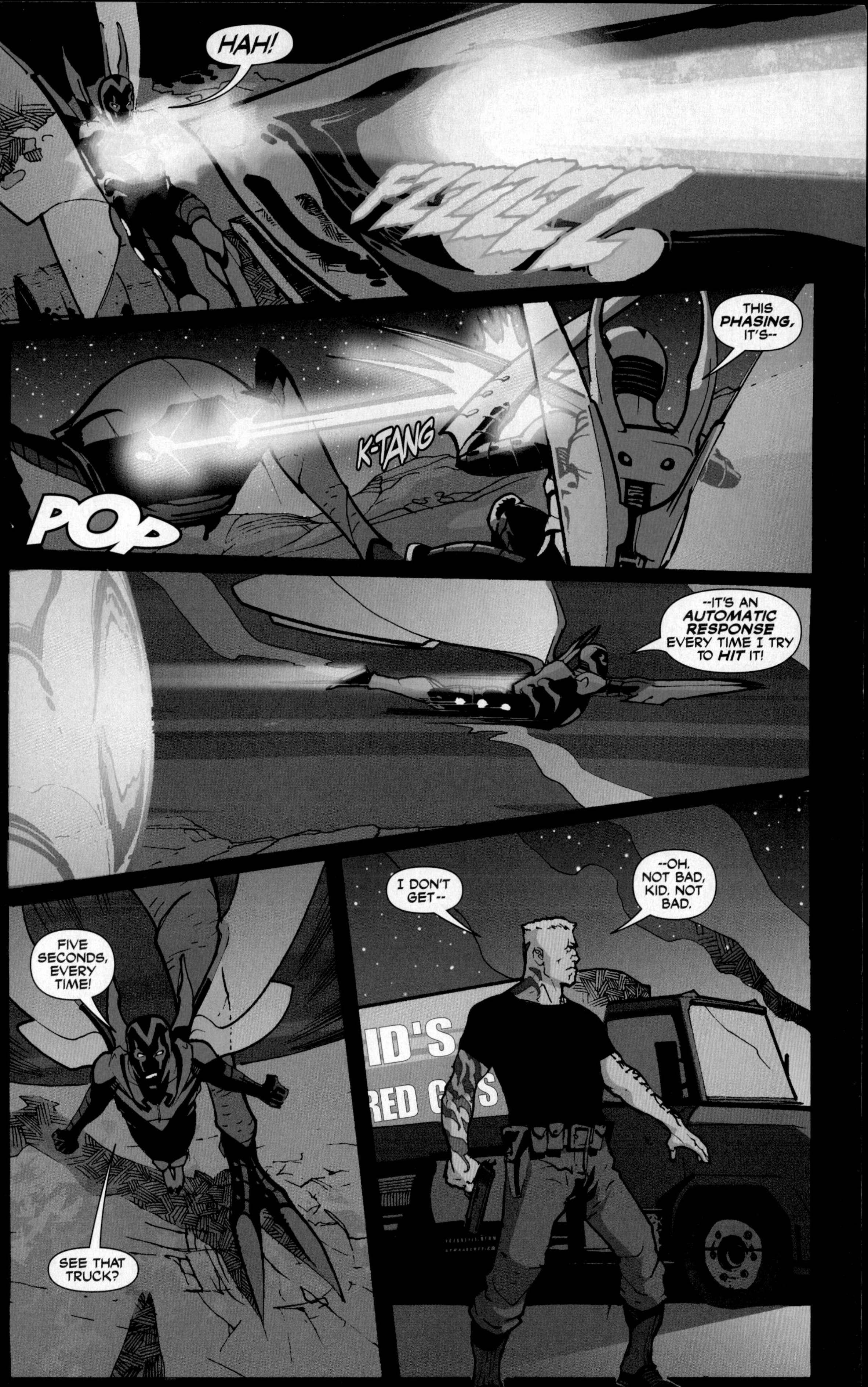
HAH!
FZZZZZZ
THIS PHASING, IT'S--
K-TANG
POP
--IT'S AN AUTOMATIC RESPONSE EVERY TIME I TRY TO HIT IT!
FIVE SECONDS, EVERY TIME!
SEE THAT TRUCK?
I DON'T GET--
--OH. NOT BAD, KID. NOT BAD.
ID'S
RED G S

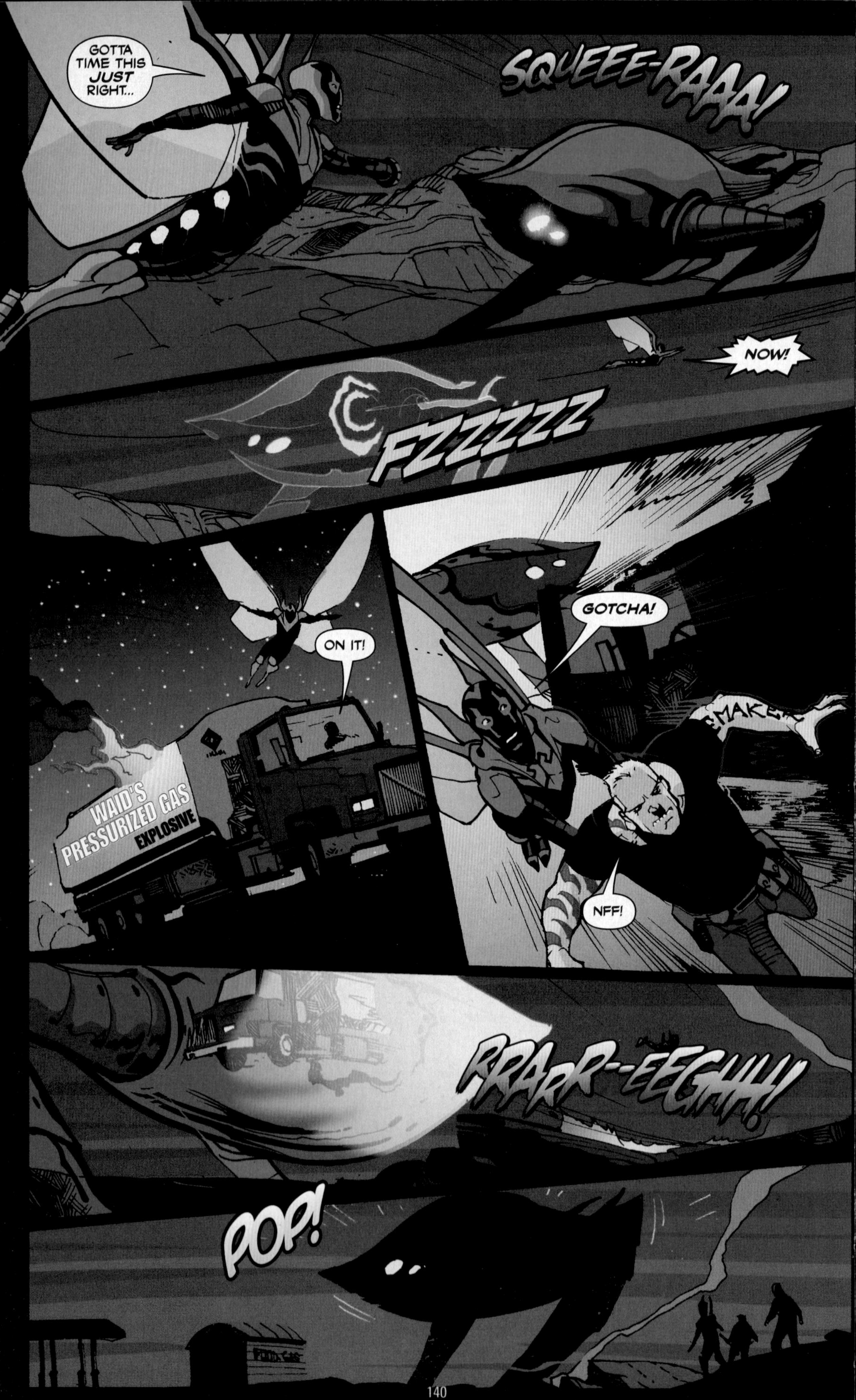
GOTTA TIME THIS JUST RIGHT...
SQUEEE-RAAA!
NOW!
FZZZZZ
ON IT!
WAID'S PRESSURIZED GAS
EXPLOSIVE
GOTCHA!
NFF!
RRARR--EEGHH!
POP!

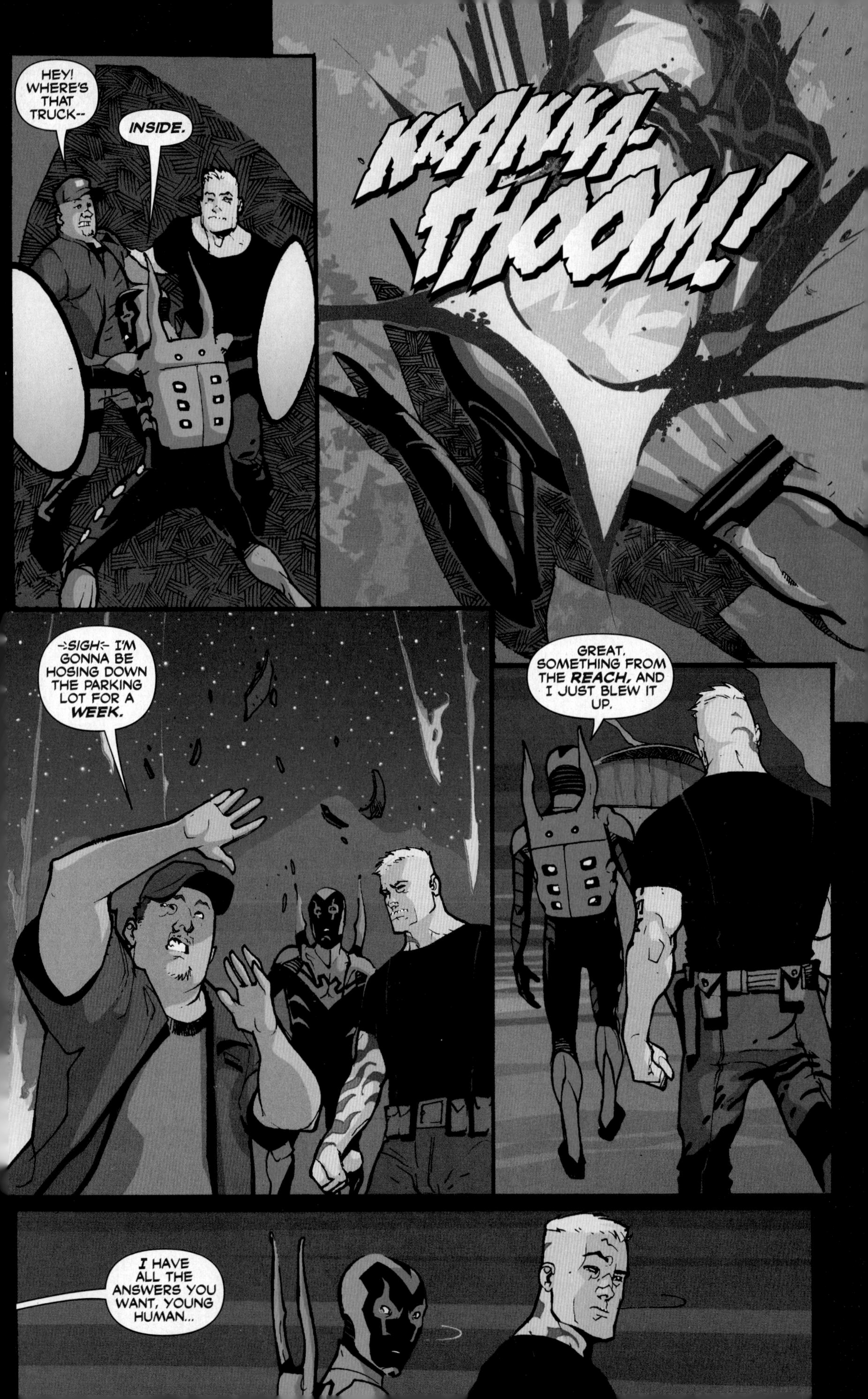
HEY! WHERE'S THAT TRUCK--
INSIDE.
KRAKKA-THOOM!
-SIGH- I'M GONNA BE HOSING DOWN THE PARKING LOT FOR A WEEK.
GREAT. SOMETHING FROM THE REACH, AND I JUST BLEW IT UP.
I HAVE ALL THE ANSWERS YOU WANT, YOUNG HUMAN...

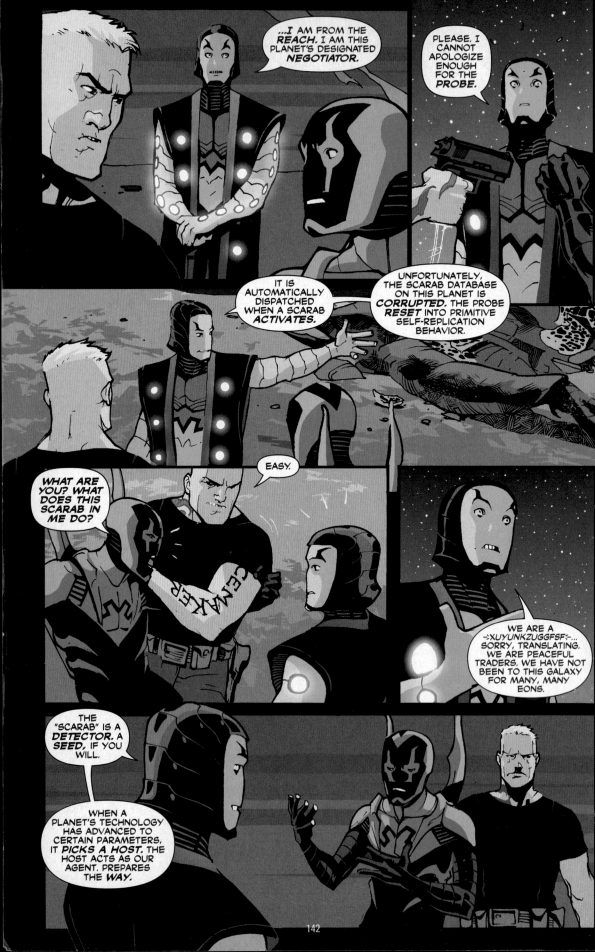

...I AM FROM THE *REACH*. I AM THIS PLANET'S DESIGNATED *NEGOTIATOR*.

PLEASE. I CANNOT APOLOGIZE ENOUGH FOR THE *PROBE*.

IT IS AUTOMATICALLY DISPATCHED WHEN A SCARAB *ACTIVATES*.

UNFORTUNATELY, THE SCARAB DATABASE ON THIS PLANET IS *CORRUPTED*. THE PROBE *RESET* INTO PRIMITIVE SELF-REPLICATION BEHAVIOR.

WHAT ARE YOU? WHAT DOES THIS SCARAB IN ME DO?

EASY.

WE ARE A →*XUYUNKZUGGFSF*←... SORRY, TRANSLATING. WE ARE PEACEFUL TRADERS. WE HAVE NOT BEEN TO THIS GALAXY FOR MANY, MANY EONS.

THE "SCARAB" IS A *DETECTOR*. A *SEED*, IF YOU WILL.

WHEN A PLANET'S TECHNOLOGY HAS ADVANCED TO CERTAIN PARAMETERS, IT *PICKS A HOST*. THE HOST ACTS AS OUR AGENT. PREPARES THE *WAY*.

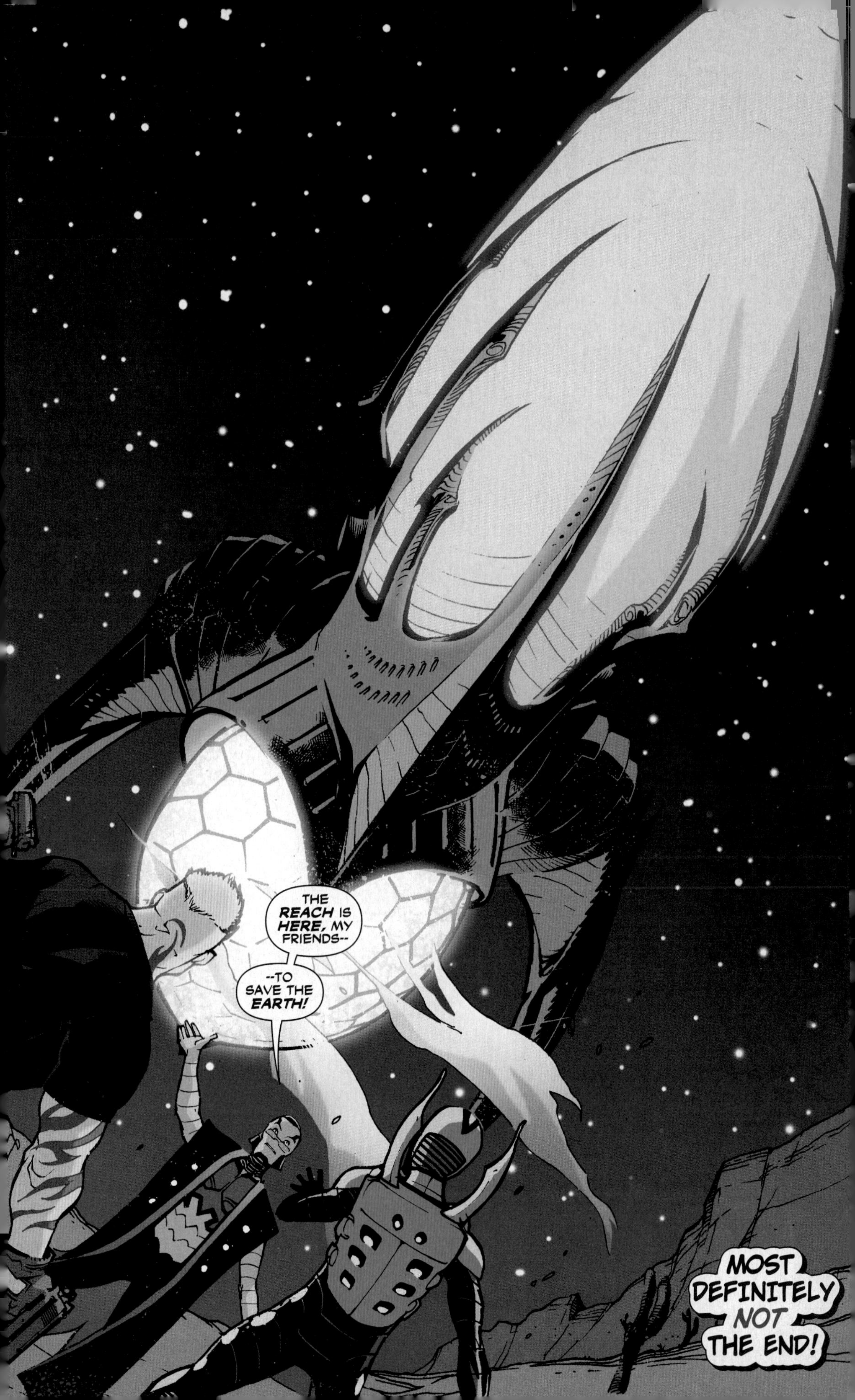
THE REACH IS HERE, MY FRIENDS--
--TO SAVE THE EARTH!
MOST DEFINITELY NOT THE END!

READ MORE ADVENTURES OF YOUR FAVORITE HEROES IN THESE COLLECTIONS FROM DC COMICS:

KINGDOM COME

THE GREATEST SUPER HERO EPIC OF TOMORROW!
KINGDOM COME
Mark WAID
Alex ROSS

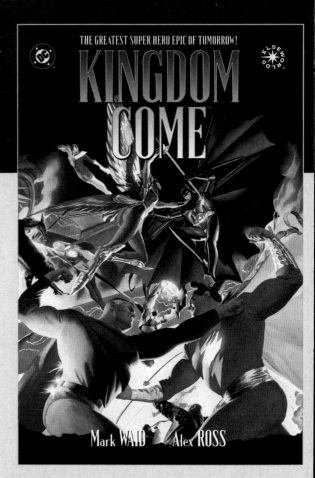

Mark Waid and **Alex Ross** deliver a grim tale of youth versus experience, tradition versus change and what defines a hero. KINGDOM COME is a riveting story pitting the old guard — Superman, Batman, Wonder Woman and their peers — against a new uncompromising generation.

WINNER OF FIVE EISNER AND HARVEY AWARDS, INCLUDING BEST LIMITED SERIES AND BEST ARTIST

IDENTITY CRISIS

NEW YORK TIMES BEST-SELLING AUTHOR OF THE ZERO GAME
BRAD MELTZER
RAGS MORALES MICHAEL BAIR
IDENTITY CRISIS
Introduction by JOSS WHEDON, creator of BUFFY THE VAMPIRE SLAYER and FIREFLY

BRAD MELTZER
RAGS MORALES
MICHAEL BAIR

CRISIS ON INFINITE EARTHS

CRISIS
ON INFINITE EARTHS
MARV WOLFMAN
& GEORGE PÉREZ

MARV WOLFMAN
GEORGE PÉREZ

DC: THE NEW FRONTIER VOLUME 1

DC: The New Frontier
VOLUME ONE
BY DARWYN COOKE WITH DAVE STEWART

DARWYN COOKE
DAVE STEWART

SEARCH THE GRAPHIC NOVELS SECTION OF

www.DCCOMICS.com

FOR ART AND INFORMATION ON ALL OF OUR BOOKS!